# AMERICAN HEBRAIST

# DIMYONOT דמיונות

## Jews and the Cultural Imagination

**Samantha Baskind, General Editor**

EDITORIAL BOARD

Judith Baskin, University of Oregon

David Biale, University of California, Davis

Katrin Kogman-Appel, University of Münster

Kathryn Hellerstein, University of Pennsylvania

Laura Levitt, Temple University

Ilan Stavans, Amherst College

David Stern, Harvard University

*Volumes in the Dimyonot series explore the intersections, and interstices, of Jewish experience and culture. These projects emerge from many disciplines—including art, history, language, literature, music, religion, philosophy, and cultural studies—and diverse chronological and geographical locations. Each volume, however, interrogates the multiple and evolving representations of Judaism and Jewishness, by both Jews and non-Jews, over time and place.*

OTHER TITLES IN THE SERIES

David Stern, Christoph Markschies, and Sarit Shalev-Eyni, eds., *The Monk's Haggadah: A Fifteenth-Century Illuminated Codex from the Monastery of Tegernsee, with a prologue by Friar Erhard von Pappenheim*

Ranen Omer-Sherman, *Imagining the Kibbutz: Visions of Utopia in Literature and Film*

Jordan D. Finkin, *An Inch or Two of Time: Time and Space in Jewish Modernisms*

Ilan Stavans and Marcelo Brodsky, *Once@9:53am: Terror in Buenos Aires*

Ben Schachter, *Image, Action, and Idea in Contemporary Jewish Art*

Heinrich Heine, *Hebrew Melodies*, trans. Stephen Mitchell and Jack Prelutsky, illus. Mark Podwal

Irene Eber, *Jews in China: Cultural Conversations, Changing Perspectives*

Jonathan K. Crane, ed., *Judaism, Race, and Ethics: Conversations and Questions*

Yael Halevi-Wise, *The Multilayered Imagination of A. B. Yehoshua*

David S. Herrstrom and Andrew D. Scrimgeour, *The Prophetic Quest: The Windows of Jacob Landau, Reform Congregation Keneseth Israel, Elkins Park, Pennsylvania*

Laura Levitt, *The Afterlives of Objects: Holocaust Evidence and Criminal Archives*

Lawrence Fine, ed., *Friendship in Jewish History, Religion, and Culture*

Hassan Sarbakhshian, Lior B. Sternfeld, and Parvaneh Vahidmanesh, *Jews of Iran: A Photographic Chronicle*

J. H. Chajes, *The Kabbalistic Tree / האילן הקבלי*

# American Hebraist

Essays on Agnon and Modern Jewish Literature

BY ALAN MINTZ

EDITED BY BEVERLY BAILIS AND DAVID STERN

The Pennsylvania State University Press
University Park, Pennsylvania

Library of Congress Cataloging-in-Publication Data

Names: Mintz, Alan L., author. | Bailis, Beverly, 1971– editor. | Stern, David, 1949– editor.
Title: American Hebraist : essays on Agnon and modern Jewish literature / by Alan Mintz ;
    edited by Beverly Bailis and David Stern.
Other titles: Dimyonot (University Park, Pa.) ; v. 15.
Description: University Park, Pennsylvania : The Pennsylvania State University Press, [2022] |
    Series: Dimyonot : Jews and the cultural imagination ; 15 | Includes bibliographical
    references and index.
Summary: "A collection of fifteen essays by Alan Mintz (1947–2017) on the Nobel Prize winner
    S. Y. Agnon, modern Jewish and Israeli literature, and the Holocaust. Includes a critical
    introduction by David Stern and an epilogue by Beverly Bailis"—Provided by publisher.
Identifiers: LCCN 2022019035 | ISBN 9780271092386 (hardback)
Subjects: LCSH: Agnon, Shmuel Yosef, 1887-1970—Criticism, interpretation, etc. | Jewish
    literature—History and criticism. | Hebrew literature, Modern—History and criticism. |
    Israeli literature—History and criticism. | Holocaust, Jewish (1939-1945), in literature. |
    LCGFT: Essays.
Classification: LCC PJ5017 .M56 2022 | DDC 892.4/09—dc23/eng/20220602
LC record available at https://lccn.loc.gov/2022019035

*For Susanna Morgenthau*
*Amira Morgenthau-Mintz and Avital Morgenthau-Mintz*
*With much gratitude for all their support and help*

# CONTENTS

ACKNOWLEDGMENTS

The following essays first appeared in these journals and volumes. We are grateful to their publishers and editors for allowing us to reprint them here.

Alan Mintz. "Agnon in Jaffa: The Myth of the Artist as a Young Man." *Prooftexts* 1, no. 1 (January 1981): 62–83. Reprinted with permission of Indiana University Press.

———. "Agnon Without End." *Commentary Magazine* 89, no. 2 (February 1990): 57–59.

———. "Ahad Ha-am and the Essay: The Vicissitudes of Reason." In *At the Crossroads: Essays on Ahad Ha-am*, edited by Jacques Kornberg, 3–11. Albany: State University of New York, 1983.

———. "Haim Gouri at 90." *Jewish Review of Books* (Summer 2014): 36–39.

———. "Hebrew in America: A Memoir." In *What We Talk About When We Talk About Hebrew (and What It Means to Americans)*, edited by Naomi B. Sokoloff and Nancy E. Berg, 211–26. Seattle: University of Washington Press, 2018. Reprinted with permission from University of Washington Press.

———. "In the Seas of Youth." *Prooftexts* 21, no. 1 (Winter 2001): 57–70. Reprinted with permission of Indiana University Press.

———. "Israeli Literature in the Minds of American Readers." In *Translating Israel: Contemporary Hebrew Literature and its Reception in American*, 1–44. Syracuse: Syracuse University Press, 2001.

———. "Knocking on Heaven's Gate: Hebrew Literature and Wisse's Canon." In *Arguing the Modern Jewish Canon: Essays on Literature and Culture in Honor of Ruth R. Wisse*, edited by Justin Cammy, Dara Horn, Alyssa Quint, and Rachel Rubenstein, 23–35. Cambridge: Center for Jewish Studies, Harvard University, 2008.

———. "Modern Hebrew Literature and Jewish Theology: Repositioning the Question." *Orim* 3, no. 1 (Autumn 1987): 93–109.

————. "On 'The Sense of Smell' by S. Y. Agnon." In *Reading Hebrew Literature: Critical Discussions of Six Modern Texts*, edited by Alan Mintz, 126–34. Hanover: Brandeis University Press, 2003.

————. "Reading 'HaHazanim,'" *Ayin Gimel: A Journal of Agnon Studies* 2 (2012): 93–107.

————. "Sefer ha'aggadah: Triumph or Tragedy?" In *History and Literature: New Readings of Jewish Texts in Honor of Arnold J. Band*, edited by William Cutter and David C. Jacobson, 17–26. Providence: Brown University, 2002.

————. "Viva Voce: Vicissitudes of the Spoken Word in Hebrew Literature." In *There's a Jewish Way of Saying Things: Essays in Honor of David Roskies*, edited by Avraham (Alan) Rosen and Jillian Davidson. *In Geveb*, June 2020, 1–9.

————. "Writing About Ourselves: Jewish Autobiography, Modern and Premodern." *Jewish Quarterly Review* 98, no. 2 (Spring 2008): 272–85.

Beverly Bailis, "Packing Up an Office: The Work of Mourning and the Creation of an Archive." *Prooftexts* 37, no. 3 (2019): 451–62. Reprinted with permission of Indiana University Press.

# American Hebraist

*An Introduction*

DAVID STERN

Alan Mintz (1947–2017) was a singular figure in the American Jewish literary landscape. The leading scholar of modern Hebrew literature in his generation in America, he was also one of the few Americans in the field to command equal respect and authority in Israel among his contemporaries there. Beyond his academic specialization, Mintz was a major figure in Jewish Studies more generally, as a public intellectual, and as an authoritative voice in all matters of modern and contemporary Jewish culture here and abroad. A mentor to many junior scholars in modern Jewish literature, in America and abroad, he was known for his generosity, support, and magnanimity. He was a founder and coeditor of two seminal literary journals, *Response: A Contemporary Jewish Review* and *Prooftexts: A Journal of Jewish Literary History*. *Response* was a herald of the Jewish countercultural movement of the late 1960s. It is no exaggeration to say that *Prooftexts* reinvented the academic study of Jewish literature, from the Bible to the modern period, and in all languages, in America and in Israel.

Mintz's own scholarship ranged over the entire length of Hebrew and Jewish literature, from the Bible to contemporary Israeli fiction, and he brought to all his writing an extraordinarily sophisticated and rich worldliness, born out of a deep knowledge of Western literature and culture.

Indeed, out of that worldliness, Mintz fashioned a uniquely rich literary critical voice that was unlike any other in either America or Israel. Neither confessional nor academic in tone, Mintz's style possessed a precision and elegance that made virtually every sentence instantly recognizable as his own. A close reader of texts with an unusually subtle and insightful eye, he was able to connect language in all its details and nuances with the personally relevant issues animating a writer's imagination and, at the same time, connect those issues to the dominating, overarching concerns of the age, to the larger social context, and most importantly, to the arc of Jewish history.

Mintz was the author of six books of his own, each of which became a definitive monograph on its subject. He also wrote many scholarly articles unrelated to the subjects of his books, and throughout his career he contributed numerous reviews and essays to literary journals including *The New Republic*, *Commentary*, *The New York Times Book Review*, and in the last decade especially, *The Jewish Review of Books*. Scattered in miscellaneous volumes and publications, these writings reveal sides of Mintz's scholarly personality that are not always evident in his books. In this volume, we have collected fifteen of these scholarly articles and more occasional essays. This introduction will situate these previously uncollected writings within the larger frame of Mintz's intellectual career. The volume concludes with a personal essay on packing up her teacher's office by Beverly Bailis, my coeditor, and the last student to complete a doctorate under Alan Mintz.

Alan Mintz came to the study of modern Hebrew literature through a path that was not entirely typical of his contemporaries. When Mintz entered Jewish Studies in the late 1970s, it was an established field in the American university. Many of his peers, whatever their specific fields of specialization, had been trained in doctoral programs in Jewish Studies; some had also completed undergraduate majors in Jewish Studies. There was also a substantial number of graduates of rabbinical schools, especially the Jewish Theological Seminary, who entered doctoral programs after receiving ordination, and even then, there were students who had studied in yeshivot and other post–high school or college educational programs in Israel. Mintz had done none of those things.

Born in Worcester, Massachusetts, Mintz grew up in a Conservative Jewish community and received his early Jewish education in a synagogue Hebrew school which was still under the sway of the American Hebraist movement. American Hebraism—about which Mintz would eventually write a monumental book, *Sanctuary in the Wilderness*—was a movement created by mainly Eastern European immigrants to America in the first decades of the twentieth century. These Hebraists were self-styled heirs to Bialik and his generation of Hebrew literary pioneers, who sought to establish in America what Mintz called a "Republic of the Hebrew language." As Mintz would later describe their core ideology, Hebrew for these Hebraists was *the* guarantee of cultural continuity, *the* matrix for the construction of Jewish identity.

By the time Mintz entered Hebrew school as a boy in the 1950s, Hebraism as a movement was already in steep decline, but it was still powerful enough to leave an impression upon a few young students. Alan was one of those few. From the time of his first exposure to Hebrew, he appears to have taken an unusual pleasure in learning the language and to have found in it a personal key for unlocking the meaning of Judaism and his own Jewishness. By the time he was a teenager he had already acquired a fluency in the language impressive for an American his age. As a counselor at summer camp he was able to speak Hebrew to his campers, and when he became national president of USY, the Conservative youth movement, his mastery of Hebrew was a clear strength. Throughout high school, he attended the Prozdor Program at the Boston Hebrew College, one of the last real bastions of Hebraism in America, whose principal was Eisag Silberschlag, an American Hebraist poet whom Mintz would later write about in his book. As Mintz acknowledged, the personalities of these Hebraists had an impact upon him as powerful as the subjects they taught.

When he enrolled in Columbia College in New York City, Mintz continued to take courses in Jewish Studies at the Jewish Theological Seminary, among them a class in modern Hebrew literature taught by Avraham Holtz in which he wrote his first paper in Hebrew; its subject was a story by S. Y. Agnon, a not incidental fact, as we shall see. Over the course of his undergraduate years, however, Mintz's literary interests increasingly shifted to English literature, and when he graduated from college, he was admitted to Columbia's doctoral program in English literature to study the Victorian novel, one of its powerhouse specializations. Eventually, he completed his doctorate with a dissertation on George Eliot that later became his first published book, *George Eliot and the Novel of Vocation*. The two directors of his dissertation were Steven Marcus and Edward Said. Both were eminent scholars who used literature as a tool of cultural criticism, and both had truly eclectic interests that ranged far beyond conventional literary topics, two qualities that had a clear impact upon their students including Mintz. (Marcus was already famous for a book on Victorian pornography; Said had not yet written *Orientalism,* but he was already known as one of America's leading post-structuralist theoreticians).

*George Eliot and the Novel of Vocation* was a prophetically timely first book—prophetically timely, that is, in terms of Mintz's own career. The argument of the book, in short, was that in the late Victorian period, a new subgenre of the novel emerged, a subgenre of fictional narrative that explored the ways in which work became more than simply what one did for a living or a matter of duty. Work, the task of labor, was transformed from being a livelihood or the ethical responsibility of a gentleman and became instead a vehicle for self-realization and self-definition. Work became a vehicle through which an individual could fulfill personal ambition and simultaneously serve greater, selfless causes in the service of society at large. If the idea of vocation had previously been akin to a theological calling, it now became a secularized dilemma that challenged how a person chose to live, and thereby a fitting subject for the novel to explore.

As Mintz was writing this dissertation on the transformation of the conception of work, he was in the process of finding a vocation for himself, his own calling. As he later wrote in an autobiographical memoir, "My Life in Hebrew," it was during his third year in graduate school that Mintz came to the realization that he could no longer see himself committing to a lifelong career as a professor of English; he wished to do something that would contribute to "Jewish culture." Exactly what in Jewish culture he did not yet know. Mintz was initially attracted to classical Hebrew literature—midrash, medieval Hebrew poetry, *piyyut*—but these fields, he realized, required an immersion in classical Jewish texts—of the sort gained only by growing up in a traditional background or by studying for years in a yeshiva or rabbinical school—that he felt he could never acquire. After spending several years studying and retooling himself at the Hebrew University in Jerusalem and at Harvard University in Cambridge, Mintz finally (and happily) fixed upon modern Hebrew literature. In retrospect, this may seem like an almost painfully obvious choice for him to have made, if only because of his previous training in English literature and literary theory, but the key fact is that it was a decision he had to make for himself. Like much else in

Mintz's intellectual life, it was a considered choice, made out of deliberation and reflection, not an inevitability.

Mintz's first academic position was as an assistant professor at Columbia University, and during his time there he wrote several articles on Agnon, Berdichevsky, and Feierberg; the latter two would later become part of his second book. But the inspiration for his first book in the field of modern Hebrew literature arrived from a different source. In his own memoir about their personal and professional friendship, David Roskies, Mintz's close friend and the cofounder with Mintz of *Prooftexts*, related the story. In the late 1970s, Roskies, on the faculty of the Jewish Theological Seminary of America, organized and led a course with guest lecturers on Jewish responses to catastrophe from the Bible to the Holocaust. The course was a huge success and led Roskies himself to write his own prize-winning book on responses to catastrophe in modern Yiddish literature and culture, *Against the Apocalypse*. Mintz audited the lecture course, and for him, too, it had a consequential impact. As Roskies tells the story, Mintz came to him and broached the question as to whether he, Mintz, could carve out a discrete area of the huge topic—namely, the response to national catastrophe in the Hebrew literary tradition—and write his own book on that specific tradition. The two decided amicably to each pursue their own scholarly path, and thus *Hurban: Responses to Catastrophe in Hebrew Literature* (1984) was born.

As both Roskies and Mintz acknowledged, their two books were at once complementary and different. The underlying argument of *Against the Apocalypse* was to identify a genre of Yiddish literature that Roskies called "sacred parody," by which he meant a chain of Jewish literary works that deliberately inverted and subverted tradition. In contrast, Mintz was more interested in showing how successive generations of authors in Hebrew literature—from the Bible to Aharon Appelfeld—used the literary imagination to reinvent paradigms to explain the ever-surpassing magnitude of each new catastrophic horror as it exceeded and exhausted previous paradigms. The arguments behind both books, however, were conceived in opposition to a regnant trend in the emerging field of Holocaust studies. This trend, epitomized in the works of literary critics like Lawrence Langer and Terence des Pres, viewed the Holocaust as a unique event, singular, sui generis, whose burden of meaning resided exclusively in the darkness of the death camps, ultimately resisting all representation. Both Roskies and Mintz rejected this approach precisely because it eliminated the specificity of the

Jewish element which, they argued, lay not in the ultimacy of victimization but in the creative responses that Jews took to avail their survival, whether or not their strategies had been successful. Both Roskies and Mintz, each in his own way, sought to prove that the Jewish response to the Holocaust, far from being unique, had grown out of a lengthy tradition of Jewish responses to earlier national traumas.

At the time of their initial publication, both *Hurban* and *Against the Apocalypse* were important for pushing back against what Mintz would later call the "exceptionalist" view of the Holocaust as an irreducibly singular event with no precedents in Jewish history. Looked at today, however, almost forty years later, an equally lasting contribution of *Hurban* may have been to the study of Hebrew literature as much as to Holocaust literary studies. *Hurban* worked through the canon of Hebrew literature, from the Bible to the Holocaust, dwelling upon watershed texts that responded to catastrophe—the Book of Lamentations, Eikhah (Lamentations) Rabbah, medieval Crusader Chronicles and martyrdom poems, Tchernichovsky, Bialik, Uri Zvi Greenberg, and Aharon Appelfeld. Each of these works had of course been studied extensively by scholars in the past, and Mintz had worked through the scholarship—there was nothing naïve or uninformed (let alone misinformed) about his analyses—but his own chapters were not burdened by the earlier scholarship. They focused on close, highly nuanced readings of passages within deeply contextualized and historicized discussions that showed how each text represented a new and fresh creative response to the challenge of catastrophe and yet built upon its predecessors even when it was discontinuous with them. Through the very sweep of the texts it treated—from the Bible to contemporary Israeli literature—*Hurban* demonstrated a tangible commitment to the full continuity of Hebrew literature, an oft-repeated slogan to which lip service has been paid countless times, but rarely put into such full and effective practice, at least in the recent past.

No book of Hebrew literary scholarship quite like it had been written before in the second half of the twentieth century, and no book like it could have been written by a literary scholar or critic educated anywhere but in America in the late 1960s and '70s, in an American liberal arts college and in a doctoral program like Columbia's English department. At Columbia College, Mintz had begun his undergraduate education with the famed Literature Humanities Core course, in which students ploughed through the canonical classics of Western literature from Homer to Virginia Woolf, exclusively reading and analyzing the primary texts, with no commentaries or footnotes, as it were. Throughout his undergraduate training, and even through his years as a graduate student, Mintz maintained a strong allegiance to reading the primary texts first and foremost. While he was schooled in theory and could avail himself of it when he wished, his literary approach was indeed much closer to the cultural criticism of Lionel Trilling and Steven Marcus. And what Mintz had learned from others at Columbia, from Said in particular, was that no form of literary discourse was immune or unsusceptible to literary analysis. This enabled him to move effortlessly from Bible and midrash to medieval martyrological poems and chronicles to more familiar modern poems and novels.

*Hurban* was an exceptionally bold and ambitious project, and an especially courageous one for a young scholar entering a new field in which he had not received a formal degree and had no official credentials. Mintz must surely have been aware that *Hurban* could have been dismissed as dilettantish or merely popularizing by more traditional and conventional literary scholars. This did not deter him. The literary voice of the book—confident but not arrogant or presumptuous, learned without being pretentious, and wearing its erudition in world literature as well as in Jewish tradition very lightly—was a fresh one in Hebrew literary studies, unlike any other in the world, and it established Mintz as a serious figure in the field to be reckoned with.

One of the reasons why Mintz did not consider the Holocaust to be the irreducible rupture in modern Jewish experience was because he, and others, knew that the true rupture in Jewish existence had already definitively taken place—in the middle to late nineteenth century, when the full weight of the eighteenth century and the crushing blow of the Enlightenment to traditional Judaism and Jewish existence had finally sunk in. It was to this moment of climactic rupture that Mintz turned in his second monograph, *"Banished from Their Father's Table": Loss of Faith and Hebrew Autobiography* (1989). A far more concentrated study than *Hurban*, this book focused on a group of writers—Mordecai Ze'ev Feierberg, Mica Yosef Berdichevsky, and Yosef Hayyim Brenner—who together invented what Mintz called the narrative of apostasy, a genre that began in autobiography and ended, with Brenner, in autobiographical fiction. Like George Eliot's novel of vocation, the apostasy narrative gave literary expression to a specific moment of radical change in the larger culture. For the novel of vocation, that moment of cultural change had been the transformation of work from a job or a duty into a calling and the source of a meaningful life. For the apostasy narrative, it was a moment of crisis in the emergence of modern Judaism, the pain and upheaval felt by the individual as the structures of traditional belief collapsed. In both instances, Mintz sought to show how a literary mode of imaginative expression could provide a vessel unlike any other for the honest and relentless exploration of life lived at a moment of extreme change.

Mintz's third book, *Popular Culture and the Shaping of Holocaust Memory in America* (2001), was, in a sense, a postscript to *Hurban* inasmuch as it dealt with two topics that he had not touched upon in the earlier work, namely, American Jewish responses to the Holocaust and the effects of the Holocaust on popular culture. Originally delivered as the prestigious Stroum Lectures at the University of Washington in 1996, the book was finally published in 2001. The book's second chapter, "Two Models in the Study of Holocaust Representation," presents the most sophisticated exposition of the theoretical framework within which *Hurban* was conceived (along with Roskies's *Against the Apocalypse*), contrasting what Mintz calls the "constructivist" approach he and Roskies espoused with the "exceptionalist" position they had rejected. Yet what stands out about the chapter and Mintz's presentation of the framework is not only its eloquence but its fairness to both opposing viewpoints. He was fully alert to the degree to which the debate involved issues that went beyond academic differences. More than any other of his books, *Popular Culture* is a work of practical criticism, explicitly addressing the impact of its concerns to American Jewish culture—the Jewish educational curriculum, the preservation and attention given to archives of survivor documents, the growing number of Holocaust museums and other institutions curating Holocaust memory. Mintz felt very conscious of his duties as a Jewish public intellectual to address these matters. Indeed, during this period, he was not only teaching courses on Holocaust literature at Brandeis, where he was now a professor; he was also leading National Endowment of the Humanities summer institutes on the Holocaust for high school and college teachers that drew national audiences and sought to draw wider attention to views he felt important enough to deserve greater exposure.

During the period that Mintz was working on *Popular Culture* and for the following ten years, Mintz was involved in several side projects as well. He edited a volume, *The Boom in Contemporary Israeli Fiction* (1997), and published a volume of his own review—essays on Israeli writing entitled *Translating Israel: Contemporary Hebrew Literature and Its Reception in America* (2001). A few years later, he edited a volume that came out of an acclaimed symposium of literary scholars he ran at Brandeis, *Reading Hebrew Literature: Critical Discussions of Six Modern Texts* (2003). And some five years later, he published an expanded version of a collection of stories by S. Y. Agnon that he had earlier coedited with Ann Golomb Hoffman, *A Book That Was Lost: Thirty-Five Stories* (2008, originally published in 1995).

His true preoccupation during this period was the monumental book I mentioned in passing earlier, *Sanctuary in the Wilderness: A Critical Introduction to American Hebrew Poetry*, which he published in 2012, after working on it for over a decade. In one sense, Mintz's study of the American Hebraist movement and its poetry was a partial payment for the personal debt he felt he owed for the education he had received in Hebrew school as a child in Worcester and especially as a teenager when he attended the Prozdor program run by the Boston Hebrew College. But his investment in Hebraism was more than a sentimental debt. As he wrote in the preface to the book, the actual spark that ignited the project was "the exhilaration and frustration" he had come to feel after teaching Hebrew language and literature in American universities for a number of years, when he began to ask himself what it meant to teach Hebrew in America. Most specifically, what did it mean to be immersed in a language and literary culture at a geographic remove from its center in Israel? He was well aware of the deficient state of Hebrew literacy in America, and of the typically American belief that everything can be conveyed in translation. What did that mean for Jewishness? In seeking answers to these questions, Mintz was reminded of the Hebraists, *tarbut 'ivrit* as they called their movement, and their attempts to create a vigorous Hebrew culture in America. Even though their project had not succeeded, as Mintz knew well it had not, its failure might shed light on our current situation.

The achievement of *Sanctuary in the Wilderness* was not a solution to the predicament of Hebrew in contemporary America, but the retrieval of an entire chapter in the history of modern Hebrew literature that had been all but lost. This was no small accomplishment. In a book over five hundred pages long, Mintz wrote substantial essays on the literary careers of twelve American Hebrew poets as well as separate chapters exploring thematic clusters—with titles such as "California Gold," "In the Tents of Cush"—that dominated their poetry. The lead essay in the volume is an extended analysis of an extraordinary poem, "Ḥaquqot otiyyotayikh" ("Engraved are thy letters"), an ode to the Hebrew language, by the poet Abraham Regelson, in which Mintz explored the eroticized passion that the American Hebraists felt for Hebrew, "a religious—libidinal attachment" to the language that was the "motor of desire" behind American Hebrew poetry. What emerged from this passion, as Mintz demonstrates, was a vision and conception of the Hebrew language and of Hebrew literature that was markedly different than the one developed by Zionist writers in Mandate Palestine and later the State of Israel during the same period. For the latter, Hebrew was a medium for national reinvention in their own land. For the American Hebraists (who were no less Zionist than their peers on the other side of the Mediterranean), Hebrew was the DNA of Jewish culture, the secret of Jewish continuity, a bridge between religiosity and secularism, between Jewish values and American materialism. What the American Hebraists represented, in other words, and what Mintz's book sought to recover, was an alternative vision, a path not taken for modern Hebrew literature, but certainly one to be known, remembered, and appreciated.

Mintz's next project—the last he completed before his untimely death—consisted of several parts. This project, too, was an act of retrieval, and its origins also went back to the beginnings of Mintz's career as a student of modern Hebrew literature. It will be recalled that the first paper Mintz wrote in Hebrew—while he was a college student in the courses he took at the Jewish Theological Seminary—was on S. Y. Agnon. That Agnon remained his *ahavat ne'urim*, his first love, is demonstrated by our decision to publish the series of essays on Agnon that Mintz wrote throughout the length of his career. This new project was also an act of correction on Mintz's part for an omission he had made in the course of writing *Hurban*. While researching and writing the last section of the book on responses to catastrophe in modern Hebrew literature written in Israel (either during the Mandate period or after the establishment of the State), he had accepted the consensus view that, with a few notable exceptions—Uri Zvi Greenberg, Dan Pagis, and Aharon Appelfeld—the most important Israeli novelists and poets had avoided the Holocaust as a subject. Agnon, he acknowledged, was a partial exception inasmuch as he had written a few stories that touched upon the Holocaust, but within the totality of the Agnon corpus, Mintz still felt justified in arguing that the Holocaust was not one of the writer's major preoccupations.

In the intervening years since writing *Hurban*, Mintz realized he had been wrong. The Holocaust, the destruction of European Jewry, *had been* a dominant obsession of Agnon's literary imagination from the middle of the 1950's until his death in 1970. In the course of those years, Agnon wrote but never completed a massive compilation of intertwined stories called *'Ir U-Melo'ah* ("A City in Its Fullness"). This compilation served as a memorialization of Buczacz, the city in Galicia (in present–day Western Ukraine), in which he had been born and grew up. In these stories, Agnon re-created the daily lives of the city's vibrant Jewish population from its formation until the outbreak of the Holocaust. This imaginative re-creation—Agnon himself described it as "building a city"—was the great writer's response to the Holocaust, and it was this project of re-creation that also turned out to be the subject of Mintz's own final project.

The project in its entirety actually proceeded in three stages. It began with a pilot experiment he conducted with Rabbi James Diamond, a Ph.D. in Hebrew Literature and adjunct professor, who was also a brilliant translator and a scholar of modern Hebrew literature with a particular fascination with Agnon. This first project featured a key novella from "A City in Its Fullness," translated by Diamond, along with a lengthy essay about the novella written by Mintz, published under the title, *A Parable and Its Lesson*. Satisfied with this initial success, the two embarked on translating the greater part of *A City in Its Fullness*. Tragically, midway through the project, Diamond was killed in a car accident. Mintz ultimately decided to complete the project by enlisting numerous colleagues from America and Israel to finish the translations, and *A City in Its Fullness*, coedited with Jeffrey Saks, was published in 2016. The third and most important part of the overall project was Mintz's own study of *'Ir U-Melo'ah*, a monograph entitled *Ancestral Tales*, published in 2017.

Although many of the volume's stories were published serially throughout the 1950's and 60's, *'Ir U-Melo'ah* was first published in 1973, three years after Agnon's death, edited by Agnon's daughter, Emunah Yaron, following her father's plan for the volume. The book's initial reception was mixed. While Agnon enthusiasts predictably greeted its appearance with great excitement, the larger Israeli critical establishment did not quite know what to make of it; the stories seemed old-fashioned, sentimental, too old-worldish, especially amid the anxious tribulations following the Yom Kippur War. And so, the book languished. More recently, closer to the time Mintz began working on the novel, some critics and scholars had begun to pay greater attention to it. In Spring 2015, Mintz organized a distinguished working group at the Institute for Advanced Studies at The Hebrew University in Jerusalem consisting of leading scholars of literature and history from America, Israel, and Eastern Europe to study the book collaboratively in its different aspects.

The guiding inspiration behind the working group was Mintz's intuitive grasp of 'Ir U-Melo'ah as a genuine response to the Holocaust, indeed as a *modernist* response. One of Mintz's most original and compelling points is his demonstration of how Agnon—because of the constraints and requirements of the material he was working with—had to relinquish the autobiographical narrative persona he had developed through the course of his career and fashion a new narratorial voice. This new narrator was a thoroughly modernist creation: at once authoritative, omniscient, and unreliable.

Mintz's reading of 'Ir U-Melo'ah as a response to the Holocaust had multiple effects. For one thing, it redefined the genre of Holocaust literature, for this novel was not about the Destruction itself, but about the world that had been destroyed, narrated from a point *after* the destruction. Viewing Agnon's re-creation of Bucacz in its fullness as a response to the destruction also served to reintegrate Agnon's "late" work into the complete Agnonian oeuvre, and in effect redefined its overall shape. Mintz's intention clearly was to make it difficult, if not impossible, for future readers of Agnon to overlook, let alone miss, A City in Its Fullness when evaluating Agnon's literary career. In this respect, Ancestral Tales was analogous to what Mintz had accomplished in Sanctuary in the Wilderness, since both of these works of literary criticism altered the accepted canon of modern Hebrew literature.

This was not, however, the end of Mintz's deep involvement with Agnon. In the brief period after he completed Ancestral Tales, Mintz turned to another project on Agnon, one that he hoped would have a more personal, autobiographical dimension. The idea was to write a literary biography of Agnon drawing upon the writer's autobiographical fiction but also invoking the actual places, persons, and events from which the fictions derived. And Mintz himself was to play an active role in this biography as its narrator. Unfortunately, he was able to complete only the first chapter of this book, a remarkable chapter about Agnon's childhood based on Agnon's autobiographical stories. It is the first selection in our volume, and we are proud to be the first to publish it.

The subsequent five essays in this volume all deal with different texts by Agnon. We have sequenced them in the order of their publication to give a sense of how Mintz progressed in his views about the writer and because the essays themselves often reflect self-consciously upon his changing views. The first essay, "Agnon in Jaffa: The Myth of the Artist as a Young Man," is a study of three early stories Agnon wrote when he first emigrated to Palestine. These stories do not fit neatly into the persona that Agnon fashioned for himself as a mature writer, and Agnon revised them later in his career. Mintz's essay deals with these revisions, Agnon's refashioning of himself through the act of rewriting, a subject that had deep personal interest for Mintz himself, as we shall see shortly.

The second essay in the series is a review of the English translation of *Shira*, the first of Agnon's novels to be published posthumously. The review is an important statement by Mintz about Agnon's late work as a writer when it is read together with *Ancestral Tales* as twin studies of *'Ir U-Melo'ah* and *Shira*. The third essay, "In the Seas of Youth," is a fascinating study, and not only because it offers an original reading of an important novella, *In the Heart of the Sea*. This novella was also the subject of the very first essay that Mintz wrote in Hebrew for Avraham Holtz's Hebrew literature class at the Seminary when he was an undergraduate at Columbia, and it was also the subject of the first essay he published in English on Agnon, which was in fact a revised and expanded translation of the original Hebrew paper (it was published in the first issue of *Response* in 1967). Mintz used his essay on *In the Heart of the Sea* as an occasion to explore both the novella and how his own relation to the novella, its reading, and to Agnon more generally, had changed over nearly forty years of reading Hebrew literature.

The fourth essay, "On 'The Sense of Smell' by S. Y. Agnon," which analyzes a short narrative by the same name, came out of the symposium Mintz ran at Brandeis in 1999 that eventually produced the book called *Reading Hebrew Literature*, mentioned earlier. The essay is a classic example of *explication de texte* and displays Mintz's mastery of the academic genre. The final essay in this Agnon section, "Reading *Haḥazanim*," is the first article Mintz wrote about *'Ir U-Melo'ah*, and it allows the reader to see how he began working out his ideas about the new narratorial voice that Agnon eventually developed for this collection.

The next group of five essays deals with different moments in modern Hebrew literature—moments that Mintz either did not deal with in one of his monographs or that treat other aspects of topics he had written about. The first of these essays was written as a lengthy review about a book on Haskalah autobiography. This was of course the subject of Mintz's monograph, *Banished From Their Father's Table*, but Mintz used the review essay as an occasion to situate the literary question of autobiographical writing within a larger theoretical frame and chronological context that included premodern quasi-autobiographical accounts as well as Holocaust memoirs and contemporary autobiographical Israeli fictional texts. The ultimate point of the review essay is to explore the meaning and place of autobiographical writing in modern Jewish literature. The second essay in the section deals with Ahad Ha-Am's singular use of the essay as a genre and how he used the literary form as a tool to mediate between classical and modern Jewish traditions. The third essay treats Bialik's classic anthology, *Sefer Ha-Aggadah* (The Book of Legends), from the perspective of two key works the poet wrote in the aftermath of completing the monumental collection—his late poem "*Lifnei Aron Ha-Sefarim*" ("Before the Bookcase") and his essay, "On Anthologizing the Aggadah." As Mintz shows, in the essay Bialik set out both the goals and challenges he and his coeditor Yehoshua Hana Ravnitzky met in compiling their anthology, while in the poem he articulated the emotional and spiritual price he paid in giving up poetry for the work of anthologizing. In this way, Mintz sought to show how the two literary statements lay bare the deep cleavage in the modern Jewish literary imagination between personal and national projects of creative literary salvation.

The fourth and fifth essays in this section both deal with contemporary Israeli literature. "Israeli Literature in the Minds of American Readers," originally appeared as a stand-alone essay in 1997, and was later revised and expanded into the introduction to his collection, *Translating Israel* (2001). Even twenty years after its publication, it remains strikingly perceptive, and one of the very few full accounts of the reception of Israeli literature in America. The fifth and final essay in this group is a lengthy celebration of the Israeli poet Haim Gouri that appeared in the *Jewish Review of Books* on the occasion of Gouri's ninetieth birthday. Among the most important literary figures of his generation in Israel, Gouri was (and remains) much less known in America, but he was a writer for whom Mintz felt an especially close personal rapport, and one whom he felt needed to be introduced to an American audience. The essay displays Mintz's truly intimate familiarity with the Israeli literary world. Colleagues in Israel consider it one of the best portraits written about Gouri in any language.

The final group of four essays in the volume deal with Hebrew literature and larger thematic issues. The first article in this group, "Viva Voce: Vicissitudes of the Spoken Word in Hebrew Literature," deals specifically with the representation of spoken speech in modern Hebrew literature, particularly in comparison to the role spoken speech plays in contemporaneous Yiddish literature, but the particular topic leads Mintz to range over a wide spectrum of topics, from the roots of spokenness in the Oral Torah of the Rabbis to the ubiquity of monologues (and the relative absence of dialogue) in modern Israeli literature. The second essay, "Knocking on Heaven's Gate: Hebrew Literature and Wisse's Canon," is ostensibly a pointed critique of Ruth Wisse's attempt to construct a canon of modern Jewish literature, but it raises far more interesting questions about the place of modern Hebrew literature within that canon and the question of translatability, canonization, and readership, particularly in America. The third essay in the section, "Modern Hebrew Literature and Jewish Theology: Repositioning the Question," was originally written for a conference in the mid-1980s. It explores a connection that was at the heart of some of his earliest efforts in Jewish Studies, including a chapter he wrote for the landmark Jewish literary guidebook, *Back to the Sources* (1984), that dealt with the liturgy and prayerbook and their theological significance. In this essay, Mintz sought to show that modern Hebrew literature could serve as an untapped source of theological insight, both for its critique of the false ideologies of modern Jewish (and specifically Israeli) culture and, by virtue of its detachment from the tradition, because of its honest and forthright depiction of the struggle between faith and apostasy.

Mintz's final essay in this volume, "Hebrew in America: A Memoir," is remarkable in several respects. For one thing, it is one of the few openly autobiographical essays that Mintz wrote. In general, Mintz did not write about himself, at least not explicitly. He honed a literary voice that was immediately recognizable as only his, possessed of a richness of language and detail and the kinds of insights that come only from the intense personal experience of reading literature closely, even intimately. But he never used this voice as a medium for self-advertisement. In "Hebrew in America," he wrote very frankly about his insecurities as a scholar of modern Hebrew literature (in particular as an American in the field), but he also attempted to give a very fair evaluation of his accomplishments and his motivations in becoming a student and teacher of modern Hebrew literature.

I want to conclude this introduction by placing Mintz's career as a scholar of Jewish Studies within a larger frame. Since its inception in *Die Wissenschaft des Judentums*, Jewish Studies (as many have recognized) has always been driven by two impulses. One impulse has been a desire to serve the Jewish people, either by using the academic study of Jews, Judaism, and Jewish culture to effect reform or revitalization or renewal (and for some, alas, to give Judaism "a decent burial," in Moritz Steinschneider's famous formula). The other impulse has been a more individualistic one on the part of Jewish Studies scholars: as a path of identity, for their own personal fulfillment and self-realization as Jews in place of the more traditional models which had ceased to work for them. Both impulses have always been active in the field, but it is fair to say that while the first—the impulse to use Jewish Studies to contribute to the future of Jewish culture—was predominant in the earlier phases of Jewish Studies, the second impulse has become more dominant over the last half-century.

Mintz was a kind of throw-back to the earlier phase of Jewish Studies. He put aside the Victorian novel for modern Hebrew literature because he wanted to make a contribution to Jewish culture. Like his American Hebraist predecessors, he always saw the Hebrew language—and by extension, Hebrew literature—as the key to the survival of Judaism in America. Mintz liked to say that Hebrew was the DNA of Jews; it was certainly part of his DNA, as was service. It was these twin commitments to Hebrew *and* service that led him, in 2001, to leave Brandeis and join the faculty of the Jewish Theological Seminary of America in New York City as the Chana Kekst Professor of Hebrew Literature, so that he could create a Hebrew Honors Program for undergraduates and make his vision of Hebrew literacy a reality.

Scholarship, too, for Mintz was a form of service—to the community, to Jewry at large, perhaps even to God. So, too, was Mintz's personal and professional generosity, his collegiality toward all, and his unflagging support, both to colleagues and students. All his friends knew of his great culinary skills, as a master chef who loved to cook and prepare elaborate and delicious meals with extraordinary skill and true brilliance. But what Mintz loved most about cooking was *serving* the meals, feeding his guests, giving them pleasure. And this was why he felt that scholarship could serve the purpose of service—because it could nourish and sustain. And for this reason, devotion to scholarship as service, he was repeatedly led back to Agnon. In "Hebrew in America," he explained why he felt Agnon was so important, especially for Jews in America. Agnon, he wrote, ". . . provides a bridge that teaches in two directions. It connects Zion and the Jewish State to the culture of the Diaspora, and it connects modern Hebrew writing to the Talmud, the Midrash, *piyyut,* medieval philosophy, Hasidic tales, and the other producers of premodern Jewish civilization. For us American Jews, Agnon's expansive embrace is particularly relevant because, unlike our Israeli counterparts, we did not have the great either/or between religion and secularity forced upon us."

More than any other modern Hebrew writer, Agnon—Mintz believed—could contribute to the future of American Jewry, if only there were a scholar who could translate Agnon's message into the American idiom, who could be the bridge between the Hebrew text and the American reader. I am certain that Mintz had much more to articulate, both to himself and to others, as to what exactly Agnon could teach and contribute to American Jewry, how that writer's uniquely expansive embrace and imaginative genius could demonstrate the relevance of literature in a beleaguered and dim time like ours. There is not a doubt in my mind that had Alan lived longer, he would have succeeded fully in elaborating his vision of Agnon's importance and meaningfulness to our lives. This is only a small part of the loss we sustained with his untimely death. *Yehi zikhro barukh.*

NOTE

I want to thank Beverly Bailis, David Roskies, Barry Holtz, Jeffrey Saks, and Kathryn Hellerstein for reading earlier drafts of this introduction and offering many helpful suggestions as well as providing me with important biographical information about Alan Mintz's life and intellectual career.

# CHAPTER 1

# Agnon's Childhood

The day I visited Buczacz in 2012 happened to be August 24th, the Ukrainian national day, the day that marks independence from the Soviet Union.[1] Blue and yellow flags hung over the shops, and women in embroidered peasant blouses and men carrying hampers strolled with their children in the fair weather on their way to picnics and celebrations. Buczacz is a small city in the Ternopil Oblast, about 90 miles southeast of Lviv. It has always been a market town for the surrounding agricultural hinterlands. Buczacz has its charms. The River Strypa, a tributary of the Dniester, runs among the hills upon which the town is built, and several distinguished buildings recall Buczacz's earlier rulers. For centuries the town was wholly owned by a single Polish noble family, the Potockis. After the Partition of Poland in 1772, it passed into the hands of the Austrians as part of the province of Galicia. It remained an eastern outpost of the Austro-Hungarian Empire until World War I, when it was incorporated into the independent state of Poland. During World War II, Buczacz changed hands several times between the Red Army and the Nazi Army, and then emerged after the war as part of the Ukrainian Soviet Socialist Republic. It remained under Soviet rule until the August day in 1991, whose 21st anniversary was being colorfully celebrated around me.

The citizens of Buczacz are descendants of the Ruthenian peasants, who were colonized by Polish nobles, called magnates, in the sixteenth century. The Jews were brought in to administer their great estates, market agricultural produce, import manufactured goods, and, as contractors called arrendators, to help the magnates profit from the lumber in their forests, the mill power of their streams, and, most famously, the grain of their fields, which was turned into alcohol and sold to the peasants. The Ruthenians occupied the bottom rung of a three-tiered social structure in which the Jews were in the middle, with the Polish nobles on top. The three groups were differentiated by extremes of wealth and literacy, as well as by different languages, religions, and political prerogatives. Most Ruthenians were serfs whose labor was owned by the local magnate; Jews constituted a corporate estate with limited protections and onerous tax burdens; most Poles enjoyed wide privileges constrained only by the will of the magnate, whose word was law. When the Kingdom of Poland was dissolved toward the end of the eighteenth century, a fourth rung was added: Austrian provincial officials, who administered laws promulgated from Vienna. The powers of the magnates were curbed, and in 1848 serfdom was abolished. In the final decades of the Austro-Hungarian Empire, the Ruthenians of Galicia came to see themselves as Ukrainians pursuing national ambitions in intense competition with Polish national ambitions.

Over the course of the long, bloody twentieth century, this pyramid was inverted. During World War I, the Jewish communities of Galicia were decimated by widespread pogroms, and during World War II, the Jews of the region were murdered by the Nazi mobile killing units aided by local Ukrainian helpers. Most of the Polish nobles were killed by the Soviets in 1939–1941, and the general Polish population of the region underwent ethnic cleansing by Ukrainian nationalists at the end of the war. By 1947 there were almost no Poles left. The town, which had once been the easternmost outpost of a European empire, was now on the westernmost border of the vast Ukrainian state. With independence from Moscow in 1991, Ukrainians had come full circle after centuries of subjugation and became their own masters. The vulnerability of that independence, however, was demonstrated by the Russian annexation of the Crimea in 2014.

As I wander around Buczacz on this August day, it is this uniform Ukrainianness that I find so striking. True, there are visible reminders of earlier regimes. The ornate Rathaus or Town Hall and the massive Basilian

Monastery were erected by Count Mikolaj Potocki in the mid-eighteenth century. The stolid Gymnasium was built by the Austrians. But when it comes to the Jews, aside from an overgrown cemetery, there is no trace. The Great Synagogue, a monumental building in its own right, was torn down together with the study houses and other communal buildings. Where they once stood in the town center there is a sprawl of small shops and petty enterprises today. As something of a Jewish nationalist myself, I can understand the pleasure the Ukrainians take in speaking their own language and practicing their own religion on their own land. What is harder for me to fathom is that Jews lived among them for over four hundred years, yet now it is as if they had never existed. When it comes to the young families gathering lazily for celebrations of their national holiday, one cannot expect them to recall what took place over seventy years ago. But their elders have found it convenient to make the presence of the Jews—and the Poles, for that matter—into a passing episode, a matter of foreign bodies that the rich Ukrainian soil has opened up and swallowed. The strolling couples might be surprised to know that in 1870 Jews comprised 67.9% of the town's population and that the mayor of Buczacz, from 1879 to 1921, was a Jew named Bernard (Berish) Stern.

I've come to Buczacz in search of Agnon. Here he was born in 1887 and he lived here until he was twenty, when he left for Palestine. Although this is my first visit, Buczacz has been in my head for many years. Many of Agnon's stories and two of his novels are set in this town, and recently my academic work has focused on a great cycle of stories about Buczacz that Agnon wrote during the last fifteen years of his life. The stories were published as a book called *A City in Its Fullness*, three years after his death. During the course of the research, my imagination was taken over and colonized by those stories. As a young reader I lived vividly within Stevenson's adventure novel *Treasure Island* and came to know each craggy hill and mysterious cove on the island traversed by Jim Hawkins and Long John Silver. In a similar way, the town of Buczacz laid itself out, and became a richly detailed virtual reality long before my visit to this spot in Ukraine. My adolescent reading days are long behind me. But Agnon's Buczacz tales satisfied in me a similar need, a long existing desire to be catapulted backward in time and allowed to peer into the world of my forefathers in Eastern Europe, long before modernity and emigration. As a grown-up reader it was not adventure that I craved but authenticity. The stories delivered that commodity in abundance, as well

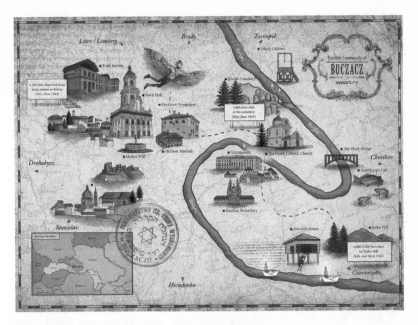

FIG. 1.1  Literary Map of Buczacz. Map used with permission from The Toby Press LLC, from *A City in Its Fullness*, ed. Alan Mintz and Jeffrey Saks (Toby Press, 2016).

as offering the tang of great fiction. In their epic abundance, they created an imaginative world of their own, a world I was happy to lose myself in.

A truly imagined world demands a map like the one I had found in *Treasure Island*. When I was preparing an English edition of the Buczacz stories, I sat down with a graphic designer in Jerusalem to draw a literary map of Buczacz (fig. 1.1).[2]

The map projects onto a spatial plane the tales that crowded my mind's eye. There is the Icarus-like figure of the architect, Theodore, trying to escape from the tower of the great Town Hall he has designed and in which Count Potocki has locked him up to die to prevent him from creating any grander building. There are the gallows on which the innocent youth, Yekele, was hanged by the Austrian authorities because of the whim of a Jewish oligarch he had insulted. There, at the bottom, is the one-room house on stilts built by Feivush, the thug who collects the loathed candle tax from his fellow Jewish townspeople. Above it, to the right, are the frogs that consummated the humiliation of a wealthy man who sought to circumvent the community's boycott against the high price of fish. And, speaking of fish, there is the mightiest finned creature to ever swim the waters of the Strypa, and it is wearing the *tefilin* of a gluttonous money lender. There, on the Strypa, float candles stuck in paper boats to light the way for drowned martyrs to recite penitential prayers in the weeks before the New Year. And, jumping ahead to the middle of the twentieth century, there are the cemetery, the Fedor Hill and the train station, where the Jews of Buczacz were murdered or deported.

Because for so long Buczacz has been living vividly in my mind's eye, seeing the real place is disorienting and dispiriting. Everything is small and shabby! The mighty Strypa is a mere stream, and it looks as if you could leap over it if you got a running start. The commercial center, where the Great Synagogue once bordered the marketplace, is a hodgepodge of graceless shops. After hearing Agnon so often refer to Buczcacz as *'iri*, my city, I see with my own eyes that it is really a very small town. Topography provides some small comfort, though. I'm moved to see the Strypa, even if diminished, as well as the famous hills surrounding the town, especially the Fedor Hill. The land endures, even if the Jews who once walked upon it are no more. I knew that the disappearance of those Jews would weigh on me, but I had hoped that the genius of the place would still speak to me.

The true source of my letdown, I realize, is the inevitable gap between an intensely evoked fictional world and the reality of place. I probably would have found even the Caribbean atoll that served as the model for *Treasure Island* to be a disappointment. The same dejection set in when I visited Dublin after having avidly consumed *Ulysses*. I walked by the slate grey Liffy and lay in a hotel bed on Eccles Street while the rain poured down and wondered, "Is this it?"

It might seem laughable that Dublin comes to my mind when I think about Buczacz, but I see an essential connection. Both Joyce and Agnon are writers who exiled themselves from the cities of their birth and youth only to spend the rest of their lives writing about them. In both cases, the motive was neither nostalgia nor obsession but rather a fundamental modernist paradox: Universal truths about the human condition can be grasped only by drilling down into the bedrock of particularity. There are no shortcuts. We have to find out ALL about Dublin before we can get at the themes of sonship, fatherhood, language and compassion. And when it comes to Buczacz, we have to learn ALL about the customs and the controversies and the rabbis before we can understand the essence of Galician Jewry in its greatness and in its decline. It would of course be silly to say that the two cities are comparable. Dublin won a place in the literary firmament because of Joyce, but it remains a formidable presence even without him. Without Agnon, however, Buczacz would have little claim on our attention.

Yet the fact is that Agnon chose Buczacz, and I'm fascinated by the power of that act. Of the dozens and dozens of Galician cities and towns of equivalent or greater stature, Agnon chose Buczacz and endowed it with a kind of immortality. Standing amidst the hills of Buczacz on this August day, my mind generates an even more heretical analogy. I think about Worcester, Massachusetts, the community in which I was born and raised until I left at about the same age that Agnon left Buczacz. At their heights, both Worcester and Buczacz had Jewish populations of about 10,000, and like Buczacz, Worcester was just one of a number of modest New England cities like Springfield, Hartford and Providence that existed in the shadow of a metropolis, Boston. If I had greater talents, and if I placed them in the service of bringing to the Jewish community of Worcester in all its universality and particularity life on the page, would Worcester live forever in the minds of readers? The comparison is fatuous, I know, and not a little deluded, but it helps me to establish a point of personal contact as I gaze at the Ukrainian landscape. I understand that Agnon's decision to ennoble Buczacz was not first and foremost an homage to his native town. Buczacz was being built up and reinforced so that it could bear the weight of standing for a civilization as a whole. And also, so that it could serve as a suitable cradle for the birth of the artist who gave it imaginative life.

The sleight of hand concerning the date of Agnon's birth is an excellent introduction to the author's lifelong devotion to shaping and reshaping his autobiographical persona. Shmuel Yosef Czaczkes (later Agnon) was born on the 18th of Av, according to the Hebrew calendar, which was August 8 in 1887. Yet throughout his life, he averred that he was born on the 9th of Av, the summer fast day commemorating the destruction of the Jerusalem temples called Tisha b'Av.[3] Why would one choose to identify with such a doleful occasion? The answer is that according to a talmudic tradition, Tisha b'Av is the birthday of the Messiah because the darkest point of catastrophe contains within it the seed of deliverance. Agnon was never shy about his genius and its significance. He not only synchronized his personal history with the fate of the Jewish people but viewed his art as necessary to its redemption.

Is this a sign of delusional grandiosity or assured self-assessment? This is a question that Agnon's life and work force us to return to again and again.

Agnon was the eldest of five children born to Shalom Mordechai Halevi Czaczkes (1859–1913) and Esther Farb (1864/5–1908). Esther was born in Buczacz, the daughter of Yehudah Farb, a merchant in furs and leather and a supplier of manufactured goods to distilleries. The family was well off, and Yehudah Farb played an important role in the leadership of the community as well as being renowned for his devotion to Talmud study. Agnon's father, Shalom Mordechai, originally came from Zalozhtsy near Ternopil and settled in Buczacz when he married Esther. He was a promising Torah scholar, who received rabbinic ordination, but when he married, he gave up thoughts of the rabbinate and became a merchant in furs like his father-in-law. He maintained a shop in Buczacz and traveled widely in order to market his furs and acquire new merchandise.

In order to understand Agnon's early life and education it is necessary to grasp the uniqueness of Galician Jewry at the end of the nineteenth century. When Poland was partitioned in 1772, the Russian Empire and the Austrian Empire each suddenly found itself for the first time ruling over large populations of Jews. Most of the images we have of East European Jewry from this time come from life under the increasingly autocratic and xenophobic regime of the Tsars: economic privation, censorship, exclusion from public life and higher education, and pogroms. The Habsburg monarchs, on the other hand, were enlightened absolutists who affirmed the multi-ethnic nature of their empire. True, there were conversionary pressures exerted on the Jews, as well as the imposition of special taxes; and the refusal to invest in the industrialization of Galicia left the province poor. But Jews, like other minorities, were granted religious freedom and, in 1867, the franchise to vote in regional elections. There were no pogroms. Jews enjoyed free movement within the empire and were allowed to settle in Vienna, which, over the course of the nineteenth century, became a great metropolis with a large Jewish community. The universities in Vienna were filled with Jewish students who had come from the provinces. Anti-Semitism in its modern racialist form was a force to reckon with. But it did not prevent Jews from becoming leading figures in the arts and a range of professions. Let the career of Sigmund Freud, whose family had roots in Buczacz, serve as evidence.

This meant a degree of security and stability for the Jews of Buczacz, who made up a majority of the town and were represented on its town council. Within the Jewish community this was also a time of eased tensions. Early in the nineteenth century, Galician Jewry had been torn apart by sectarian conflict. The long-established regimes of Talmud study and synagogue custom and communal authority had been challenged and undermined by the propulsive spread of Hasidism and its popular, enthusiastic spirituality. The rabbinic establishment, whose members were called *mitnagdim* (sing. *mitnaged*), was attacked from a different angle by small groups of modernizing intellectuals called *maskilim* who sought the inclusion of history, science, and languages into the traditional Jewish schoolroom, and who, above all, abhorred what they viewed as the superstitious obscurantism of the followers of Hasidism (*Hasidim*). That strife, which in its time convulsed communities and split families apart, had subsided into entente and accommodation. Take the Czaczkes family, for example. Agnon's maternal grandfather, Yehudah Farb, was a confirmed *mitnaged* and a stalwart of the Old Beit Midrash, a man for whom the study of the Talmud was the sole pinnacle of Jewish learning. Agnon's father, on the other hand, in addition to being an accomplished Talmudist, was a Hasid and a follower of the Chortkiv Rebbe (Chortkiv is about 23 miles east of Buczacz). Agnon would accompany his father to the local Hasidic prayer house and on occasion took trips to the Rebbe's court in Chortkiv. But the boy would also pray with his grandfather in the Old Beit Midrash. He could do both without conflict because the old battle lines had receded, and the two camps had made common cause against the forces of modernization and westernization that were threatening the world of traditional study and observance.

These boundaries were more permeable than we might imagine today. Despite the piety of Yehuda Farb's household, his daughter, Esther, was allowed to learn German, and she became very fond of German poetry, especially Schiller. Her own daughters, Agnon's sisters, were sent to a Polish-language school, without apparent protest by her father, the Talmudist. There was a curious double standard in place that allowed girls an exposure to gentile culture, whereas boys were expected to hue to the curriculum of classic Jewish studies, at least publicly. Agnon read German poetry with his mother and was given a private tutorial in German with a teacher from the local Baron de Hirsch school. Altogether, from our vantage point in the twenty-first century, it is not easy to grasp the nuances of Jewish life in Buczacz in the 1890s. We tend to see an intensely learned and believing traditional community that is the opposite of our acculturated, multicultural world with its fringe of ultra-Orthodox Jews, who maintain a connection to that pre-enlightenment world of centuries ago. This picture is inaccurate at almost every level. But rather than trying to correct the perception of a whole era, I seek to be precise about Agnon's Buczacz.

Most all the Jewish families of Buczacz remained traditional. The term Orthodox does not truly apply because, in contrast to Germany, there was no Reform movement that dissented from the communal consensus. Most all Jewish boys were educated in a *ḥeder*, in which the language of instruction was Yiddish and only Jewish subjects were taught. Most all Jewish males owned a seat in one of the town's synagogues and appeared there every Sabbath, if not every day. Nevertheless, these same Jews—men and women alike—were very aware of great changes in the larger world and at home. Yiddish and Hebrew newspapers, which began to circulate widely in mid-century, reported on world politics and the fate of far-flung Jewish communities, as well as the Galician scene. Zionist clubs and organizations were active in Buczacz, and the whole community closely followed Theodore Herzl's proclamations and diplomatic maneuvers; his death in 1904 occasioned anguished communal mourning. Smaller groups of Jewish anarchists and socialists advocated their positions and tried to win souls among servants and the working classes. Since the granting of the franchise in 1867, party politics became a noisy, messy, and sometimes violent affair in Buczacz, especially in the run up to the elections to the regional assembly.

When it came to languages, Buczacz had its private and public spheres. In home life and worship, each group had its own language. The Poles spoke Polish among themselves and listened to the service in Latin and the sermon in Polish in their Roman Catholic churches. The Ukrainians spoke Ukrainian/Ruthenian, prayed in Church Slavonic and listened to their sermons in Ukrainian in their Greek Catholic churches. The Jews spoke Yiddish to each other and studied Hebrew/Aramaic sacred texts in Yiddish and recited prayers in Hebrew; well-educated men knew Hebrew and could read Hebrew newspapers and write letters in Hebrew. Despite these separate domains, the marketplace and the public square were of necessity a babel of languages. A Jewish man or woman who operated a shop would need to know enough Polish and Ruthenian to do business, and communal leaders would conduct their transactions with the government in German. Young men who studied in the gymnasium, many Jews among them, studied their subjects in Polish and were taught by teachers with strong Polish nationalist allegiances. Ambitious young men who sought a university education had to make a choice between the competing German and Polish cultural spheres. Members of a previous generation were likely to look in the direction of Vienna, as was the case with Agnon's older relation and Buczacz native, David Heinrich Müller, who became a professor of oriental languages at the University of Vienna. Polish universities were beginning to attract students as well, as was the case with another, younger relation of Agnon's, Emanuel Ringelblum, also a native of Buczacz, who went to Warsaw to obtain a doctorate in history and sociology and who later organized the famous Oyng Shabbos archive in the Warsaw Ghetto.

This is the hybrid world into which Agnon was born. He was raised within a family sphere that was strongly traditional and saturated with pride in scholarly ancestors. Piety was taken for granted and Torah learning deemed the highest value. At the same time, the boundaries of this sphere were permeable. As he grew up, he was increasingly exposed to contending non-Jewish cultures in Buczacz itself and to the assertion of modern political ideologies in the wider world.

This is what we know of Agnon's schooling. He began *ḥeder* at age three and was a pupil in three different *ḥadarim*. At age nine, he ceased studying in a classroom full of other children, and instead was tutored privately by his father. Because of his father's varied intellectual interests, the education received by the young Shmuel Yosef was broader than the norm for families in similar religious circles. To the usual concentration on Talmud, the father added exposures that reflected his own passions. Shalom Mordechai Czaczkes was attracted to the *aggadah*, the legendary and narrative sections of the Talmud, and not just to its legal portions. He had a lifelong devotion to the works of Maimonides and left a scholarly manuscript on the subject when he died. He read some poetry with his son, and he made him aware of Galician Hebrew writers. When he was twelve, Agnon studied for a year in the Old Beit Midrash with Rabbi Shmuel Yisakhar Shtark, an author of books on *halakhah* and *aggadah*.

Then he was free. After his bar mitzvah, Agnon studied on his own in the Old Beit Midrash. There were German lessons with the teacher from the Baron de Hirsch school, occasional sessions reading German poetry with his mother, and chances to sit with his father reading Hasidic texts in the prayer house of the Chortkiv Hasidim. But otherwise, Agnon was left to his own devices to make use of the extensive library in the Old Beit Midrash and educate himself. This freedom, so at odds with our usual notions of the restrictive regimen of yeshiva education, requires some explanation. The practice of sending academically gifted young men away to centers of advanced learning, such as the famous yeshivot of Volozhin and Slobotka, far to the north in Lithuania, was not the custom in Galicia, where students studied closer to home. In Agnon's particular case, the freedom he enjoyed was an expression of the trust his parents placed in him. They could trust him to apply himself assiduously to the study of the canon of rabbinic learning. That canon was understood broadly in Agnon's family, and that liberality gave him license to range freely over the highways and byways of Jewish classical writing. He was like a graduate student granted access to the open stacks of a great university library and allowed to follow his interests wherever they led him. After discharging his debt to his Talmud studies, on a given day he could pick up the *Yeven Metsulah* and indulge a fascination with the Khmelnytsti persecutions of the seventeenth century or devote himself to the study of kabbalistic customs in the *Ḥemdat Yamim* or lose himself in the allegorical stories of Nahman of Bratslav. And then there was European literature itself, which he would read at home rather than in the beit midrash. He could manage some reading in German, but by the end of the nineteenth century, not a small number of the classics of German, French and English literatures had been translated into Hebrew or Yiddish. When Agnon was eleven, one of the first books he purchased with his pocket money was E. Salkinson's Hebrew translation of *Othello*. And then there was the growing library of modern literature written originally in Hebrew by M. H. Luzatto, M. Y. Levenson, A. Mapu, Y. Perl, and Sh. Y. Abramovitch.

From this formative period of free study, we can observe the emergence of three continuities in Agnon's life. To begin with, he had the soul of an autodidact. He was elusive of teachers and prescribed courses of study. Reading on his own and following his own interests fitted him perfectly. During his long sojourn in Germany, he read widely and voraciously, but he had no interest in the venerable universities that attracted so many other Jewish students from the East. Second, Agnon moved back and forth between sacred studies and modern literature with no feeling he was crossing a heretical boundary. He internalized the trust extended to him by his parents by trusting himself. He believed that all the artifacts of culture he consumed, sacred and worldly, were being distilled in the alembic of his art for a higher purpose. Third was his chronic, incurable bibliophilia. During World War I, Gershom Scholem, ten years Agnon's junior, came across Agnon going through the card catalogue of the Jewish library in Berlin. Asked what he was doing, Agnon answered, "I am trying to find a book I have not read." Agnon was a lifelong collector and *amateur* of Hebrew books. The formative trauma of his life was the destruction by fire of the library he had lovingly assembled in his home in Bad Homburg in 1924.

Of the titles of the books Agnon consumed during late childhood and adolescence with such intense and free-ranging curiosity, we know next to nothing. Our ability to make conjectures and to reconstruct something of his intellectual itinerary comes from the poems and stories that he himself wrote during these years. The fact he was writing literature means that he was reading literature and, like all fledgling writers, learning to write by imitation. Agnon started writing early. In a 1927 letter to M. A. Jacques, Agnon expresses delight and pride in his precociousness:

> When I was nine years old I wrote a ballad about a boy who lit candles and floated them on the river on the first night of *seliḥot*, which was the custom when I was a child, and about a water sprite in the form of a girl who took him away. Even before that I wrote a poem about missing my father when he was away on a journey. From then on I was like an unstinting fountain. Every day I wrote a formidable poem.[4]

Portrait of the artist as a young *graphomaniac*? Agnon is exaggerating only a little. From the time he turned sixteen in 1903, to his departure for Palestine five year later, this teenager published sixty items in the Hebrew and Yiddish press. He wrote many times that number, because for every piece that was accepted for publication many were rejected and many more held back and never submitted.

More surprising than this juvenile profusion is the very fact that this Talmud student, this denizen of the beit midrash, should be writing literature altogether. Make no mistake: Agnon was not writing liturgical poetry or pious tracts but literature in the modern secular sense we use the term. He was experimenting with writing not merely as a mode of self-expression but as a vocation, as a life's work. And we know from the fact that he succeeded in becoming a great writer that this was a defining moment in his young life. The hundreds of poems and stories he wrote during his adolescence, almost none of which he later chose to include in his published works, were in the service of a consolidating resolve to become a writer.

Agnon was not alone in this resolve. By the turn of the twentieth century, the emergence of a Hebrew writer from the chrysalis of a Talmud student was not an unprecedented phenomenon. Moshe Leib Lilienblum, Hayyim Nahman Bialik, Michah Yosef Berdichevsky, Mordechai Ze'ev Feierberg, Yosef Hayyim Brenner, and Uri Nissan Gnessin—in fact nearly all the pioneers of modern Hebrew literature—had made the same journey. They were raised in fervently devout homes and immersed in religious studies in their youth before turning to Hebrew writing. Yet Agnon's path was fundamentally different, and it is this difference that sets him apart from the course of Hebrew literature in the twentieth century and constitutes his greatness. It is therefore crucial first to understand the general paradigm in order to understand Agnon's distance from it. The collective biographical, generational experience of these young writers was rooted in rejection and rebellion. At a time when the authority of traditional society was already crumbling, these young Talmud students were secretly exposed to Enlightenment ideas and then to the new Hebrew writers. Unbeknownst to parents, in-laws, and wives, they underwent a crisis in which the plausibility of traditional faith and the observance of the commandments collapsed. For some, this crisis of faith was experienced as a loss, a vertiginous fall into a vacuum of meaning; for others, it was a welcome rite of passage and the sloughing off of an old skin. In all cases, the crisis inevitably triggered banishment from family and community and self-exile to the metropolis and the challenge of belatedly acquiring the rudiments of a secular education. Writing Hebrew literature became a way—often a tortured, existential way—of finding a modern voice outside the walls of the tradition but within the fold of the Jewish people. These writers were co-opted by the Zionist movement as pioneers in a national renaissance, but they themselves felt far from reborn. They were wary of ideological movements and doubly suspicious of the presumption of ideology to fill the role of religion.

How Agnon stands apart from his generation is a question of great complexity and great importance. It is one of the purposes of this biography to comprehend it. At this early stage, it can be said in the broadest strokes that Agnon's turn to Hebrew writing and his decision to leave Buczacz were different from the negations of the Hebrew writers of his generation. Surely there was much in the social and religious fiber of Buczacz as a provincial town in decline that elicited his antipathy and judgment and made it unthinkable as a staging ground for his literary career. Yet beneath and behind the compromised present, Agnon discerns in the traditions of learning and piety deep reservoirs of spiritual value. By virtue of his turn to writing and to the vocation of art, Agnon had become a citizen of modernity. Yet he understood his role as a modern Hebrew writer as restorative rather than rebellious. He would tell the truth about the depleted present, but he would also reimagine what was most enduring in the hoary religious civilization of Polish Jewry.

Here, then, is the fundamental difference. Agnon understood his turn toward Hebrew writing as an extension of his family heritage rather than as a rejection of it. By acceding to his vocation as a Hebrew writer, he was not fleeing from his duty to Jewish faith and learning but fulfilling it. This awareness must have been inchoate at this early point in Agnon's life. But it's worth jumping ahead for a moment to a much later stage in his career to see where this trajectory is leading. In the 1937 story, "The Sense of Smell," and again in his Nobel Prize acceptance speech in 1966, Agnon stressed his family's descent from the biblical tribe of Levi, whose task it was to care for the holy objects in the ancient Jerusalem sanctuary, and to sing sacred songs to accompany the temple service. When the Temple was destroyed, the vocation of sacred song was passed on to the great liturgical poets, the *payyetanim*, and later to the great *ḥazzanim*, the synagogue cantors. In the fallen age into which Agnon was born, song and poetry have been replaced by prose and storytelling. His art, therefore, is the perpetuation of his levitical lineage within the world of modernity.

To be sure, there is something self-serving in this schema. In one stroke Agnon succeeds both in minimizing the degree of breakage in becoming a modern writer and in elevating the role and bringing it on par with the great practitioners of the sacred arts from the past. Later in life, as Agnon disappeared into his persona as a pious sage, the master modernist sought to normalize and harmonize his relationship to religious tradition. In his eyes, writing modern fiction, as least in the way *he* practices it, is a continuation of the tradition of Jewish learning and sacred song fitted to the needs of the era. Now, even if we make adjustments for the later Agnon's grandiose sense of his place in Jewish history, we can learn something useful about Agnon the adolescent. Deciding to become an artist, instead of a rabbi or a learned shopkeeper, indeed meant taking a contrary and provocative stance toward the world of his birth, a stance that would inevitably require him to leave it behind. Nevertheless, both for Agnon himself and for those close to him, this provocation was muted by several factors.

The family, to begin with, delighted in his cleverness. The capacity to write verses was considered a gift rather than a satanic transgression. Agnon's father had written some poems, and there was a cousin named Hayim Czaczkes who published frequently in the Galician Jewish press. There was no necessary reason to think that writing verse was a heretical or irreligious act. In the summers, when Agnon would spend his days reading and writing in the forest, the family circle would gather in the evenings to hear him read aloud what had been written that day. Even his pious grandfather, Yehuda Farb, was gratified to see his grandson's writing appear in Yiddish and Hebrew newspapers. Another factor was the hospitality of the publishing venues. There were many regional and local Jewish newspapers in Galicia, most in Yiddish and some in Hebrew. The flourishing of a Jewish press was one of the major developments of the second half of the nineteenth century, and in Galicia there were none of problems with censorship that bedeviled publication efforts across the border in Russia. These newspapers were hungry for material from young writers, especially from traditionally minded writers like Agnon, who could provide seasonally appropriate stories and poems about Purim and Hanukah and other holidays. The exhilaration of seeing his name in print at such a young age could not help but make Agnon feel that he was talented and that even greater success would be his as he grew older and mastered his craft. The very plausibility of a life in letters was embodied by several figures who encouraged the young writer. Yitzhak Fernhof, a leading figure in the renaissance of Hebrew writing in Galicia, made his living as a teacher in Buczacz, and befriended the young Agnon. In 1906, Elazar Rokeah, the colorful descendent of a rabbinical family from Safed in the Galilee, began to publish a weekly called *Der Jüdische Wecker* in Buczacz and made Agnon his assistant. A much grander opportunity presented itself in the winter of 1907 when Agnon was invited to Lemberg to become the salaried assistant to Gershom Bader in putting out a new Hebrew weekly called *Ha'et*. Agnon spent two months in the great metropolis meeting other writers and Zionist leaders, in addition to performing his editorial duties and contributing his own writing. By March, however, *Ha'et* had failed, and Agnon returned to Buczacz unpaid. Nevertheless, the taste for the literary life had been acquired, and returning home must not have been easy.

A year later, Agnon boarded a ship in Trieste bound for Jaffa. He would return to Buczacz only twice over the course of his life. Yet before we let the young man proceed to the next station in his journey, it is worth pausing to reflect on how little we know about his childhood. We understand something of the family and its lineage against the background of the times; we have the outline of his schooling; we see his juvenile successes as a writer. Yet in the sixty or so precocious poems, stories, and sketches Agnon published before he left Buczacz, in Yiddish and Hebrew, there is almost nothing about himself, no self-portraiture, nothing that would open a portal to his inner experience as a child. Those early literary efforts are of considerable importance to Agnon scholars, who have turned them over to find early preoccupations that were developed in later works. The earlier writings are mostly imitative, and there is little there that would portend the emergence of a great talent. Agnon's own retrospective judgment on them was severe. In the 1926 letter to Jacques mentioned above, he writes, "The Lord be praised that from the verse I wrote as a child not one word has survived." (This statement was, however, false and Agnon knew so at the time.)

Yet, Agnon did not leave us empty handed. Between 1923 and 1938, Agnon wrote a series of extraordinary autobiographical stories that visit key moments in his childhood and adolescence. The publication dates of the stories from early to late follow the development of the autobiographical protagonist from early childhood to adolescence. The stories were placed as a unit by Agnon in the volume of his collected works titled *Eilu ve'eilu* ("These and Those"). It is to those stories we will now turn to seek a deeper look at Agnon's childhood. This act of looking backward, our looking backward at Agnon looking backward, is a gesture that will repeat itself in each stage of the author's life. This is because Agnon's autobiographical reflection takes place only at a remove in time and place from the lived experiences. Just as the treatment of childhood is deferred, the years spent in Ottoman Palestine are not returned to until Agnon arrives in Germany, and portraits of the artist in Germany do not arrive until the 1950s. This deferred autobiographical retrospect will form an essential component in our attempt to take Agnon's measure in each of the stations of his life. First the facts and then the belated refashioning of them.

Before turning to the stories of childhood, I will offer several gener-alizations about these retrospective fictions of self. They are, everywhere and always, just that: fictions. Agnon does not write memoir or "straight" autobiography, which are separate modes of writing in which historically real authors endeavor to describe their earlier historically real selves or render an account of episodes in their earlier lives. He is writing stories that do not aspire or pretend to be an objective portrayal of events. Neither do they aim to deliver a solely psychological truth that comes from an archeological exploration of the self and its earliest traumas and formative experiences. Rather, Agnon returns in his fiction to earlier stages in his life in order to fashion and elaborate his own self-myth. By the term self-myth, I do not mean the narcissistic management of image and reputation; I mean the purposeful construction of a symbolically laden narrative about the writer's life. This is the story of the writer's life he fashions and conveys to us, and its telling, with him squarely at the center, is justified not because he has achieved fame but because his life has representative importance. It has the potential to tell us something deep and universal about what is, or should be, most important to us.

The new Hebrew literature was replete with depictions of childhood, and it is only against this background that Agnon's stories come into their own. Bialik, Feierberg, and Brenner, together with Mordechai Aaron Ginsburg and Sh. Ben-Zion and others, wrote influential representations of child-hood (read: boyhood) that were all, in one way or another, extensions of the critique of traditional Jewish society. Singled out for excoriation was the *ḥeder* as a site in which the child's natural curiosity is quashed and his self-esteem, as well as his body, abused by boorish teachers. Performance and rote memorization confer approval rather than understanding and acuity. The sphere of religious experience is suffused with dread and superstition. Everyday life means suppressing the exuberance of childhood in order to avoid falling victim to the demonic forces of sin and impurity. The more promising a boy is as a budding scholar, the greater the likelihood that he will be treated like a valuable piece of merchandise, married off around the time of his bar mitzvah, ripped from his family and placed in the clutches of an acrimonious mother-in-law. If this is what early life is about, who could emerge from it unmaimed? Who would not rebel against it? Who would not revile the society in which it was rooted?

For his part, Agnon would not. But he does succeed in finding a place to stand apart from this nightmarish vision and to offer a more affirmative understanding of traditional Jewish experience. He manages this in part by avoiding the *ḥeder*, the synagogue, and the stringencies of ritual discipline, that is, those areas in which boys portrayed in the writing of other authors felt repressed, constrained, or abused. Agnon also makes the fundamental move of prising apart the degraded reality of Jewish society from energies and values that remain nurturing to the spirit. Furthermore, by availing himself of the child's point-of-view and its unique capacity for wonderment, Agnon is in fact able to reverse the oracles and elicit from childhood something very different from abasement and terror. The construction of childhood is always, in some fundamental sense, a retrojection of adult attitudes. The generality of Hebrew writers, who lost their faith during adolescence and rejected the claims of religious tradition, portrayed childhood as already shot through with the kind of delusions and interdictions that made apostasy all but inevitable. Agnon was speaking from a relationship to that tradition that was complex and ambivalent but certainly not hostile and rejecting. His conception of a childhood that led to his identity as an adult would therefore be very different from that of the other members of his generation. Finally, Agnon was lucky in his origins. He was born into a family that was financially comfortable and secure in its religious commitments yet not fanatical. He was an admired and trusted eldest child. Much trouble was taken over his early education, after which he was given freedom to pursue his own course. Buffered from the worst excesses of a contemporary Jewish childhood, Agnon was thus in the fortunate position of being able to assess his early life without the rancor and deprivation that were the lot of others.

The earliest memories of childhood in Agnon's autobiographical stories are connected to books as material objects. In the 1923 story, "My Grandfather's Talmud," the eponymous object of the title is the more-than-twenty oversized folios of the Babylonian Talmud. Yehudah Farb, Agnon's maternal grandfather, was renowned in Buczacz for the extraordinary feat of having completed the study of the entire Talmud eight times. The Talmud volumes that rested on the highest shelf in his bookcase were printed in Lemberg by Avraham Yitzhak Menkes, an edition known for its wide margins, good paper, and elaborate frontispiece illuminations. The grandfather ordered ten sets of this Talmud. As each tractate was printed, the narrator of the story delights in telling us, ten sets of unbound folios were shipped to Buczacz.

When all the folios had arrived, two bookbinders were summoned to take up residence for a week in the grandfather's home to assemble the sets, enclose them in sumptuous leather covers, and apply the gold leaf lettering for the titles. One set he kept for himself and installed on the uppermost shelf of the bookcase, and the remainder he donated to the *batei midrash* of the town.

It is not the mother and her breast that form the first memory but the bookcase and its contents.

> This bookcase was one of the first memories of my childhood. I remember when I was an infant being placed on the floor to crawl around on all fours. I once got myself to the bookcase, opened its doors and felt around inside. I sat there astounded to realize that what I thought was a single bloc was actually divided into many pieces. I didn't calm down until I had pulled out one volume after the other and the grown-ups caught on and took me away. From that moment on I was drawn to the bookcase, and no other objects could compare to it. I even used it to measure my height. When I grew tall enough to reach the highest shelf, which held the *gemarot*, I was filled with joy and I cried out, "Look at me. I'm a *gemara* lad!" (216)[5]

Set down on the floor to play, the infant makes his way to the bookcase because it is a focus of adult interest, and he wants to know what it is all about. From a distance, the rows of books seem like a formidable and unbroken preserve kept from the child behind glass doors. The great discovery, exciting in its intensity, is that these revered objects are many rather than one, and therefore they can be handled and played with. The child's intrepid curiosity at once diffuses the aura of the books and appropriates them for his pleasure. Being whisked away only intensifies the attraction. In time he learns that the Talmud resting on the highest shelf has been invested with more sacred prestige than any other object in his world, and it is by this standard he measures his physical growth. The joy he expresses when he finally reaches the high shelf encapsulates the duality of Agnon's presentation of himself as a child. While the objects of Jewish life engage and enchant him, his pleasure depends on an assertion of his ownership over them.

We see this again later in this same brief story. In the meantime, the grandfather's set of Talmud becomes invested with more and more value. When the grandfather is sitting at study over these volumes, a sense of beneficence descends on the house, and the wafting of fragrant spices is released each time the bookcase is opened. It is next to this bookcase and from this set of volumes, rather than in the *beit midrash* and its library, that the narrator is later tutored by his father. But before that, when the infant has grown into a young child, we are given another scene of appropriation:

> When my father or grandfather was in the house, I would sit and learn. But if they went out, I would practice forming the letters of the *Gemara*. Often I would copy the ornamental scrollwork on the opening page of the volume or the filigreed frame that surrounded the first letter of the tractate, and from these I would create a *mizrah*. In those days if someone had told me there were more beautiful drawings than these, I would not have believed them. It's also true that there was no one to whom it would have occurred to say such a thing. (219)

The moment parental oversight is lifted, the boy shifts his attention from studying the text to imitating its visual materiality. Looking at the frontispiece of tractate *Beitsah* from the Menkes printing of the Talmud (fig. 1.2), it is easy to see what attracts him. For a boy brought up in a world that frowns upon the making of images, this elaborately reticulated ornamentation is a feast for the eyes. But it is not enough to ogle it; he has to make it his own. He is training his hand to draw the letters and the decorative motifs so that he can create an art object of his own. A *mizrah* is an illuminated plaque placed on the eastern wall of a home—*mizrah* simply means east—in order to orient the worshiper toward the direction of Jerusalem. Even though it has a religious purpose, a *mizrah* is not a holy object that requires the official calligraphy of a scribe, and thus the boy is free to try his hand at it.

He is suffused with pride in his accomplishment. It is a revealing detail for the retrospective narrator of the story to include. His delight discloses not a glimmer of regret about having abandoned his studies the minute the grown-ups leave him alone. Turning to the drawing may be a little naughty, but in the boy's mind, doing so is not a dereliction of his religious duty but a fulfillment of it on a different and perhaps higher level. The key feeling is proprietary joy. He has made something of his own that is an extension of the text, and he asserts that he would not believe someone who said there were drawings more beautiful than these. The acknowledgment, even the approbation, of others is important to him, and he is confident in his success in obtaining it. If the last sentence of the passage (". . . there was no one to

FIG. 1.2 Photograph of the frontispiece of tractate *Beitsah* from the 1861 Menkes edition of the Talmud. Photograph by Alan Mintz.

whom it would have occurred to say such a thing") is deflationary, it is only in the ironic retrospect of the adult narrator. When he had the experience as a child, his confidence was unchallenged.

The effort to establish the "I" and the willingness to pay the price for doing so are at the center of the next story of childhood, "My Bird" (Tsipori, 1926). The story is beguilingly charming in a way that demonstrates how Agnon's stories take on meaning by making struggle visible beneath a delightful surface. The boy, who bears the author's own name Shmuel Yosef, takes care of a bird that has been caught between the double windows of his house and becomes exhausted from struggling to free itself. Over several days, the boy parries his mother's concern that he is neglecting his religious duties, brags to his friends about his possession of the bird, and protects it from the house cat. Danger, though, comes from a different quarter. Just as he is about to set the bird free, it dies after flying too close to the flame of his mother's stove.

Although there are no explicit markers, it is clear enough that the bird is a metonym for the boy's soul. Like his soul, the bird is small, fragile, and delicate; its essence is freedom and flight, although it is now constrained. The connection is strengthened by the delight the boy takes in the bird as well as by his sense of ownership. As the title of the story makes clear, it is *his* bird to be admired by his younger sister and envied by his school friends. His devotion to the bird—it is not clear whether he is rehabilitating it or imprisoning it—makes demands on him. He cuts off a button from his jacket to thank the family's handyman for building a cage for the bird. He endures the ridicule of his friends, who resent his possession of such a tiny wonder. Most of all, he lies to his mother, who views the bird as a distraction from his studies and his prayers. Deception is one of the motifs of the story. The boys in school at first accuse the narrator of lying about the existence of the bird, and then they lied when asked about why they are running as a group to the boy's house.

The worst of it comes on the Sabbath eve when the mother is making pancakes filled with raisins and cheese for breakfast. Morning prayers must be said before eating, according to Jewish law; but the boy demands his portion before he has prayed:

"Mother, give me my breakfast." She says, "But you haven't prayed."
And I said, "So I'm to be suspected of eating before praying! Give me

my portion." My mother gave me two pancakes and some cake filled with raisins. I picked out the raisins and gave them to the bird. (235)

The lie turns out to be only half a lie because the gruff urgency is exerted on behalf of the bird; his own portion will be eaten, *comme il faut*, after he prays. Yet the break with the mother and the parental order she enforces are palpable. To protect his relationship to the bird and his right to delight in it the boy has been forced to confront the divergence between his ideal self, the obedient boy who performs the will of his parents and God, and the self that desires recognition and possession even at the cost of deceiving others.

This is also the self that identifies with the bird's ability to take flight—at least in the best of times. The bird's death during its final flight does not come from its perennial antagonist the cat, but from the realm of the mother and her oven. This is hardly an encouraging premonition about what the boy will have to do in the future to escape the same fate. For the meantime, the boy is crushed by the bird's death. In an effort to deny this painful reality, the boy's mind goes to the tales from the early prophets being studied in the *heder* that summer. He remembers the story in the fourth chapter of Second Kings in which Elisha resurrects the son of the Shunamite woman. In his pocket there is a coin that he had meant to give to charity but diverted to the needs of the bird. Now he puts the coin in the charity box and, with the magical thinking of a child, he hopes for a miracle.

This is the child's first encounter with the finality of death, and he is bereft. His sister silently understands his loss and sews a tiny set of shrouds for the bird. An improvised ceremony of burial provides a modicum of closure, but the bird continues to occupy his thoughts for many days to come. The true gravestone for the creature, the narrator tells us, is in his heart, and it consists of the memory of pain. *Tsipori*, "my bird," is the single word on a single line with which the story concludes (237). Standing there starkly by itself, the word embodies the resonating persistence of the loss. Subtly, the word puts a proprietary stamp upon the experience: my bird, my loss, my painful memory. There is no light between self and object. The delight in the bird's life and the grief over its death take their importance from their role in the formation of the tender "I" of the young boy.

The same insistence on ownership is noticeable in the title of the next story in the sequence: "The Beautiful Story of My Prayer Book." The boy is older here. He is not yet a bar mitzvah, but he already feels a tingling of anticipation in the places on his forehead and arms where the black leather straps of the *tefillin* will be wrapped. The occasion for the story is a small siddur, a prayer book, which his father brings him as a gift upon his return from a trip to a commercial fair. The father's return takes place on Friday afternoon, the one time in the week, aside from Shabbat, when the boy is free from *ḥeder*. The story consists of his rapturous thoughts as he turns to sections of the siddur and conjures up the feasts and holy days of the Jewish year. The premise is a clever device for accomplishing an ambitious goal: to render the inner spiritual life of a boy of about ten years old as he experiences Jewish time. Because the siddur contains prayers related to all of the year's holidays, Agnon can dispatch the mind of his young narrator to multiple points on the liturgical calendar, while he sits in one place and dips into the cherished gift brought to him by his father.

Now, Agnon's Hebrew readers, be they religious or secular, already know the lay of the land. The Jewish holidays are familiar to all, perhaps too famil-iar. The new territory Agnon is exploring is how sacred time registers on the emotional life of a boy, and we find out that it is different from the way adults experience it. The discovery is not startling or subversive but rather fresh and delightful. We cannot experience the joy at the root of these holidays because we have traveled too far into adulthood to believe in enchantment and because the Enlightenment has poisoned the well and conflated true religious experience with superstition and exilic degeneration. Agnon stakes his success in this story on making enchantment genuine and credible.

The boy is intoxicated by the instant access given him by the siddur to the entire cavalcade of the Jewish year. "I was like a man who had entered a garden of delights. Just as he picks one fruit and eats it and then picks another and eats, so I took my siddur in hand and read around in it" (237). The first holiday his fingers take him to is Hanukah. Because the Hanukah blessings and hymns are located at the end of the standard siddur, this is clearly a not-so-random destination to which his fingers are itching to take him. "Right away all the letters of the siddur began to glow before me like the candles on the menorah, and the whole page began to sing *Ma'oz Tsur*." It is as if the siddur has become a magic box or a zoetrope; touching the right buttons, projecting the right slides, makes the drama of the holiday come alive. He can smell the latkes, he can see his father distributing Hanukah gelt and his friends visiting to spin the dreidl. All is animated and vitally present. And then in a heartbeat, the scene shifts to Purim with all its holy pandemonium, its costumes and masks, and its culinary treats. How is it possible, the boy wonders, to jump from Hanukah to Purim, skipping the many weeks and Torah portions that intervene? The answer is on the page before him. For in the standard siddur, the Purim blessings are printed immediately following the Hanukah blessings at the end of the volume, both being postbiblical holidays. The contiguity of the holidays in the text of the siddur is not the same as their occurrence in real calendar time. This is a saving difference, one that enables the younger owner of the siddur to summon up the delights of these holidays whenever he wishes rather than waiting for the slowly revolving circuit of the year to bring them around.

As the child narrator proceeds to conjure up the holidays, we realize that he is passing them through a filter. He is filtering *out* the fast days that commemorate national catastrophes as well as the Days of Awe (Rosh Hashanah and Yom Kippur), with their focus on sin, contrition, and punishment. And when it comes to the major festivals, he is filtering *in* only those aspects that are entrancing and gratifying to him as a child. His "editing" of Passover is a good example. There is nothing about his mother's back-breaking labor in cleaning the house and converting it for the holiday, nor, for that matter, about the back-breaking labor of the Israelites under their Egyptian taskmasters. Instead, the boy is consumed by his father's angelic presence. "Every time I see him dressed in white he appears to me like an immortal angel who stands before the Holy One and recites hymns and praises" (239). When the father begins the seder with the Kiddush, the blessing over the wine, something miraculous takes place. As the leader of the seder, he thanks God for "having chosen us and raised us (*romamtanu*) from among all the nations." As the words are being recited, the boy has the sensation that "the whole world is being raised up and we are being raised above the world" (ibid.). The boy's astonishment comes less from the power of the holy moment than from its source. "I am amazed that on the strength of one word uttered by my father the whole world is elevated and we are elevated above it."

It is no coincidence that the site of all the boy's favorite rituals is the home and not the synagogue. Shavuot is the exception that confirms the rule. The *kloyz*, the Hasidic prayer house in which his father worships, is a poor affair, with holes in the wall, broken windows and peeling walls. But on Shavuot, in honor of the giving of the Torah on Sinai out of doors, the spaced is so transformed by an abundance of tree branches and plantings that it resembles a forest rather than a synagogue. And again the boy experiences the enchantment of the world: "Especially beautiful is the holy ark surrounded by beautiful trees. When the wind blows and they tremble, do you think it is because they are cold? No, it is because they are whispering to each other and saying, 'Although we did not merit being used in the construction of the holy ark, in the future we will heat the stove on winter nights for students studying Torah'" (242).

There is so much joy and allure in the circuit of the Jewish year for this boy with a receptive imagination how could anything possibly be lacking? But there is something, and the boy gives away what's on his mind when, playing with his new gift, he opens up the siddur and chances upon the laws of 'eruvin, the wires and poles used to demarcate an area within which it is permitted to carry objects on the Sabbath. His mind goes to the birds that pause to sit on these wires before taking wing to trackless climes. "Master of the Universe," the boy then opines, "this little creature is free to take itself to wherever it wants, but if I even leave the house I'm immediately asked where I'm running to!" (ibid.). He owns up to a longing to escape his bonds and journey into the world, and the next prayer he "inadvertently" happens upon is *Tefilat Haderekh*, the traveler's prayer. He turns down the edge of the page so he can find it in a hurry when the time comes.

Agnon is having a good time playing with concepts of time and space. The boy has been happily absorbed in the sacred cycle of the liturgical year and its pleasures, when all of a sudden he begins thinking about leaving home. Where can he be thinking of going? He has no distinct destination in mind. For a boy so immersed in Jewish lore, "away" can only mean going off to study Torah at a great center of learning, or crossing the mythic Sambatyon River to find the lost tribes and arouse the thirty-six hidden righteous to implore Elijah to bring the Messiah, who, in turn, will end the Exile and return the Jews to Zion. So the journey away is in truth part of the ancient messianic desire to escape time and break out of the orbit of history into eternity.

But in the meantime, which is part of the long meantime that interposes itself between the present and the Redemption, the boy has his life to lead. The merchants have shuttered their shops, and the town is preparing for the Sabbath. When the boy brings the siddur with him to the *kloyz* for prayers, he exposes his precious new possession to the scrutiny of his schoolmates and friends, who know that his father will have brought a gift back from his journey. At first the siddur is praised for its beauty and quality, and its possessor is puffed up with pride. But soon enough the pack of boys begins to tell scary stories about ghostly prayer books and to denigrate the boy's gift for having been printed in the Russian town of Petrikov rather than in Jerusalem. His pride deflated, he prays in his heart, "Master of the World, in Your great mercies erase the word that has caused me grief and shame and replace it with 'Jerusalem'!" (246). The magical aura of the siddur apparently does not extend to the fulfillment of personal wishes, and its exilic place of publication stubbornly refuses to disappear.

In the end, the boy withstands the test of his friends' raillery and recoups the proprietary joy he has taken in the siddur. The story concludes with a singular experience that is both ecstatic and cathartic. As the boy's heart begins to jump, the prayers in the siddur become animated and begin to jump up and down too, and he sees that they are all straining to ascend to the Land of Israel. The Passover Haggadah is also contained in the siddur, and when he reaches its concluding words, "Next year in Jerusalem!" he burst into tears of joy. "The tears drop down on the letters until the letters are swimming in tears, as if the siddur itself was weeping with me" (247). Jerusalem rebuilt is the ultimate destination in Jewish time and space, and the story ends with the consolation of imagined arrival.

Let us now pause and take stock of what we have learned so far about Agnon the child from these three autobiographical stories. First, the boy's development is presented through his relations with objects rather than persons. Whether it's the set of Talmud or the bird or the siddur, he is alone with it, and the parents are in the background. Two of the objects belong to the textual tradition and one is a creature of nature, and it is from these two realms that the child's self-formed. The next story in the sequence, "Two Pairs," deals with another important object, *tefillin*, the black leather boxes and straps donned after a boy becomes a bar mitzvah. Second, the stories present the child unapologetically as a robust narcissist. It is *his* bird and *his* siddur. He appropriates the bookshelf with the Talmud at the top as the yardstick of his growth. He asserts that no one could deny that the drawings he made are beautiful. He is a child who is confident about his place in the world. To explain the pride he has in his siddur, he states, "A person naturally cherishes what is his own." The adultified sagacity of this utterance illustrates the third point: Although the world of the stories is focalized through the sensibility of a child, it does not always sound like it is a child who is doing the telling. There is an implicit and unelaborated relationship between an adult narrator who is "staging" the telling of the story and the voice and viewpoint of the child, whose "I" is both the subject and the object of the action. Finally, there is the vital connection between the inner world of the child and the symbols and experiences of Judaism. That connection is intimate and interlocking and stands in contrast to the general picture in Hebrew literature of zealotry and superstition filling the empty vessel of the child's mind with dread. In Agnon's construction of childhood, the child is possessed of a unique receptiveness to the wonder of creation, and this openness is nurtured by the tangible rituals of Judaism rather than being crushed by them. It's the very tangibility of these ceremonies—their concreteness, their appeal to the senses, their base in family ties—that make them fitted to the emotional intelligence of the child. It is as if Agnon is implying that before the modern age the great richness of Jewish religious culture could be experienced by all Jews. But now it is only children who have access to this potent plenitude.

This bounteous feast, this garden of delights—what will be its fate when the child is no longer a child? This is the subject of "The Kerchief," one of Agnon's greatest stories and the consummation of his treatment of childhood. It is the story that comes next in the sequence both in terms of when it appeared and the stage of development it depicts. It is quintessentially a bar mitzvah story. The climax of the tale takes place on the day on which Agnon's child stand-in turns thirteen and is called up to the Torah for the first time. The story is divided into thirteen sections, and it was printed as a special presentation gift to mark the bar mitzvah of 13-year-old Gidon Schocken, the son of Agnon's patron, Salman Schocken.

In "The Kerchief," Agnon finally brings the parents into the picture and constructs an ambitious analogy between the family and the sacred history of the Jewish people. The analogy is founded on the resonances of the word *bayit*, the Hebrew term for house and home. In its homeliest sense, *bayit* stands for the immediate family circle; in its grandest sense, *bayit* stands for the Jerusalem temple (*beit hamikdash*). In the child's mind at the beginning of the story, the two are the same. The father's absence during a prolonged business trip casts a pall upon the family akin to the mourning and trepidation that mark the days leading up to the Fast of Av, which commemorates the destructions of the Temple. In the father's absence, the boy sleeps in his bed and dreams about the Messiah. When the father returns home safe and bearing gifts, it is as if the Messiah has come. This (con)fusion in the boy's mind between family home and national home and between father and Messiah is precisely what "The Kerchief" sets itself to undo.

It is not that the two realms are not related or that it is perfectly natural for a child to conflate them. Agnon insists on prizing them apart because not to do so encourages denial and irresponsibility, which in turn lead away from Redemption rather than toward it. Renouncing messianic fantasies and accepting responsibility for acting in the world become the new definition Agnon proposes for arriving at the age of mitzvot and entering Jewish adulthood. The autobiographical narrator successfully negotiates this passage by the end of the story, but how he gets there is clear. There is a certain sleight of hand in the narration of the events. For most of the story, the boy seems young, perhaps the age of the narrator in "The Beautiful Story of My Prayer Book." He is beside himself with joy over his father's return and the gifts he brings; he happily mistakes the ends of his mother's silk kerchief grazing his cheek for the wings of angles; he wants to stand on the Sabbath table and shout out "The earth is the Lord's and fullness thereof!" Then quite abruptly at the end of the story, the boy goes to the synagogue to celebrate becoming a bar mitzvah, and on the way home he has an encounter with a beggar that demonstrates his coming of age.

The process whereby the boy arrives at this maturity is not Agnon's point, nor could it be within the compass of a short story. In fact, he wants to keep the two stages of development apart so that we can feel more poignantly what it means to renounce childhood. The earlier stories in the sequence already have established the synergy between the boy's sensitive inner life and the rich nourishment provided by symbols and experiences of Judaism. "The Kerchief" now expands the picture to include the family. This includes the boy's relationship to his father, the focus in the first half of the story, as well as the relationship between father and mother, the focus in the second.

The boy's fantasies about the Messiah illustrate the powerful analogy between his golden childhood and the divine favor enjoyed by the Jewish people while the Temple still stood. Agnon presents two versions of what happens on the nights the boy sleeps in his father's bed while he is away. Both center on the talmudic legend that represents the Messiah, disguised as a miserable beggar, as tarrying at the gates of Rome, the locus of impurity and the antithesis to Jerusalem. In the first version, the boy, not yet asleep, has a reverie about the coming of the Messiah, which is all wish fulfillment: all the Jews will go up to the Land of Israel, his father will not travel away from home, and he himself will be liberated from *ḥeder* and free to play before the Lord in the courtyard of the Temple. He prides himself in the fact that while others might despise the beggars surrounding the Messiah for their poverty, *he* would give them honor because the Messiah is among them. But on another night, the reverie turns into nightmare when his eyes close and sleep allows the unconscious to emerge. A great bird appears, and the boy ties himself to its wings with the fringes of the *tsitsit* and commands it to take him to Father. Instead, the bird flies him to Rome and lowers him into the company of poor men surrounding a beggar binding his wounds.

> I turned my eyes away from him in order not to see his suffering. When I turned my eyes away, there grew a great mountain with all kinds of thorns and thistles upon it and evil beasts grazing there, and impure birds and ugly creeping things crawling about it. (57–58)[6]

Now Father appears and saves him by wrapping him up in his tallit and bringing him to safety. The boy wakes in the morning to find that the father's return from the fair has been hastened by a day.

As a child, the boy is entitled to a childlike conception of the Messiah as a kind of superhero, who throws off his beggarly tatters and fulfills every wish. Yet while his waking mind declares his readiness to stare at suffering without blinking, his unconscious betrays his inability to admit the existence of misery and impurity. "I turned my eyes away from him in order not to see his suffering." Again, he is only a boy, and he should hardly be expected to come to terms with the existence of evil in the world. But the moral agenda has been laid down. If he wants to come of age, this is the reckoning that awaits him. Theologically, his magical Messiah will have to be exchanged for a sober conception of Redemption, one that understands that the coming of the Messiah depends upon the recognition of evil and the readiness of each individual to take steps against it. That is where the story will take us. On the fateful day of the bar mitzvah the boy will succeed in making the leap by sacrificing something very precious to him.

The achievement of that moment can be grasped only if we appreciate the value of what has been given up. The boy, Agnon's juvenile self, cannot grasp it in the throes of experiencing it. That its significance can only be understood in retrospect is one of the key points made by all the autobiographical stories. Throughout the discussion of these stories, I've avoided referring to the boy as the narrator even though they are written in the first person. True, we see the world through the enchanted eyes of a child, but at the same time we know that it is the adult the child has grown into who, many years later, is reconstructing the child's viewpoint and choreographing his experience. The simultaneity of these two planes of perception, boy and man, is perhaps characteristic of all "literary" stories of childhood. Yet in "The Kerchief" Agnon endows this duality with a particular eeriness, because when the boy mentions his father or mother, beginning with the first line of the story, he appends the Hebrew epithet used by children when speaking of their deceased parents: "of blessed memory" (*zikhrono leverakhah*) for the father and "peace be with her" (*'alehah hashalom*) for the mother. The loss of his parents is far in the boy's future, yet he speaks as if his orphanhood were already an accomplished fact.

How to explain this strange effect? A passage toward the middle of the story gives something of an answer. Father has just that moment walked in the door, back from his travels. Enormous in his son's eyes, he bends down, picks him up and kisses him.

> I look about me now to try and find something to which to compare my father when he stood together with his tender children on his return from afar, and I can think of many comparisons, each one finer than the next; yet I can find nothing pleasant enough. But I hope that the love haloing my father, of blessed memory, may wrap us around every single time we come to embrace our little children, and that joy which possessed us then will be possessed by our children all their lives. (59)

Reading through "The Kerchief," one might easily take this passage in stride as another sweet sentiment about childhood. But even as an experienced reader of this story, every time I come upon these lines I'm jolted, and I feel as if a scab has been pulled off a wound. Throughout these stories, Agnon has labored to place us within the perceptual world of the child with its awestruck and wonderfully literal view of Jewish experience and to sustain that illusion. Here, however, Agnon suddenly pulls the curtain aside and shatters the illusion. When he writes, "I look about me now," the "now" is the present time of the writing, some thirty years or more after the events themselves. I see Agnon sitting at his desk in Jerusalem—the story appeared in 1932—at work on a story about his childhood when all of a sudden his forward progress is blocked. He looks up and reflects on the obstacle that has confounded him, and we hear the voice of the adult speaking.

Something is happening to him. The process of writing about his childhood and giving it artistic shape has unexpectedly triggered a visceral memory of the grace and protection he felt in his father's love. As a writer, he is used to reaching for the metaphors appropriate for his purposes. But in the case of an experience so powerful and vivid there are no words. This is not an admission of frustration or failure but a recognition of the modesty of language, wielded even but such a one as he, in the presence of what is truly ineffable.

It is his response to this potent recollection that is most revealing. He turns from the memory of the plenitude of his father's love for him to his own situation as a father. Agnon married Esther Marx in Germany in 1920; his daughter was born there in 1921 and his son in 1922. If we assume that Agnon, now settled in Jerusalem, wrote "The Kerchief" in the year or two before it appeared, then his children were about the same age as his autobiographical persona in the story. The memory of what he felt upon his father's return home so long ago provokes a fervent wish concerning his relationship with his own children. If we look closely we see that two related but different wishes are being uttered in this passage. One concerns the speaker's capacity and the other concerns its effect on his children. Agnon, as the adult narrator and implied author, first wishes that he could extend to his children the same *hesed* ("unconditional love") he experienced when his father embraced him. He then wishes that the transaction be successful and that his children be the beneficiaries of the same *simhah* ("joy") he received from his father's embrace. *hesed* is the quality he hopes to be given, and *simhah* is the experience he hopes to transmit.

Now, some readers might take these wishes for granted as prayerful aspirations. I hear them more equivocally, even darkly. If these wishes were indeed prayers, as we might expect from the persona of a religious writer, they would be addressed to God and they would begin with some version of the conventional pious formula, "May it be Thy will oh Lord our God that . . ." Yet the term used here is the very peculiar Hebrew word *halevai*, which is not exactly "I hope" and closer to "Oh that it were!" Grammarians call this an utterance in the "optative mood," which expresses a desire for a situation to come into being that does not presently exist. It is this wistfulness I hear in these wishes. Agnon suspects, even knows, that it is not in his character to be the parent his father was. His absorption in his own genius makes it difficult for him to make room for the lives of others; he further knows that, whereas he was raised in a world of faith, his own children have been born into a different age, and the fact that they cannot be held close by the Tradition affects the joy that can be given them. *Ḥesed* and *simḥah* are not, by their nature, qualities that can be granted upon request. And to request that they be present "every single time" and "all their lives" betrays an unspoken desperation. I hear in Agnon's *halevai* a sigh of resignation.

The narrator refocuses the story after this brief but remarkable interruption. Having described the love between the father and his children, he turns his attention to the bond between husband and wife. In terms of Agnon's childhood stories this is new territory, and it is signaled by the eponymous kerchief of the story's title. The father has brought back gifts from his journey for all the members of the family; they include a siddur for the narrator, presumably the same siddur that figures in the story discussed above. For the mother he has brought a silk brocaded kerchief adorned with flowers and blossoms. Precise attention is accorded to this beautiful object. The mother puts on the kerchief on Sabbaths only within the home; for the synagogue she wears a hat with feathers. The exception is Rosh Hashanah and Yom Kippur, when she wears it both at home and at synagogue. In the child's mind, the kerchief is part of his enchanted world. When he sees the ends of the kerchief quivering as the mother stands before the Sabbath table as her husband recites the ode to the Woman of Valor, the boy knows that it is the effect of "the Sabbath angels moving their wings and making a wind" (62). The kerchief remains miraculously unstained despite years of wear and the splatter of cherries falling from cakes. The kerchief is a luminous symbol of the holiness of the family, its harmony and unfading durability. By adding the love between the parents to the father-child axis, the family becomes a triangle that is not only holy but stable and enduring.

It is just this wondrous object that is lost at the climactic moment of the story. And the fault is wholly the boy's: "But for me she would have kept the kerchief all her life long and would have left it as an heirloom" (64). To explain how this happened, the story leaps ahead from childhood to the day of the boy's bar mitzvah. In one of the several symbolic transfers central to the story, the mother ties the kerchief around his neck. When he returns from the synagogue, the kerchief is gone. The explanation for the loss concerns the appearance of a new beggar in town, and it circles back to the boy's fantasies about the Messiah as he lay in his father's bed.

Many beggars pass through Buczacz, and the town boasts networks of hospitality to assist them. This particular beggar is an exception. He is in tatters and sick with running sores, and his appearance is so frightening to children and grown-ups alike that he is pelted with stones and driven from the marketplace. He is even chased out of the synagogue and denied Sabbath hospitality. The boy observes all this and is confounded because he knows the people of his town to be righteous and charitable. In order to hold on to that belief he is forced to take recourse in magical thinking. "The ministers of Satan," he is forced to conclude, "used to accompany that beggar and pull a veil over Jewish eyes so that they should not perceive his dire needs" (ibid.).

Now we the readers are tempted into our own magical thinking. We recall the figure of the Messiah among the poor at the gates of Rome from the boy's nights in his father's bed, and from Hasidic stories and folktales we recall that Elijah, the Messiah's herald, disguises himself as a beggar and tests the readiness of the righteous. So we think, Aha!, Agnon is rewriting one of those wonder tales in which the Redemption would have come if only the holy figure could have been recognized behind the loathsome appearance.

But it is we who have fallen into a trap. The point of the story is that the repulsive beggar is nothing more than a repulsive beggar and not the Messiah in disguise. The great test that is put to the narrator on the day of his supposed maturity is whether he can put away magical thinking, recognize the beggar for what he is, and reach out to him instead of looking away. Agnon is not thumbing his nose at the notion of the Messiah and calling it juvenile. He is making a deeper theological point. The Messiah represents the Redemption, and the only way the Redemption can be hastened is not by miracles but by small acts of kindness that contribute to a process of repairing the world.

The boy does not look away, and, indeed, looking and being seen is the essence of the encounter. The narrator returns home from the synagogue "dressed like a bridegroom" and pleased with himself that he was now putting on tefillin. When he meets the beggar his appearance is as gruesome as ever. "He looked at me as well. The sores on his face seemed like eyes of fire." The boy's heart stops, his knees begin shaking, and his eyes grow dim. "But I took my heart in my hand, nodded to the beggar, and greeted him, and he returned the greeting." Still agitated, his throat choked by tears, he feels a sensation of sweetness taking possession of his limbs. He reopens his eyes and beholds the beggar. "I took off the kerchief and gave it to the beggar. He took it and wound it around his sores" (65–66).

The encounter with the beggar is a classic test in which a child must overcome an obstacle in order to arrive at adulthood. The Jewish version of this passage is of course the bar mitzvah, and "The Kerchief" is in every respect a bar mitzvah story from the circumstances of its writing as a presentation gift to Gidon Schocken to its composition in thirteen chapters to the climatic event that takes place on the day the boy first dons tefillin and is called up to the Torah. Yet the representation of the bar mitzvah in this story is astonishingly different from the gala party and choreographed synagogue ceremony we know as the bar mitzvah in recent times. Part of the difference is due to time and place. In traditional circles in Eastern Europe before the war (this story takes place around 1900), when a boy turned thirteen, he simply went with his father to the synagogue on a Monday or Thursday—when the Torah is read—put on tefillin for the first time and was called to the Torah. The father might bring a bottle of brandy and raisin cake to share with the other worshippers after the early-morning service, and that was that. How the bar mitzvah grew to become what it is in America and Israel today is its own story. The modesty and minimalism of the ceremony in Agnon's telling are therefore not the essence of the radical revisionism. In conventional religious terms, becoming a "bar mitzvah," means literally becoming a "son of the commandment" and incurring all the obligations of an adult Jew. Agnon has minimized these legal and ritual dimensions and replaced them with an inward, moral-psychological understanding of the passage to adulthood. The boy can arrive only if he gives up his magical thinking, acknowledges the existence of suffering in the world and takes steps toward alleviating it.

Magical thinking is only the primitive face of the deep experience of the enchantment of the world. Agnon's childhood stories calibrate a precise resonance between a child's capacity for wonder and amazement and the mythic world of Jewish observance. The legends are alive for the child; the ritual objects and even the holy texts are present to him in their sensuous concreteness. The Hebrew letters on the page dance for him; the holidays—but only the joyous ones!—pop up from the siddur and dramatize themselves with hologram-like vividness. The key the father uses to unlock his traveling case to retrieve the children's gifts smiles at the boy, and the Sabbath angels rustle his mother's kerchief. Satan makes the beggar invisible to the townspeople. This is the Edenic world the boy has to take leave of in order to move forward. It is a necessary sacrifice, but Agnon insists that this was not a world of folly or error. To the contrary, the boy's sensitivities were fully engaged in absorbing—on his wavelength, as it were—the best of what Judaism had to offer him at that age. It has to be left behind as such, but these experiences have penetrated deeply. They have left their deposit and fashioned him. Yet the enchanted world of childhood has to be left behind because it necessarily ignores the existence of evil, suffering and the flawed nature of human life.

The kerchief has to be given up as well. This beautiful, delicate object was given in love from husband to wife and then from mother to son. Its voluntarily forfeiture defines the boy's coming of age. Like Chinese lacquer, Agnon has applied layer upon layer of meaning until the kerchief becomes a radiant symbol of family holiness. What, then, does it mean to give it away? Here things get complicated. It is clear that a significant renunciation is being made, but the nature and degree of the renunciation are less clear. I see in the boy's encounter with the beggar a parallel to another test: the Akedah, the binding of Isaac narrative in Genesis 22. Abraham passes the ordeal imposed on him by God by displaying his readiness to sacrifice his son without, in the end, having to carry it out. In Agnon's story, the boy is ready to give up the familial love that has held him so tightly, and he divests himself of the material symbol of that love. But that does not mean that he is bereft. Still buoyed by the sweetness that had flooded his limbs, he returns home to his mother and suddenly realizes what he had done with the precious kerchief she had given him. The story concludes thus:

> Ere I had asked her to forgive me she was gazing at me with love and affection. I gazed back at her, and my heart was filled with that same gladness as I had felt on that Sabbath when my mother had set the kerchief about her head for the first time.
>
> The end of the story of the kerchief of my mother, peace be with her. (66)

Is this sacrifice without payment? Does the narrator pass the test without giving up something real? The story's laconic ending does not give us much to go on. But one thing is clear: His action has not alienated his mother's love, and the concluding words, "my mother, peace be with her," gesture toward a bond that has persisted into his adulthood long after her death.

At the conclusion of "The Kerchief," I see Agnon as a lad, no longer a boy, who is beginning the process of separating from his parents and from a childlike experience of Judaism. He is taking the love and trust given to him by his parents and internalizing these affirmations toward the day when he will be sure of his own decisions, even if it means disobeying their wishes. In the case of the commandments, he has given up a need for their enchanted, mythical aura and stored them as fundaments of his being. He continues as a student devoted to his studies in the *beit midrash,* but those studies, now unsupervised, will lead him in a widening gyre of intellectual curiosity, and at a point not too far away he will abandon the *beit midrash* for the forest.

## NOTES

Printed with permission from Susanna Morgenthau.

1. We would like to thank Jeffrey Saks for suggesting corrections to this essay and helping to fill in incomplete notes.

2. Alan created this map with his coeditor Jeffrey Saks and the graphic designer Elad Lifshitz of the Dov Abramson Studio, in Jerusalem. It appeared as the endpapers of *A City in Its Fullness* (Toby Press, 2016).

3. Dan Laor, *S. Y. Agnon: A Biography* [Hebrew] (Jerusalem and Tel Aviv: Schocken, 1998), 19.

4. *Me'atsmi el 'atsmi* (Jerusalem and Tel Aviv: Schocken, 1976), 7.

5. For the full English translation of the stories "My Grandfather's Talmud," "My Bird," and "The Beautiful Story of My Prayerbook," see *A Dwelling Place of My People: Sixteen Stories of the Chassidim by Samuel Joseph Agnon,* trans. J. Weinberg and H. Russell (Edinburgh: Scottish Academic Press, 1983). While Alan consulted the translations in this book, he reworked much of the language of these translations into more modern and colloquial English. All page numbers for citations from these stories correspond to the original Hebrew stories in Agnon, S. Y., *Eilu veilu* [Hebrew] (Jerusalem and Tel Aviv, 1966).

6. All citations of "The Kerchief" are taken from I. M. Lask's translation that appears in *A Book That Was Lost and Other Stories by S. Y. Agnon,* edited and introduced by Alan Mintz and Anne Golomb-Hoffman (New York: Schocken Books, 1995).

# CHAPTER 2

# Agnon in Jaffa

## *The Myth of the Artist as a Young Man*

I wish to begin this study of certain of Agnon's early writings by placing in apposition two facts, one concerning the status of Agnon's career in midlife and the other concerning the nature of a group of texts Agnon wrote as a young man.

Agnon's "institutionalization," by which term I mean the process whereby a writer is raised to the status of a national resource, dates, according to Arnold Band, from the early 1930s. By that time, in his middle forties, Agnon had made a series of choices which were to determine his situation for the remainder of his life. He permanently returned to Palestine after a prolonged sojourn in Germany; now married with a family, he established his home in Jerusalem rather than in the Jaffa of his youth; he reconfirmed his commitment to Orthodox practice; and he gathered and revised his writings for a multi-volume edition of his collected works. In the broader life of the Yishuv, Agnon was accorded the status of a sage: the recipient of innumerable literary prizes, the subject of a half-dozen jubilee volumes, the preferred eulogizer of political and cultural leaders. Writing in the last years of Agnon's life, Band aptly describes Agnon's passage from "person to persona."

In the last three decades Agnon has been gradually fading as a real personality.... The real Agnon has merged with the mythical Agnon who is partly the product of popular imagination, and partly the persona who speaks in the various novels and tales published under the name Agnon.[1]

Yet the reader of Agnon who comes across certain of the early works, stories written well before the consolidation of the classical persona, is left with a sense of the young writer that is jarringly at odds with the later aura of the artist-laureate. In 1907 at the age of nineteen Agnon left his native Galicia for Palestine and lived there for six years, mostly in Jaffa. During this time he wrote such stories as *Agunot* ("Chained Souls") and *Vehayah he'akov lemishor* ("And the crooked Shall Be Made Straight") that seem roughly continuous with the writer's mature style in their use of traditional Jewish symbols, folk motifs, and the conventions of the hasidic tale. Other stories surprise us: They are almost entirely secular; they have contemporary settings of Jaffa of the Second Aliya; and they are broadly autobiographical in spirit, concerned as they are with young Hebrew writers recently arrived in Palestine. What takes us most unawares in these tales is both their extravagantly expressive style (in contrast to the allusive classicism of the later works) and their thematic preoccupation with erotic love. *Be'era shel Miryam* ("Miriam's Well," 1909), for example, the earliest of these stories, is an unhappy conflation of several narratives, which together make a statement about the death of the beloved as a necessary condition for poetic creativity, a statement that teeters on the brink of the gothic and the necrophiliac. The short tale *Aḥot* ("Sister," 1910) contrasts the easy flirtations of a young Lothario, a clerk by day and a poet by night, with the Laingian madness of his sister, to whom he is deeply attracted. *Tishrei* ("Tishrei," 1911) tells the story of how an unconscious desire on the part of the young artist for a pretty though uneducated and materialistic young woman ends by crippling his will and undermining his art. The last story of this group, *Leilot* ("Nights," 1913), is the most abandoned in its sensuality; it concerns the efforts of the artist-hero to resist the solicitations of a young girl in order to remain available for a series of ecstatic, dreamlike encounters with the shadowy Salsibylla.

I have juxtaposed Agnon's institutionalization with a cycle of his early stories in order to support a speculation as to Agnon's dilemma as a writer in the late 1920s and early 1930s. Now a family man in his forties, resettled in Jerusalem, reconciled with Orthodoxy, already a public figure, Agnon was faced with the decision of what to do with these youthful tales, already available to the world in published form, as he set about fashioning the edition of collected works that would do so much to promote him to the status of a national sage.

There were strong reasons for suppressing the Jaffa tales as there were for conserving them. Against the stories were the romantic effusiveness of their style, with which Agnon no longer identified nor did he employ, and the bathos of the characters' engulfment in extreme and *outré* states of feeling. What must have been most disturbing was the inevitability of an autobiographical reading of the texts. For like his heroes, Agnon too was a son of a comfortable family, neither German nor Russian, who divided his time between his writing and various clerkships and who lived in the same neighborhoods in Jaffa. Regarding his religious behavior at this time, we have no certain knowledge; it is generally accepted that during these years Agnon, like his characters, abandoned the Orthodox practice and dress to which he had adhered throughout his upbringing in Bucacz and participated equally in the teeming life of the Second Aliya. Moreover, these are the only writings in Agnon's oeuvre in which the autobiographical connections seem explicit and comprehensive; including them in the canon of his collected works would have been tantamount to authorizing an official account of his life and times as a young man.

Yet a great writer cannot easily leave the question of his origins entirely unanswered. One of the obligations of a writer who has been raised to the status of a national institution is to supply the nation with an account of his artistic beginnings: how a callow young man with the hopes and delusions of all young men becomes a great writer. Agnon of course could have suppressed the Jaffa tales altogether, but then he would have had either to forego offering a myth of beginnings, or to invent a new one. To take either course would have meant repudiating the stories and the experiences they represent absolutely. In addition to a writer's natural reluctance to silence his creations, there was something else. It is fair to imagine that no matter how imperfectly realized or how discontinuous with his later identity, there must have been some truth of experience embedded in these stories to which Agnon felt a sense of fidelity. To give them up would have been to give up a part of who he had been.

The way out of this dilemma involved, in the end, a combination of suppression, conservation, and revision. Here we can move from speculation to fact. Of the four stories, only *Be'era shel Miryam*, with its maudlin morbidity, was put aside altogether, though parts of it were later used for other purposes.[2] The remaining three stories—*Aḥot, Tishrei* (now renamed *Giv'at haḥol* "The Sand Dune") and *Leilot*—were substantially revised.[3] Although the characters and the sequence of actions remain basically unaltered, there are other changes of great significance. In style, there is a move from a decorative, atmospheric, expressionist use of language to a spare economy of modifiers and detail that is rigorously subordinated to the thematic intentions of the works. In theme, the figure of the artist and his development are brought more squarely into the foreground and the mode of presentation of this thematic shifts from romantic sentimentality to irony and ridicule. The most interesting change has to do with an adjustment in the connections among the three stories. In their original form the stories are related by a common milieu and a common character-type, but beyond this the links are shadowy and indeterminate. In the revisions of the 1930s the connections become considerably clarified by the addition of new cross references, such that the stories, with *Be'era shel Miryam* eliminated, form stations in a clear narrative sequence moving from *Aḥot* to *Giv'at haḥol* to *Leilot*. What emerges is a triptych whose panels are episodes, admittedly episodic, in one essential movement of spirit.

There are two ways to approach the Jaffa tales. By comparing the original versions with the revised ones much can be discovered about the evolution of the structures of the individual stories and in general about Agnon's way of working and about the changes in his imagination over time. This path has been taken productively by Arnold Band and Gershon Shaked, especially in reference to *Giv'at haḥol*.[4] The second way, the one I propose to follow, would put aside the early versions and concentrate on producing a reading of the revised texts of the three stories as a sequential whole. To read in this way would be to grasp the larger revisionary myth of beginnings that Agnon, the ascendant writer pausing in mid-career, sought to affix to his fictional enterprise. We shall be able thereby to come closer to Agnon's self-understanding in this period and to his struggles with such issues as the representation of sensuality, the relationship between experience and art, and the balance between the symbolic self-sufficiency of the text and its dependence upon allegorical solutions.

The difficulty in producing a comprehensive reading of this chain of stories lies in the difficulty of its last link, *Leilot*. While the relative accessibility of *Aḥot* and *Giv'at haḥol* has fostered a respectable body of interpretation, *Leilot* has received almost no attention, and this either because the hermetic quality of narrative seemed not to repay analysis or because its shimmering fabulistic texture seemed to separate *Leilot* from the more seriously "novelistic" tale *Giv'at haḥol*, from which it may have been regarded as an atmospheric spin-off. For Agnon too the tale was troublesome. The story first appeared in *Bentayim* (ed. Y. Feldman, Jaffa) in 1913 and was revised in the form we read it now by 1931 and published in *Aḥdut ha'avodah*, but unlike *Aḥot* and *Giv'at haḥol*, *Leilot* was not included in the collected works of that year, and it was not until 1941 that it was brought into the Agnon canon altogether, and not until 1953 that it appeared in its present grouping, along with the two other Jaffa tales in the volume in which it presently appears, *'Al kapot haman'ul*.

The difficulty of *Leilot*, I believe, results from its being read out of the sequence in which it is embedded. If returned to its place, it can not only be made to make sense but to disclose the full meaning of the segmented structure of which it is a consummation. I propose now to review this myth of beginnings as it takes shape in *Aḥot* and *Giv'at haḥol* and to suggest the rather surprising turn of events that takes place in *Leilot*.

Naaman, the twenty-year-old hero of *Aḥot*, works by day as a clerk in a Jaffa office. By night he writes poetry. He is attracted to women and they are attracted to him. Since he has left his parents' home in Europe and breathed the freer atmosphere of Jaffa, he has taken his pleasures in many dalliances. He is helped by his position as a clerk. While as a poet he may find his work distasteful, for the girls of Jaffa such respectable employment raises him above the run of destitute scribblers and makes him sought after, and this even though they realize that he does not intend to marry.

The story opens on a note of loathing. Confronted at the end of a long day with a stack of letters still to be copied, Naaman writhes in his confinement. His work requires him to be the quintessence of secondariness, a mere copyist of the work of others, and he despises it. The alienation of his position is further exposed by the recollection of recent sensual encounters; memories of flesh, desire, agitation, and release embitter his servitude. He forces his mind back to his work, finishes the letters, and leaves the office. Once outside he discovers that it is not as late as he had thought, and the question of how best to spend the evening presents itself. The choice is between settling down to a serious session of poetry writing and seeking pleasure in the arms of the girls of Jaffa. Naaman does not even consider the first, and we are told that not infrequently does it happen that the muses are pushed aside for other kinds of feminine charms. As he strides into the street he weighs the question of which woman might most sweeten his evening. Would it be Adah, whose mysterious form drew him to her even before they met, or Tsilah, whose full, bare arms will wildly embrace him snakelike? What a fearsome dilemma, Naaman thinks to himself jocularly, surely what I am experiencing must be the throes of love!

Naaman's manner, the names of his lovers, and the nature of their charms constitute what amounts to an anatomy of a pose. Adah and Tsilah are the two wives of Lemach to whom he addresses his taunt song in Genesis 14. Like Lemach, Naaman is cast as a *miles gloriosus*, the mock-epic figure of the braggart soldier. Though in reality he is only a clerk-poetaster who prowls Jaffa for his amatory conquests, he comports himself like the sun in Psalm 19, which strides "the land in glory like a warrior running his course." The reptilian imagery for Tsilah's lovemaking suggests the physicality of Naaman's sensual play. He experiences women not at a level of deep erotic encounter but amidst an episodic tangle of limbs. Naaman is a master of dalliance; he savors and plays and withdraws uncommitted, having never been deeply engaged to begin with.

What happens to Naaman in the second part of *Aḥot* is the undermining of his epic swagger, the undoing of his pose. This comes about in his encounter with his sister. His sister is his double. Both have been cut off from their family and planted in the teeming life of Jaffa; but whereas Naaman has flourished in his freedom, she has withdrawn into herself and lapsed into melancholic depression that presages a drift toward early death. In the dark shuttered room she sits immobilized, dressed in an overcoat in the middle of the summer, surrounded by piles of unread books. Unlike Naaman, who runs from embrace to embrace to escape an awareness of temporality, his sister is denied the least slip of insulation against this awareness; in every gesture of experience she is condemned to feel the full rush of time toward death. As Naaman struggles with himself in the silence exuded by her presence, he glimpses the truth of this knowledge for the first time and he weeps, shedding his tears not out of pity for his sister but in mourning for what he himself has lost. The story, however, does not end on a note of loss. The shining of love at the end is a breakthrough of sorts, if one hastily produced; this love is not the play of dalliance but a deeper form of eros made possible by the consciousness of time, and it carries with it a possibility of eventual usefulness to the higher purposes of art.

When in *Giv'at haḥol* we next meet the artist-hero he is named Hemdat and he has left off pursuing women and withdrawn from the gay life of Jaffa. There is no doubt that he is a version of the hero of *Aḥot*, for Hemdat too has acquired a reputation as a great womanizer and is even compared to Rembrandt in his restless appetites (pp. 453–54). But now he has given up the chase and no longer seeks out stolen kisses (pp. 452, 455). He keeps to his house, which he has set up neatly to provide for all his needs, and he writes. This house of Hemdat's, which is the central presence of the story, is a version of the romantic topos of the artist's ivory tower. In *Aḥot*, when we saw the artist in pursuit of sensual experience, we saw him in relation to the antithetical topos: the sacred fount of life, from which the artist must drink in order to create. But just as there was something *manqué* and faintly ridiculous in Naaman's Byronic pose, so in *Giv'at haḥol* Hemdat's creative isolation is seriously flawed. Hemdat's retreat is so tidy, comfortable, and well-provisioned that he seems much less like the august Yeats in Thoor Ballylee than simply a *ba'al habayit*, the traditional figure of the householder, the proprietor of his own physical and mental homestead.

Hemdat's domesticity is manifested in his careful husbandry of his life. The young men of Jaffa live squalidly in boarding houses, nap all day, and fritter away time between meals in endless chatter. Not Hemdat. He has been well bred, a *ben tovim*. He has his own room; in the room stands a writing table and on the table sheets of fresh paper. In every sense he provides for himself. Within reach is a well-stocked larder and a spirit burner for coffee. He prepares his own food; he measures his time into useful units and he writes poems. He may indeed be a householder, but in his household he is the only member and it is all he can do to provide for his own needs. A closed system of self-sufficiency guarantees his composure; when he is surprised by the presence of another person his response is retention, a panicked holding on to what is his. He used to joke garrulously with the girls of Jaffa but now Hemdat saves his words for his poems, and when he finds himself in company he becomes nearly speechless, managing only fragments of utterance.

When in one episode in *Giv'at haḥol* Hemdat is confronted with demands on his sexual resources by one of the freer women of Jaffa, his reaction is likewise retention (p. 462). Into this domestic preserve there intervenes a disruptive presence: Yael Hayyut (Chajes, in the European pronunciation), a Jaffa girl whom Hemdat tutors and then unwittingly falls in love with. Yael is the figure of the *yored*, the person of good family who has become impoverished. At first inspection, Yael seems to be simply a spoiled girl down on her luck, an object of pity. She has ended up in Palestine by accident and her assimilated background has left her Jewishly unlettered, so she has turned to Hemdat, who has volunteered to give her Hebrew lessons. Vacant and unintellectual, an indifferent student, she is nonetheless bemused to be in the company of a poet. She comes and goes unpredictably until she finally settles down with a medical student from a well-off family.

Yet the unremarkableness of Yael's behavior is belied in fact by a set of gestures and details involving hair, teeth, dismemberment, and hunger that associate her with a dire quality of animality. Yael, as her name announces (*ya'el* = ibex, *hayyut* = vividness, animalness), embodies physicality in both its aspects of aggression and vulnerability. Her sexual assertiveness is constant and she is rumored to have had affairs with many men. Hemdat completely misreads his responses to her and fails to understand the threat she presents. He believes he is doling out pity, when in reality he is secretly being undone by the workings of desire for her and by her predatory tamperings. In the end, his self-possession is overthrown and he is left with neither love nor art.

The disintegration of the artist's will is realized largely in a single metaphor. That metaphor, as is the case in so much of Agnon's fiction, is the figure of the house, which stands here as a spatial representation of the self's power to assert control over the organization of its being and as a version of the ivory tower to which the hero-artist has retreated after his abandonment to experience in *Ahot*. Alertness to the working out of this metaphor helps to make sense of the method of the narrative. Read as a conventional narrative, *Giv'at hahol* may justly seem episodic and unconstructed; read as a story of a progressive dispossession and dislodgment from a symbolic space (house = will), the narrative comes into focus as a carefully wrought artifice. *Giv'at hahol* becomes the story of how Hemdat begins as a master of his house, the true *ba'al habayit*, and ends sitting forlornly on a sand dune.

When Yael first comes to Hemdat for lessons he is fully the proprietor of his quarters, the patron who is opening his door to the less fortunate. He dispenses food as well as knowledge to the needy girl. The difference between master and mendicant is not maintained for long. There are times when Yael succeeds in dragging him out of the house for walks in the Jaffa night and even once to her house. As Yael's visits become less regular, Hemdat begins to let his own housekeeping slip and attends less to his own hygiene; he washes only when Yael is to come. Within his room her absence decenters his movements; no longer planted squarely at his writing table, Hemdat takes up a position by the window in a stance of perpetual anticipation of her coming. During Yael's prolonged absence from Jaffa for medical treatment, Hemdat reaches the nadir of affectlessness and depression. He abandons his room for aimless walks about the town. The Jaffa he encounters is not the city of nocturnal enchantment and shifting sands, but the city of dusty, contentious marketplaces, a jungle of commercial and sexual desires. On the eve of Yael's return Hemdat cleans and rearranges his room and prepares a festive meal for her, but when Yael comes by she refuses to come inside and draws Hemdat out of his house into the night.

Who gets to feed whom and under what conditions in *Giv'at haḥol* is an important indicator of power. At first Yael won't eat at Hemdat's house despite his urgings; later on in her visits she demands meals and dictates the menus. After returning from Jerusalem she will not allow herself to be fed in Hemdat's house but sees to it that he takes her to eat in a restaurant. The time Hemdat visits Yael's room he imagines he is given tea made from a bucket spit into by his competitor Shammai. Hemdat, for his part, begins by eating at his own table, priding himself in his discipline and self-sufficiency; by the end of the tale he is eating in rooming houses like the aimless émigrés he once made fun of. If Hemdat is left beholden to others, Yael manages, as we've seen, to secure a good life for herself by marrying a medical student. This reversal, in fact, is an element in a larger chiastic structure that takes in the whole of *Giv'at haḥol*, and this in a manner reminiscent of such tales of Nahman of Bratslav as "The Burgher and the Pauper," about which Hemdat is supposed to be an authority. *Giv'at haḥol* could be renamed "The Tale of the *Ba'al habayit* and the *Yored*."

Hemdat is of course not the only poet in Jaffa. Yael's house overflows with poets and litterateurs, who represent various currents in the young national literature of the Yishuv, most of them in some way ridiculous. There is the poet Dorban, whose nativist verse achieves its authenticity by imitating the sound of camel hooves, and the diarist Gorishkin, who is quick to give epic memoralization to the founding of every new hospital and school. Among the serious writers, Yael's gossipy thoughts probably give a version of Hemdat's critical standing. Above all towers Bialik, the great poet-sage, long a mythic figure in the national imagination. Though among Hemdat's contemporaries Hemdat himself seems to be taken very seriously, he is eclipsed by the poet Pizmoni. The greatness and innovation of Pizmoni's verse lie in its qualities of power and force, and we are meant to understand by implication that there is something in Hemdat's *bale-batishkayt* that keeps him from just such effects. The determination of whether or not Hemdat's secondariness results from inherent limitation is clearly never made. What is certain is that as we see him during the time covered by the action of *Giv'at haḥol* Hemdat lacks the one essential condition of poetic identity: poetic production. As Hemdat's obsession with Yael grows, he ceases to write entirely. To save himself from insanity during Yael's absence from Jaffa Hemdat tries to rouse himself from his passivity, but does so only enough to begin a small job of translation, and this with a pen nib that has long since grown rusty.

If his imaginative production comes to a halt, his imaginary activity does not. Hemdat allows his mind to indulge in a series of non-scriptive fantasies, ones of the sort I have elsewhere described as reveries.[5] There are five of these in *Giv'at haḥol* and they mirror both the disintegration of artistic will and the progress of Hemdat's fears and longings. Hemdat's fear of loss and his yearning for domesticity are reflected in an early reverie (p. 353) set in the forest surrounding his home village in Eastern Europe. It is a time of midsummer festivity, each tree imagined as a pole for a bridal canopy. Suddenly the joy passes and winter comes; the only voices left are those of furtive lovers seeking a melancholy tryst in the forest. Self-pity and an early premonition of loss are the essential themes of the second reverie (p. 368), in which Hemdat's mind involuntarily jumps from the thoughts of Yael in her hospital bed (where she lies at the moment) to a picture of Yael at childbirth. Hemdat sees her married well and imagines how one day he will return battered and tired from his wanderings to be greeted by a swarm of her children and by a husband who will not bother to be jealous of such a poor creature.

The remaining reveries are impelled by a growing desperation over Hemdat's poetic barrenness, and they are composed of wish-fulfilling visions of the writing life restored and of Yael's erotic threat contained. Hemdat sees himself in one reverie seated at his writing table, hard at work on his great composition, soothed by fragrances from the garden and by his familiar coffee-making rituals (p. 372). He dreams of the one chaste kiss Yael will bestow on him that will restore his composure and remove any desire for more furtive embraces; when he will become an old man people will no longer doubt the purity of his relationship with Yael (p. 375).

In the depths of his loneliness at the end of the story Hemdat slips back into the kind of bad faith in which Naaman was mired in *Aḥot*. Afflicted with nostalgia, he now longs to abandon his artistic isolation and return to his old ways, "when he would kiss the hands of mothers in public and the cheeks of their daughters in private" (p. 387). The final reverie (pp. 387–88) indicates the full extent to which real literary production has been replaced by the fantasy of production. Blessed days will arrive, according to the vision, in which Hemdat will no longer be found wandering in the streets and quais of Jaffa; faithfully stationed at his desk, he will celebrate the new season with the sacrificial offering of his poetry (*korban shirato*). The garden wafts pleasing fragrances, the sun sets, and Yael enters. "He receives her benignly and refrains from reminding her of her former wrongdoing. They sit as one on the green divan. Yes, she is his beloved."

Much about the themes and situations of *Leilot* reminds us of Agnon's other Jaffa tales. The action of the story is clearly set sometime shortly after that of *Giv'at haḥol*, so that for Hemdat, the central figure also of *Leilot*, Yael is a memory, but one recent enough still to be painful; *Leilot* continues the preoccupation with artistic sterility and its precarious relationship to sensual experience; the house has an important metaphoric function here too, as does an entire series of symbolic details: flowers, fish, hair, thorns. But despite these pronounced continuities, a simple reading of *Leilot* tells us that this is a story told in a very different mode. *Leilot* seems suspended in a timeless world, lacking any of the density of reference to the large life and problems of the Yishuv characteristic of *Giv'at haḥol*. There seems to be no "plot" to speak of, rather a sequence of romantic gestures that appear often to lack motivation and connection. The mysteriousness of Jaffa by night casts its own spell; the air is heavy with suppressed movements and desires; this is an animistic world in which the tiniest objects stir with sympathetic life. Snatches of folktales and parables hang in the air. The mysterious Salsibylla appears, vanishes, and reappears.

*Leilot* is shrouded in hermetic integuments. Because of the story's difficulty, my interpretation will proceed in two parts.[6] First through paraphrase and commentary, I try simply to follow what happens in the narrative and to understand the connections between one action and the next. "Simply" here is of course a naive term because any attempt to set out the *"peshat"* of a text is inevitably tinctured in retrospect by the thinking one has done about its larger thematic concerns. I do my best, however, to keep the two separate and to go on afterward to a more conceptual and generalized level of interpretation that deals with questions of theme and poetics.

*Leilot* opens by contrasting the serenity of Jaffa after a storm with Hemdat's increasing agitation of spirit. The waves and the shore have been reconciled in repose, but Hemdat cannot gain control of himself. His restless anxiety and unstinting tears are the result of Salsibylla's prolonged and unpredictable absence. When she suddenly appears before him, Hemdat is entirely overwhelmed. His heart pounds, he loses the power of speech and can bring himself to gaze only at her feet.

Salsibylla's godlike aura is unmistakable. Her name echoes of the Sibylline Oracle. Her sudden, unpredictable materializations resemble the epiphanies of a capricious goddess; the pleroma of her presence cannot be easily gazed upon by mortals. Her limbs seem chthonian, grown from the earth. But it is no more than the aura we see. Here, as elsewhere in *Leilot*, the text discloses virtually nothing about Salsibylla herself; we learn only of Hemdat's experience of her presence. That experience is so powerfully elemental that Hemdat loses control of himself, just as her absence earlier in the chapter causes a similar breakdown of self-possession. Hemdat's condition at the outset of the story may be summed up as follows: The effects of his relationship with the mysterious Salsibylla are such that Hemdat's life is strung between two moments, one more miserable than the other, between a state of inconsolable desolation and agitation in her absence and a state of hyperemotionality and engulfment in her presence. This is an alternation, moreover, that is ungovernable; Salsibylla appears when she appears.

Hemdat's behavior the next day in chapter 2 reveals the depths of his desperation. He sits alone in his house with his head in his hands, listening for Salsibylla's footsteps and calling out her name. Once again his thoughts race uncontrollably, and in his anguish he is astonished to discover that his hair has turned white. That night (chapter 3), he leaves the house and comes upon the grove of the seven sycamores; sitting among the sands, he calls out Salsibylla's name in vain. Her absence leads not to despair but to redoubled hope. Hemdat cuts Salsibylla's name on a tree and is cheered when a glowworm comes along and illuminates his inscription.

When Hemdat returns later that night (chapter 4), he finds his young neighbor Ruhama on his doorstep. Who is Ruhama? She is very young, an adolescent nuisance from next door who pesters her bachelor neighbor. Throughout the tale she is compared to a flower, trembling and glistening in the dew. Ruhama is in fact anything but frail and innocent. All her actions seem systematically directed toward destroying Hemdat's faithfulness to Salsibylla and replacing her in his affections. Ruhama is the figure of the neighbor, in the literal sense of the one who is nighest unto hand, the physical temptation of that which is immediately present, in contrast to a more difficult loyalty to spiritual value at a distance. She is a version of Yael in *Giv'at haḥol*, younger and more insistent, a figure in whom the qualities of sensuality, aggression and willfulness have been honed to the point of demonic resourcefulness.

If Hemdat's task is to wait in good faith for Salsibylla, Ruhama's is to invade and disrupt the space of his waiting. She interrogates Hemdat on each point of his ritual of waiting for Salsibylla: the late-night vigil, the preparations of the house, the placement of the flowers by the door. Though Hemdat keeps faith with Salsibylla and reveals nothing, Ruhama seizes on each evasion and afflicts him with its transparency. Ruhama's insistent sensuality is not, however, without its allure, and with his will weakened by the incessant questioning, he takes her up in his arms and they kiss. The kiss turns out to be a kind of vampirage in which Hemdat's warmth is drained from him and Ruhama's damp trembling is transferred to his own soul.

Chapter 5 begins with a vignette concerning a blind beggar who knocks at Hemdat's door. The housekeeper turns him away and, recognizing her voice, the beggar curses his sightless eyes, which have brought him back to a source of futility. The episode makes explicit the theme of repetition and difference which has been latent from the beginning and which will emerge later as the story's principal teaching. For Hemdat at this point the beggar's frustration is an emblem of his own past. Before his eyes were opened to the truth, he too repeated the same ungratifying act over and over again, pursuing woman after woman, and eventually finding his nemisis in Yael Hayyut.

Hemdat has made progress in his struggle to gain release from past obsessions. Salsibylla is a relational object of an entirely different order of value; his mastery of himself in the ordeal of waiting for her coming is an index of additional change. Rather than calling out Salsibylla's name in a frenzy of desperation, Hemdat sits quietly composing his thoughts in preparation for meeting her; instead of wandering through Jaffa in search of Salsibylla, he sits at home in determined anticipation. Hemdat hears a woman's footsteps approaching, but they turn out to belong to Ruhama, who has once again insinuated herself into the vacuum of Salsibylla's absence. Whether by accident or not, Ruhama breaks the lamp that Hemdat has set out as a beacon for Salsibylla. Ruhama goes on to taunt him about his nocturnal wanderings, implying that his purpose has been to station himself under *her* window. Hemdat manages to evade her probings without compromising Salsibylla and this time without yielding to her vulnerable sensuality. Instead of succumbing, he takes pity on her, as he does on all living things, even the cricket and the snake; and for these creatures he sings a song, the first of several in *Leilot*. The song is a summary of Hemdat's impasse and a hint at its eventual solution. The eye of the snake, from as far back as the description of Tsilah in *Aḥot*, is an emblem of sensual experience, while the eagles represent the asceticism of artistic detachment. Hemdat has betrayed the high road, and as a punishment his poetry has been silenced. It requires an act of grace in the form of an intervention by the Angel of Song, a creature superior to the eagles and the snakes and tied more directly to the source of art itself, to enable Hemdat to resume his song.

As Hemdat walks Ruhama home, she tells him of her violin lessons and her music teacher. Ruhama's playing betrays no sensitivity to the gentler arts. It is literally music to soothe the savage beast within herself and is an instrument to torment others. The attitude of Ruhama toward this symbol of art that is revealed at this point helps us later to decode the crucial episode on the beach when she burns her violin.

Ruhama next tries to manipulate Hemdat into stroking her hair. To keep her at bay he sings another song, a song about a mermaid who shaves her hair and places it at the feet of the king, lest another caress the hair the king has stroked. In parabolic terms the song describes the relationship of divestment, faithfulness, and obeisance Hemdat is moving toward with Salsibylla. In that spirit, after he deposits Ruhama at her house, Hemdat rushes home to wait for Salsibylla. The stars accompany him on his way as if to signal cosmic approval of this enterprise of waiting. Waiting is no longer an ordeal; indeed, Hemdat has arrived at a state of acceptance in which the act of waiting is sufficient in itself.

At this juncture Hemdat recalls some of the many women he has kissed. Hemdat used to go from one to another, he claims, because he was always seeking one love, and that is the love he now has with Salsibylla. The description of the three women is distinguished in its physicality and it is just this quality that is the subject of Hemdat's revisionary intention when they reappear in chapter 7.

At the opening of the sixth chapter, it is sunset and Hemdat is sitting in his house as the last rays of light irradiate his room. Hemdat fashions a complex trope out of this scene in which the house is likened to a violin. In its local context, the figure offers a lesson on the proper higher purposes of music in contrast to Ruhama's mean exploitation of it. As it refers back to *Giv'at hahol*, the allegorization of the house in *Leilot* serves to redeem the *idea* of the house, which in the earlier tale had represented the hero's proprietary stance of retention and insulation. The very act of fashioning the trope is significant, too. As the story progresses we see Hemdat more frequently taking given reality and transforming it through imagination. Gradually he is coming to do what a poet does: he is learning once again to sing.

In contrast to Hemdat's capacity for figurative discourse, Ruhama displays a penchant for demonic literalization. When she next arrives at Hemdat's house her head is entirely shaven, for she has undertaken to fulfill in literal terms Hemdat's parable about the mermaid and the king. She has done so, however, with a difference: instead of laying her shorn tresses at Hemdat's feet, as in the parable, she has secreted them away for herself. Ruhama's pathetic appearance makes Hemdat laugh, but he soon puts aside his laughter in order to comfort her by fashioning a new simile; he compares her shorn head to an orange and her face to the blossoms of the almond. Here again we see Hemdat not only in the act of making metaphors but also using his transformative imaginative powers to redeem the ridiculous and the grotesque by elevating them from their fallen literalness. As was the case with the simile of the house, again Hemdat is at the same time acting to redeem a theme that reaches back to *Giv'at hahol*, in which hair and its removal were signs of power and impairment.

Ruhama's confidence is shaken by the failure of her ruse to purchase Hemdat's attentions. It is clear from the efficiency of his evasions that he has gained confidence since Ruhama's earlier interrogations. He is firmly in control now and practices a kind of gnostic procedure whereby he protects the mysteries of his devotions by proffering exoteric diversions.

With Ruhama safely home, Hemdat returns to the sycamore grove. His visit here is meant to be contrasted with his visit in chapter 3, when he sought out the grove from desperation and called out Salsibylla's name continually as a way of coercing her appearance. Now, Hemdat has come here merely to savor the pleasure of awaiting Salsibylla and to worship, as it were, at the grove made sacred to her by the inscription of her name. Hemdat compares himself to the Cyclops who kissed the many women to whom he was attracted by his fleshy eyes, until a special spiritual eye grew in his forehead; thereafter he gazed on the princess and thereafter saw nothing else.

There in the sacred grove Salsibylla appears to him a second time. Again we are asked to read *Leilot* analogically, comparing this second coming with the first in chapter 1. The most striking difference here is the presence of human speech. Hemdat is not struck dumb and Salsibylla is not supernally silent. The apparatus of theophany seems to have undergone a kind of humanization; though Salsibylla is no more physically imaginable than before, she is accessible to us in her voice, whose tender responses and simple kindness reveal a sort of girlishness. What actually gets said in their exchange is less than clear. This encounter and the one that concludes the story in chapter 8 constitute two difficult points of interpretation in a text which, it should be evident by now, is not difficult once the basic ciphers have been read. What actually takes place in this scene? When Salsibylla first appears she places her hand on Hemdat's eyes and Hemdat begs her to push his eyes back in their sockets until she can see into his heart. The request to be blinded is connected to the story of the Cyclops. Hemdat wishes to be rid of his wayward earthly eyes, which once lusted after many women, and thereby have created a clear passageway through which Salsibylla may gaze into his soul and see his true faithfulness.

Salsibylla laughs at his foolishness and apologizes for having awakened him from what appears to have been his slumber. Hemdat responds by relating a parable of a king, whose bearing on Hemdat's situation is plain enough. Like the king, Hemdat has no doubt that his beloved will come, and he is prepared to wait fully alert indefinitely. The risk, however, is permanent impairment; in delaying she endangers the fullness of his eventual participation. Fully secure now, even serene in his faithfulness, Hemdat seems to be issuing a gentle, coded plea to Salsibylla not to tarry. But despite the obviousness of the parable to the reader, Salsibylla herself does not seem to get the message and she is chided by Hemdat on her obtuseness. Is Salsibylla indeed obtuse? Is she unaware of Hemdat's recent ordeal? Is she uncaring or is she simply aloof altogether? Does she know that

Hemdat's ordeal is about to be rewarded? Salsibylla's subsequent responses yield little clarification. Hemdat asks permission to touch her hair and that she give him leave to do whatever he desires. But Hemdat restrains himself from physical contact with Salsibylla. His heart glows with an inner light, transparent through his body, and he fears lest Salsibylla touch him and he be consumed. Hemdat is overwhelmed by his own illumination and he is not yet ready for a consummation, which is to come in the last chapter.

Sunk in thought the next day at home (chapter 7), Hemdat undertakes a thoroughgoing revision of his attitude to his own past in light of his transfiguring relationship to Salsibylla. In chapter 5 Hemdat had evoked the charms of his former loves in order to renounce them. Now, that is not enough. He wishes to deny their existence by arguing that these women and their embraces are not figures of real experience but only tropes: emblems in language for the *lessons* of experience. Each of the women, in this new reading, is a parable (*mashal*). The gaity of the dead Dansa is now an emblem (*mofet*) of the days of youth that are gone and buried. In the case of Wilma, he stresses not the kisses themselves but the simile in which he compared them (*dimiti*) to bees which in their frantic pursuit of pleasure forget to sting. And Thea, whose eyes were likened to the eyes of a serpent in the sun, now becomes a symbol (*semel*) of the allure of the kind of love that conceals dangers within it.

Afterward Hemdat elaborates yet another ritual in his attendance on Salsibylla. To rest his mind he goes down to the beach; there he gathers shells to place in his yard so that he may hear Salsibylla's footsteps when she comes to him. For the final time, Ruhama comes by (she is bearing her violin) to interrupt him in his act of fealty and to compel him to reveal the meaning of his behavior. But so far have the roles between them been reversed that Hemdat's subtle and fluent answers overmaster her entirely and she falls silent and begins helping him collect shells. In past encounters Ruhama's verbal aggressiveness had confused and choked him; now with Ruhama subdued, Hemdat goes on with unruffled volubility about fishermen and mermaids and the violin-like beauty of his house at sunset.

Ruhama makes a last attempt to gain control, and the stratagem she employs—trying to get Hemdat to eat food she has prepared for him, in a sense to force-feed him—recalls vividly the power-laden connotations of food and provision in *Giv'at haḥol*. Ruhama buys some live fish to grill for Hemdat and he playfully mocks her with a singsong reference to the

'Akedah: "Here are the fish but where are the skewers and fire on which to grill them? (*Hineh hadagim ve'ayeh hashipud veha'esh letsalot otam?*)" In silent determination Ruhama removes the pin fastening her kerchief and impales one of the fish. While she is occupied with her preparations, Hemdat takes the fish not yet skewered, whispers to them, "Salsibylla! Salsibylla!" (the name being uttered in a much different spirit than in the early chapters) and casts them back into the sea with a command to reveal his secret to the mermaids. In the meantime, Ruhama has failed to find wood for the fire; her determination turns demonic as she seizes her violin, the symbol of art, and burns it for fuel. As from a martyred Torah scroll, music rises from the burning instrument, as if to testify to the indestructibility of what Ruhama seeks to sacrifice.

If the body of *Leilot* is mysterious, its brief last chapter is more mysterious still. Throughout *Leilot* time and space are noted with great precision. The action is spread over five nights and four days, and in between, whether it is in the sycamore grove or on the porch of Hemdat's house, whether at sunset or dawn, we are always supplied with spatial and temporal coordinates. Yet here at the end, the text opens onto an indefinite and infinite expanse of time set not in the sands of Jaffa but in the mythic realm of heaven and earth. It is as if the text has been counting, "One, two, three . . . infinity."

It is a time of cosmic consummation. In the heavens above the angels dance and partake of the wine vinted at Creation for the delectation of the righteous in the Age-to-Come. Hemdat has been beckoned to join the celestial company but he resists ascension, choosing to remain with Salsibylla and celebrate on the earth below (there is something of a reversal here, for at the outset it was Salsibylla who seemed godlike). For Hemdat and Salsibylla it is a consummation also. They exchange endearments and Hemdat suggests a cup of wine to celebrate. In response, Salsibylla places her mouth on his, and as Hemdat picks her up "as a man would raise a goblet," they toast each other with "endless kisses."

The story concludes with a colophon that justifies the closure of discourse. "Shall I continue to tell of the good Salsibylla," the narrator wonders, "or shall I sit by myself in silent recollection of those good days?"

What is the meaning of this consummation and for what is it a reward? Why, after all of Hemdat's struggles to disengage himself from the sensual, is the final moment so intensely sensual? The answers to these questions require us to move from commentary and paraphrase to more generalized and thematic levels of interpretation. I shall discuss the meaning of *Leilot* in three different critical contexts: first, at the highest level of abstraction, the story as a parable about the nature of authentic existence; second, in the context of the two other Jaffa tales, as the solution to Agnon's dilemmas in the 1930s; third, in the context of poetics, as an attempt to establish a balance between the symbolic self-sufficiency of the text—its textuality—and its dependence on allegorical solutions.

Hemdat's ordeal in *Leilot* is actually two, one concerned with the nature of experience and the other with the nature of language. The first is reflected in the changes in Hemdat's responses to Salsibylla throughout the story. There is something powerfully redemptive about her presence; whether Salsibylla is seen as a goddess bestowing illumination, or a muse vouchsafing inspiration, or the Female Other providing oceanic ecstasy, or a messiah bringing salvation—the possibilities can be multiplied—the essential pattern is clear: by the experience of her absolute presence Hemdat is flooded with a sense of being. Salsibylla's presence was first revealed to him, we assume, some time before the action of the story begins. That experience convinced Hemdat of the shallowness and futility of the kind of sensuality represented by Yael and it reoriented his desire toward a true object. This reorientation is so complete that Hemdat feels desperate and lost in the long periods when access to her presence is denied. The problem is that no matter how redemptive her presence, its coming can be neither summoned nor predicted. Hemdat's ordeal becomes a trial of his capacity to live in absence: to be faithful, to trust in her coming, and to be sustained in the meantime by the power deriving from past experiences of presence. The test has its temptations in the person of Ruhama, who taunts Hemdat with his past foolishness and present abandonment and urges him to yield to the solicitations of the immediate. At first Hemdat does not make out well. He feels deserted; he weeps uncontrollably, he shouts Salsibylla's name in desperation, he falters with Ruhama. Gradually he masters himself, accepts the task of waiting, and discovers the joy and even sufficiency of waiting: that hopeful anticipation that purges absence of its dread. In the end Hemdat has made a successful passage from narcissistic expectation to authentic hope—and it is for this that he is rewarded.

Hemdat undergoes a deep change also in his relationship to language. He enters this story as a failed artist, whose art has been flawed both by cheap indulgence and cheap isolation. His creative capacities have shriveled; he no longer writes. But as the quality of his experience deepens by virtue of his faithfulness to Salsibylla, Hemdat begins to reappropriate a capability for literary language. We see this in several ways. As Hemdat gains control over his emotions, he first gets back the power of ordinary speech and then goes on to produce lyric songs and to fashion parables. The parables, moreover, are not ornamental in purpose and they are far from the wish-fulfilling fantasies of *Giv'at hahol*, for they serve to elevate and to redeem what is ridiculous and grotesque, especially in reference to Ruhama's self-debasements. It is in the redemption of the sensuality of his own past experience that the healing ministry of poetic discourse is most significant. It is through the transformative power of language that the flesh can be made spirit, turned into a symbol, a *mashal*—even if to begin with it is nothing more than the conventional linguistic symbol itself, the signifier. And once we know we are not talking about "real" kisses, then all is permitted; let the kisses flow— there is no danger. And so they do between Hemdat and Salsibylla, but only outside of the empirical frame of the story in the mythic place beyond time and space in the last chapter—in the Land of Pure Language.

In the context of the Jaffa cycle as a whole *Leilot* represents a movement of arrival in several ways. The image of the artist, which had been sentimentalized in the original versions of the stories and then ironized in the revisions of *Ahot* and *Giv'at hahol*, is given new and serious value in *Leilot*. The two moments of abandonment to experience (the sacred font) and retentive isolation (the ivory tower)—both modes of inauthenticity that check artistic production—are transcended by a figure whose ordeal of denial and trust is rewarded with the gift of true imaginative potency. Yet it is not with the power of art alone that Hemdat is rewarded; he is granted Salsibylla and her delights as well. Sensuality, which loomed as a mean diversion in *Ahot* and as a predatory threat in *Giv'at hahol*, is rehabilitated in *Leilot* and raised to a kind of spirituality. In negotiating a disposition of the autobiographical fiction of his youth, Agnon taught the following lesson: once sensuality is converted from experience into language it loses its threat and can be reenchanted. In having Hemdat explain his past loves as really symbols, emblems, and allegories, Agnon is playfully giving the reader a set of instructions about how to interpret the earlier stories and the original versions, how, in short, to defuse them and still retain them. Agnon could allow himself to retain these compromised images of himself as a young man because in *Leilot* he documented how he had escaped them and been reborn.[7]

The transformation in the myth of the artist in *Leilot* is inseparable from changes in the means by which the literary text produces its meaning. *Aḥot* and *Giv'at haḥol* can be placed generally within the field of novelistic discourse: the characters, their motives, actions, and thoughts, and the spaces they move through seem to be representative of the world as we see it, or at least recognizable in terms of what we know from reading other works of fiction. In *Leilot*, by contrast, the mimetic basis is considerably attenuated. The identity of the characters, the meaning of their actions, their location in time and space are not on the surface of things intelligible to us. They are strangenesses that have to be naturalized through interpretation, as I've done in commentary and paraphrase, even before they yield to questions of theme and structure. The difficulty of *Leilot*, which is the quality we remove from the text when we naturalize it, defines its specialness. The production of meaning in *Leilot* depends less on a representational correspondence between the ordinary world of experience and the elements of the text proper than it depends on the play of those elements among themselves *within* the text. *Leilot* abounds with gestural details, interweaving motifs, animate objects, atmospheric soundings which, through constant reference and cross-reference, give the text a density that makes it in itself undisplaceable. I call this quality of self-reference and self-generation textuality. Textuality is created by a process of repetition and difference that can be illustrated by an example. In chapter 1 Hemdat mentions Ruhama's pigeon, which had come to Hemdat's home and had been fed from his hand. This is a detail that seems by itself to have no particular function in the text (though an over-allegorizer like Hillel Barzel will want to explicate it and every other detail as representing *something;* here he identifies the pigeon with the Shechinah![8]); yet soon we find it related to other instances of feeding. Hemdat waters the flowers set aside for Salsibylla with his tears, while at the same time withholding water from a flower sent by Ruhama. Ruhama attempts to forcefeed Hemdat on the beach, but Hemdat repulses her and sets the fish free. Finally, in the ecstasis of the last chapter Hemdat and Salsibylla toast each other with bodies drunk like wine.

Nourishing and withholding nourishment are only one set along a larger axis of paradigmatic actions in *Leilot*. Cloaking and uncovering are another, as are piercing and incising, speaking and withholding speech, waiting and meditating, singing songs and producing figurative discourse. Along an intersecting axis of objects, we find the domain of living things (flowers, thorns, glowworms, fish, pigeons, snails), liquids (tears, the sea, wine), parts of the body. In addition, a spatial axis registers the sites of the house, the sands and the grove, the beach, and the heavens. This catalogue could be elaborated and refined. It serves only to suggest the wealth of motifs with which *Leilot* abounds. Lodged at particular moments in the unfolding of the narrative, these gestural details, of course, often play a role in the thematic movements of the text. But not always, and out of sequence, grouped in chains of association that exist statically and simultaneously, they create a sense of world rather than story; they spin a web of textuality that enables the text to seize and occupy its own space.

Yet for all its enchantment, the aura of textuality does not by itself justify our interest in *Leilot*. We would not long pause over this tale of a love-sick poet *manqué*, his adolescent neighbor, and his elusive lover if it did not hint of larger matters. And indeed, we have been able to discuss the meaning of *Leilot* in terms of conceptual categories that stand outside the text, such as the nature of experience and language and the issues in Agnon's career as a writer; and the way is open for even more extrinsic and speculative measures that would identify the characters themselves as embodiments of varieties of love or other abstractions. This naturalization of the text by recourse to a set of ideas beyond the text I call allegory, using the term in a broad sense based on its etymology, *allos*, "other" and *agoreuein*, "to speak." There is little need to elaborate on the allegorical understanding of Agnon's work because allegory is the stock-in-trade of Agnon critics and the programmed response of Agnon readers from their earliest encounters with the texts.

Of course, we cannot do without allegory. But allegory finds its rightful place only in its symbiotic relationship with textuality. The relationship is symbiotic because neither term by itself can produce the combination of aesthetic density and conceptual depth that transfigures the best of Agnon's work. The meaning of *Leilot* at the level of poetics, then, is that it is in this text that Agnon achieved the crystalline balance between textuality and allegory that became the basic paradigm in the later major fictions.

I have stressed the question of textuality because I believe that the accession to textuality was Agnon's most difficult achievement. It was not hard for him to draw away from mimetic representation when the content of experience became compromising, nor was it anything but the most natural move for a writer so steeped in classical modes of interpretation to employ allegory. But to raise anchor and allow the text to float free, powered by its own internal production, to attempt to recreate the polysemousness the rabbis accorded to the biblical text—all this must have required an ordeal of faith, attended by a fear of loss and a trial of waiting, an ordeal not so different in kind from that of Hemdat, as he separated himself from the life of dalliance and waited in trepidation and then in trusting hope for the coming of Salsibylla.

## NOTES

Originally published in *Prooftexts* 1 (1981), pp. 62–83. © 1981 Alan Mintz. Reprinted with permission of Indiana University Press.

1. Arnold J. Band, *Nostalgia and Nightmare: A Study in the Fiction of S. Y. Agnon* (Berkeley and Los Angeles, 1968), p. 28.

2. *Be'era shel Miryam* was published in *Hapo'el hatsa'ir* (Jerusalem), 11:14–18 (21 May, 3 June, 17 June, 1 July, 1909). Parts of the story were used in revised form in the beginning of the novel *Temol shilshom* and the story *Hemdat*.

3. *Ahot* first appeared in *Hapo'el hatsa'ir* (Jaffa), 1–2 (11 Nov., 1910). It was subsequently published in the collection '*Al kapot haman'ul*, 1922, in vol. IV of the collected stories of 1931, and in vol. III of the collected stories of 1953. *Tishrei* first appeared in *Hapo'el hatsa'ir* (Jaffa) V:1–5 (22 Oct., 7 Nov., 1 Dec., 6 Dec., 1911). Under the title of *Giv'at hahol*, it was published separately in Berlin in 1920. Revised again, it was published in vol. IV of the collected stories of 1931 and in vol. III in 1953.

4. Band, pp. 61–63, 68–73; Gershon Shaked, '*Al arba'ah sippurim* [On four stories], in the *Iyyunim* Series (Jerusalem, 1963) and Shaked, *Omanut hasippur shel 'Agnon* [The art of the story in Agnon] (Tel Aviv, 1973), pp. 157–76, 321, n. 3. For the beginnings of an approach that stresses yet another path, comparisons with contemporary German literature, see Warren Bargard's note in *Prooftexts* 1, no. 1 (January 1981).

5. See my "Mordecai Zev Feierberg and the Reveries of Redemption," *Association for Jewish Studies Review* II (1977), 171–200.

6. The reader is referred to the translation of *Leilot* by Hillel Halkin that originally accompanied this essay, in *Prooftexts* 1, no. 1 (January 1981), 84–95.

7. Although my purpose here has not been to compare early and late versions, I should be remiss if I did not make some mention of the major divergences between the two, which, I believe, lend strong support to the interpretations I have offered. The Agnon Archive at the National and Hebrew University Library in Jerusalem possesses a copy of the printed 1913 version with marginal notes in the author's hand (Reference Number 1:434) and a copy of the page proofs for the 1931 version, also with corrections in the author's hand (Reference Number 1:56). In the early version, the following are evident: the story is dedicated below the title to Dansa, Wilma, and Thea; the story is considerably longer and divided into thirteen chapters; there is no clear division of time into days; there are several more parables; Salsibylla appears more frequently and she and Hemdat talk and eat together; Ruhama's presence is not demonic; Hemdat does not attempt to conceal from Ruhama the reason for his nocturnal vigils, there is no pronounced movement toward inner tranquility in Hemdat and little sense of trial or ordeal; the last chapter lacks any cosmic

reference. These particular differences should be thought of together with the broader thematic and stylistic changes mentioned earlier.

8. *Sippurei ahavah shel Shemu'el Yosef 'Agnon* [The love stories of Shemuel Yosef Agnon] (Ramat Gan, 1978), pp. 85–88.

# CHAPTER 3

# Agnon Without End

The translation for the first time of a major work by S. Y. Agnon (1888–1970), the greatest writer in modern Hebrew, is sufficient cause for celebration; the fact that this work is a novel makes the event that much more interesting, but also more equivocal.[1]

Agnon, who was born and brought up in Eastern Europe and moved to Palestine for the first time in 1907, most naturally displayed his narrative genius—and gained his early fame—in short fiction which made ironic use of two traditional Hebrew forms, the midrashic vignette and the hasidic tale. When it came to writing novels, Agnon similarly constructed them by stringing together cycles of related stories. This resulted in sprawling, epic works which, despite their thematic intricacy and symbolic power, were always in danger of breaking down and breaking apart.

Agnon's transactions with the novel as a form encountered other difficulties as well. As the quintessential literary expression of the secular middle classes, novels required close attention to a particular set of themes: domestic relations, individual ambition, and, classically, adultery. This presented an immense challenge to a writer who had deliberately cultivated the persona of a pious storyteller; yet as a modern writer Agnon could hardly avoid this challenge without dooming his work to provincialism. In a novel of fairly limited scope, like *A Simple Story* (1935), Agnon's grasp of the medium is masterful. The bigger novels, *The Bridal Canopy* (1937), *A Guest for the Night* (1939), and *Just Yesterday* (1945, still untranslated), are always fascinating yet sometimes unreadable.

*Shira* is Agnon's problem novel. He began writing it in the late 1940s and published many chapters separately in periodicals; then it was consigned to his drawer. Several more chapters appeared around the time he received the Nobel Prize for Literature in 1966, and he was actively at work on the book in the years before his death in 1970. On his deathbed, Agnon asked that *Shira* be published in its incomplete form; it appeared a year later, and in subsequent editions, carrying alternative endings, one of which indicated a direction the novel might have taken but did not.

For the reader, this unrealized aspiration is no cause for lament. In the new English translation, what we have of the novel is equal to the best of Agnon and takes his writing into new thematic territory; that is no small thing. The workmanlike translation by Zeva Shapiro tends to be overly faithful to the singular patterns of Agnon's style, which has the advantage of suggesting what the Hebrew might be like, though it fails to recast Agnon as an author whose writing attains an independent embodiment in English.

*Shira* is set in Jerusalem in the late 1930s and centers on the figure of Manfred Herbst, a lecturer in Byzantine studies at the newly created Hebrew University. A scholar of considerable erudition and integrity, Herbst has bogged down in his career after the success of his first book; a new work, a monograph on the burial customs of the poor of Byzantium, lies scattered on innumerable index cards and shows few signs of ever being written and securing him his professorship.

Herbst's comfortable life—he has a protective and affectionate wife and two grown daughters—is disrupted when his wife becomes pregnant and gives birth to a new daughter. In the hospital's maternity ward, Herbst meets a nurse named Shira and begins an affair with her on the very day of his wife's delivery. Although he sleeps with her only a few times and she herself disappears midway through the novel, Herbst becomes obsessed with Shira. His work grinds to a halt; his family life becomes intolerable to him; and his psyche is delivered over to grotesque sadomasochistic dreams.

The main body of the novel in its present state leaves Herbst sucked into the downward spiral of obsession. The unfinished portion was apparently intended to lead up to the fragmentary concluding chapter Agnon attached to the manuscript, in which Shira is discovered to have contracted leprosy and to be living in a leprosarium. Herbst joins her there; embracing and kissing her, he willingly becomes infected with her disease in order to be with her always.

Adultery has been a staple of the novel since *Madame Bovary* and *Anna Karenina;* for Agnon, it serves less as an erotic theme than as a device for portraying the breakdown of a world view: the liberal German Jewish culture embodied in Manfred Herbst. Jerusalem of the 1930s as it is depicted in *Shira* is awash in German Jews—scholars, physicians, daughters of good families—who have fled Nazism only to find themselves at loose ends in an unfamiliar Zion. Their displacement is emblematized by many rare volumes and first editions of German classics that have come into the hands of Jerusalem booksellers as the impoverished refugees sell off their libraries to keep body and soul together. Although Herbst himself came earlier, before the rise of Hitler, out of vaguely Zionist motives and on the strength of an offer of a post at the new Jerusalem university, and although he has learned Hebrew and feels at home in Palestine, he remains very much the creation of German Jewish culture.

This is nowhere more evident than in Herbst's commitment to the vocation of scientific humanism as expressed in his scholarship. His researches into early Byzantine Church history are impelled by the conviction that the path to truth lies through the careful and dispassionate investigation of past events, no matter how seemingly removed from the exigencies of the present. This pursuit is undertaken in the esteemed and cherished company not of persons but of books, which become eroticized objects. (The novel abounds in vignettes of bibliomania and bibliophilia.) Yet Herbst's soul has nothing of the arid pedantry of George Eliot's Casaubon in *Middlemarch.* His mind is steeped in German romantic poetry, and he makes notes toward the writing of a dramatic tragedy of his own. Politically, his liberalism extends to an identification with the Brith Shalom group, which in the Palestine of those days favored a binational accommodation with the Arabs. Even the family circle partakes of the German Jewish ethos: an intelligent and solicitous wife who insulates her scholar-husband from the nuisances of domestic life, and strong-willed daughters raised to be useful and independent.

For all its attractiveness, however, this blossoming of late bourgeois intellectual culture curiously displaced to Jerusalem is presented in the novel as being ripe for destruction. It is being obliterated at its source as the forces of nonrationality triumph in Germany. Herbst's wife Henrietta wanders among the offices of the British Mandatory bureaucracy in a vain search for immigration certificates for her relatives at home. The Arab attacks against Jews, which intensified in 1936, come uncomfortably close to the Herbsts's house in an Arab neighborhood of Jerusalem. Unbeknownst to Herbst, his daughter Tamara has become a member of an underground group set upon evicting the British by force. Even the world of the Hebrew University, with its largely German or German-trained professoriate, is less bent on the discovery of truth, however rarefied, than it is preoccupied with jealousies of rank and reputation. The utter secularity of Herbst's world, its radical and complacent alienation from the sources of Jewish faith, is underscored obliquely by the novel's intrusive narrator, who observes his subjects from a point of view much closer to the religious tradition.

The agent who precipitates the disintegration of this world view is unlikely indeed. The nurse Shira, the object of Herbst's obsession, is neither young nor conventionally appealing. What attracts Herbst about her seems to be the mannishness of her sexuality, its freedom and nihilism. She is disdainful of religion and ideology and finds her only fulfillment in caring for the sick and suffering. In contrast to Herbst's German civility, she, who comes from Eastern Europe, fascinates him with an account of her flight naked into the Polish snows in escape from her lover on their wedding night.

As a character, Shira is both over-determined and underrealized. This touches directly on what makes *Shira* a problem novel, and on what makes the novel as a genre a problem for Agnon. We know little about the nurse. Herbst's contact with her is very limited, and midway through the novel, as I have mentioned, she disappears altogether. (The freckle-like protuberances on her skin, noticed in the first chapter, turn out to be the early signs of leprosy.) Yet the temptation to underestimate her role in the novel, to see her as, in essence, merely the exotic catalyst of Herbst's undoing, is contradicted by Agnon's naming the novel for her, by the narrator's insistence that his story is as much about her as about Herbst, and by the fragmentary conclusion in which the two are united in a leprosarium. Shira is clearly very important to what Agnon wants to do in the novel, but the nature of that importance is never entirely demonstrated.

Most critics have sought to resolve this dilemma by invoking allegory, as Robert Alter has done in his eloquently argued afterword to the new

English translation. Thus Shira, whose name means "poetry" in Hebrew, is understood as a figure for the subversive modernist fusion of eros and art; what circulates in Herbst's mind, then, is not the 19th-century poetry of sentiment, but a Nietzschean melody fueled by the darker forces of life and death. It is exposure to this troubling power that pulls down the foundations of the world built by German Jewish culture.

Such a reading of Agnon's novel, as with most allegorical solutions to literary puzzles, produces in the uninitiated reader a momentary thrill of recognition as the pieces suddenly appear to come together in a profound, overarching scheme. But the *frisson* of comprehension soon dissipates when one attempts to analyze *how* the pieces fit together. Whatever the meaning of Shira's name, it is hard to see how so perverse and sketchily rendered a character can bear the weight of such large designs.

Still, in the end we cannot do without allegory of some kind. In *Shira* one senses that the inherent limitations of Herbst's world view are being exposed by Agnon not out of any pleasure in documenting its dissolution but out of a belief in the existence of some transcendent, alternative realm. The identity of that realm is never named, but its latent power is every-where suggested. The transfiguring idea—call it what you may: art, eros, purity, spirituality—can simply not be accommodated by the this-worldly resources of the novel as a genre. For this reason I believe the novel could not be finished. Agnon's deathbed instruction to publish *Shira* in its incomplete state may thus have signaled his final acknowledgment and acceptance of that impasse.

We must be grateful, however, for his last-minute instruction, for there can be no other work of literature, however fully realized, which presents the contradictions of the modern Jewish imagination as powerfully as this incomplete masterpiece.

## NOTES

Originally published in *Commentary Magazine* 89, no. 2 (Feb. 1990). Reprinted with permission from Susanna Morgenthau.

1. This article is a review of *Shira*, by S. Y. Agnon, translated by Zeva Shapiro, with an afterword by Robert Alter (New York: Schocken Books, 1989).

# CHAPTER 4

# In the Seas of Youth

The appearance in 1934 of Agnon's novella *Bilvav yamim* (*In the Heart of the Seas*), which tells the story of the journey of a group of Hasidim to the Holy Land, marked a particular moment in his career as a writer. The novella was apparently written by 1926, and some lines from it were included in a presentation of gifts made to Franz Rosenzweig on the occasion of his fortieth birthday on December 26 of that year.[1] Agnon eventually chose to have it included in *Sefer Bialik*, the prestigious festschrift for the national poet, who died the next year. The connection with Bialik proved especially significant. Bialik himself considered Agnon's narrative not only the best thing in the volume but the best piece of Hebrew literature recently published. His high opinion of this specific story encouraged the award to Agnon of the newly established Bialik Prize two years later. The effect, according to Agnon's biographer Dan Laor, was to bestow on Agnon, who was only in his late forties at the time, the mantel of the great national writer in the aftermath of Bialik's passing.[2] Bialik's praise joined the general acclamation that greeted the appearance of *Bilvav yamim*. The novella was taken as representing the consummation of Agnon's craft, an art in which aggadic and folk materials are perfectly integrated into modern storytelling. Readers and critics were especially entranced by the heightened expression given by the text to the ideal of the love of Zion. In the midst of the Yishuv's struggles to establish itself, there was inspiration to be drawn from this tale of immaculate faith in the goal of Zion and the intrepid resolve to reach it.

The plot of *Bilvav yamim* is simply sketched. The time is the second or third decade of the nineteenth century, and the place is Agnon's ancestral town of Buczacz. The story is told by a belated narrator who, as we find out on the last, colophon-like page of the novella, has taken up the task because others have been prevented from doing so. A small group of pious towns-people decide to sell their property and belongings, put aside their business affairs, and make their way to the Holy Land to spend the remainder of their days in study and prayer. They are joined by a simple Jew named Hananya, who carries all his possessions in a kerchief and who has encountered many obstacles and privations in his longstanding efforts to reach Jerusalem. He not only completes their minyan but drives one of the wagons and provides the practical know-how that enables the faithful to negotiate the long journey across Eastern Europe to Constantinople. Along the way many Jewish set-tlements are encountered and described and many legends about the Holy Land are told. Hananya is late to the ship's departure from Constantinople to the Holy Land because he is busy releasing an *agunah*, and, unaware of his absence, the faithful embark on their tempest-tossed voyage without him. When they arrive in Jaffa, Hananya is there before them, having flown over the seas transported on his kerchief. Settled in Jerusalem, the members of the group experience a mixture of fates, and it is only Hananya who lives to a contented old age.

My first encounter with Agnon's novella took place in the framework of an introductory course on modern literature given by Avraham Holtz at the Seminary College of the Jewish Theological Seminary. It was the spring of 1966; I was a freshman at Columbia College and took occasional courses at the Seminary. I don't remember a great deal from the course beyond Holtz's infectious enthusiasm in demonstrating the unity of form and content in Bialik's short poems. The course, which was taught in Hebrew, required a paper in Hebrew, and early in the summer I submitted a paper on *Bilvav yamim*. I have the underlinings and marginal comments I made then in the volume of *Eilu ve'eilu* I still use; but the paper itself is lost, and the reasons why I chose to work on that novella, and how I came to it altogether, have only now become a little clearer to me.

The Hebrew paper, however, was to have another incarnation. During my sophomore year, I and several friends I had met as a counselor at Camp Ramah each put up one hundred dollars to publish the first issue of *Response: A Contemporary Jewish Review*, for which I acted as editor for three years until William Novak took over the job. In the inaugural issue I included two essays of my own, one of which was titled "Agnon on the Individual and the Community."[3] Using the recent award of the Nobel to Agnon merely as a pretext, the essay takes as its real occasion what it defines as the current crisis in American Jewish life: the disaffection of creative young people from the Jewish community. The issue is explored through an analysis of *Bilvav yamim* that traces the vicissitudes of the relationship between Hananya, taken as an embodiment of the free and creative individual, and the faithful, who represent the community. The essay concludes by wondering whether the creative young Jews of the present will have the courage to persevere in the face of the organized community's disregard for them. This message fitted well into the overall spirit of *Response*, whose founders felt that Judaism had been cheapened and betrayed by contemporary synagogue culture and that rescue could come only from attending to the message of young people who had rediscovered Judaism's true radical and creative nature. My other contribution to the first issue was an attempt to illustrate that betrayal; the title suggests the tenor of our attitudes at the time: "Fear and Trembling: A Retrospective Critique of United Synagogue Youth."

When I recently returned to *Bilvav yamim* for the purposes of the present essay, it was the first time I looked at the novella since writing the Hebrew paper and the English article some thirty-four years ago. This interval perplexes me. I've taught Agnon often and in many different settings; I've written reviews and articles about his fiction; I've edited (with Anne Golomb Hoffman) a major anthology of his short stories; and I've never ceased reading Agnon and expanding my familiarity with his corpus. Yet I've never revisited *Bilvav yamim*, despite its importance in the formation of Agnon's reputation. I suspect that the reason has to do with my recollection of the novella as being sentimental and belonging to what I imagined to be the cute, soppy and pietistic Agnon that I was eager to leave behind in my later quest for the properly ironic and modernist Agnon. At any rate, when the chance to participate in the "Rereadings" issue of *Prooftexts* arose, I took advantage of the opportunity to figure out why I had chosen *Bilvav yamim* as the subject for my first publication and my critical debut.

In returning to Agnon's novella I am aware of my ulterior motives. I identify with the speaker of Bialik's autobiographical poem "Lifnei aron hasefarim" ("Before the Bookcase"), who admits that he has returned to the classical texts of Judaism—the reference is to Bialik's many years of work on *Sefer ha'aggadah*—not out of a love of the books themselves but out of a desire to recapture the origins of his self, which are pressed between the leaves of the ancient tomes. Similarly, I have taken up and reread *Bilvav yamim* not out of a desire to work on that corner of the Agnon oeuvre but out of a curiosity to catch a glimpse of who I was circa 1966.

Rereading the novella proved to be much more interesting than I thought it would be. The actual experience of reading the text chapter by chapter was surprisingly pleasurable, and when I sat down to think about the work critically and to read what others have written about it, I found a great deal that interested me. When it comes to the critical issues raised by the novella, the truth be told, I see little overlap between what I find fascinating now and what I found fascinating then. Yet when it comes to the pleasure taken in the reading of the text, I sense a link between my attraction to *Bilvav yamim* as a college student and my delight in reading it today. In what follows I first contrast what I find interesting about *Bilvav yamim* now with what I found interesting then, and then I will conclude by speculating upon the continuity of the mystique the novella still exerts.

Much of what interests me now about *Bilvav yamim* is undoubtedly the result of the professionalization I've undergone as a reader over these many years. I've learned—or been conditioned—to see particular poems and stories not just in their own terms but as part of literary systems whose rules are my responsibility to attempt to understand. An example is the element of the fantastic in *Bilvav yamim* embodied in the magical properties of Hananya's kerchief. In his 1968 study of Agnon, Arnold Band presents the novella as sophisticated fantasy inviting a sophisticated reader to suspend belief and engage the text as an aesthetic rather than an ideational experience.[4] Similarly, the explosion of magic realism in European and Latin American literature and then in Israeli literature (especially in Grossman and Shalev) has led me to consider *Bilvav yamim*, written in the 1920s, as an early precursor of this technique. Whereas in fantasy the laws of nature can be wholly suspended or rewritten, in magic realism the deviation from the real is a strictly delimited element, even if it is dramatically conspicuous.[5] In the case of *Bilvav yamim*, the travelers are in no way protected from the dangers of travel, both psychological and material, especially when it comes to their perilous sea voyage from Constantinople. The only violation of the realistic conventions in the world of the novella is Hananya's magical flight over the seas to the Holy Land. It is, to be sure, a rather large violation, but its magicalness does not infect the rest of the narrative world and maintains the kind of exceptionality that we will later come to associate with magic realism.

Now, while nothing miraculous transfigures the lives of the travelers, often enough they strengthen their spirits with fabulous legends about the holiness of the Land of Israel. The novella is replete with aggadic·material from the early masters and the later masters. Whenever there is a pause in their forward journey or whenever danger besets them, the faithful immerse themselves in the legends of the Holy Land, so much so that one would have to consider this aggadic medium as often pushing to the margins the historically contingent chronicle offered by the narrator.[6] Bilvav yamim thus becomes a productive context for exploring a critical question in Agnon studies in general: How does Agnon invoke and then domesticate aggadic discourse within the novelistic discourse of the fictional text? Who is the implied reader for this genre of narrative? Is there a threshold of "literary competence," in the sense of a familiarity with the canon of aggadah, necessary to be a reader of Bilvav yamim?

As a professional reader I am given to looking for earlier narrative models against which to locate the uniqueness of the text under analysis. In the case of Bilvav yamim, at least from my retrospective vantage point, many models come easily to hand. The Hebrew chronicles of such medieval travelers as Benjamin of Tudela and Eldad Hadani shed light on the ethnographic conventions of the genre and the assumed responsibility to describe the situation and customs of unfamiliar communities. The classic send-up of the genre, Abramowitch's The Travels of Benjamin the Third, cannot be far from the Hebrew and Yiddish reader's mind. Closer still are the peregrinations among the Jewish townlets of Galicia of Reb Yudl, the protagonist of Agnon's own earlier novel Hakhnasat kalah (The Bridal Canopy), who also eventually and miraculously makes his way to the Holy Land. Widening the lens to world literature, especially medieval European Christian literature, offers the opportunity for useful comparisons between versions of the sacred quest and the ascent to Erets Yisrael as a narrative structure.

Yet it was not until I read Shmuel Werses's chapter on Bilvav yamim in his recent collection of Agnon studies that I grasped the fact that there may be not just a vague set of narrative models for the novel but *an actual source*.[7] In 1764–65, R. Simha of Zalozhitz, a town near Brody from which Agnon's own father hailed, undertook a trip to Erets Yisrael, which he described in a book titled *Ahavat tsiyon* (*Love of Zion*), which appeared posthumously in 1790. Werses brings parallel passages from the eighteenth-century chronicle and from the novella that are very persuasive in making a case for seeing *Ahavat tsiyon* as a source that Agnon had before him in the composition of *Bilvav yamim*. The parallels make the critic eager to use the source to set off systematically the particular ways in which Agnon molded his modern literary text. The pilgrimage chronicles tend to have a very linear structure, each station in the journey and each encounter being added to the previous ones. Werses astutely contrasts this combinatorial method with the elements of epic design, which he defines as the deployment of significant detail and the presentation of characters from multiple perspectives, and concludes that *Bilvav yamim* partakes of both models.

Coming to *Bilvav yamim* after being a longtime reader of Agnon also makes one keep an eye constantly peeled for the master's tricks. This does not mean that the piety of the narrator and his subjects is not sincere; it does mean that even in these holy precincts there lurks the presence of Agnonian playfulness and irony. The playfulness begins with the very fact that Agnon makes Buczacz the place of origin of the travelers and the font of all their wanderings, whereas, according to Werses, we know of no hasidic *aliyot* that came from this locality. The greatest stroke of what Band calls Agnon's mirth is nothing less than the insertion of a figure bearing his own name into the story. Rabbi Shemuel Yosef the son of Rabbi Shalom Mordechai Halevi is an esteemed member of the traveling party, and his distinction lies in his encyclopedic knowledge of legends of the Holy Land and his gift for retrieving them precisely at the moments the faithful falter and find themselves in need of spiritual uplift. Exercising his authorial omnipotence and imaginative freedom, Agnon conjures up the figure of who he might have been had he been born a century earlier during the great age of Polish Hasidism. As for irony, it makes its distinctly unmirthful presence felt at the conclusion of the novella when the narrator informs us in a tone of unruffled faith replete with honeyed martyrological overtones about the privations and humiliations suffered by the faithful once they had fulfilled their hearts' desire to reach God's city.

The playful and ironic fuse in the colophon-like concluding paragraph of the novella:

The sages and rabbis of Jerusalem have long desired that all that befell Hananya should be put on record in a book. But by reason of harshness of servitude and the urgency of livelihood, as well as because of strife and contention, the matter was deferred from day to day and from year to year; until I came and wrote all the adventures of Hananya in a book which I have called *In the Heart of the Seas*. This name I have given this book in memory of Hananya, peace be upon him, who went down into the heart of the sea and came forth peacefully. I have not left out anything I have heard and have added nothing more than my soul advised. Some will read my book as a man reads legends [*sippurei aggadah*], while others will read it and derive benefit for themselves. With regard to the former I quote the words of the Book of Proverbs: "But a good word maketh the heart glad;" a good word maketh the soul to rejoice and delivereth from care. But of the latter I say in the words of the Psalmist: "But those who wait for the Lord, they shall inherit the land."

The veteran Agnon reader has much to savor here as Agnon tweaks his or her nose in this performance of grandiosity disguised as piety. The telling of the tale is presented as the deferred fulfillment of longstanding rabbinic wishes; and it is the narrator alone who has heroically succeeded in over-coming the political and social forces that have thwarted previous attempts. The purpose of the telling is given as being devoted entirely to recording the adventures of Hananya, although he is in fact absent or marginal in much of the book's matter. The conventional assertion, with its Deutronomic echoes, that nothing has been left out of or added to the account, is teasingly undercut by the qualification that nothing has been supplemented beyond that which "the soul advised" [*mah shehaneshamah hayetah magidah li*], as though the promptings of a chronicler's soul were nothing at all. Finally, there are the two scriptural verses matching the two classes of readers the narrator envisions for his book. I've read this passage many times, and I still have no clear sense of what Agnon is up to. Despite the fact that the two classes or options are presented symmetrically, each with its accompanying prooftext, it would seem that there are ways of privileging one over the other. On the one hand, it is those who read to derive benefit for themselves [*yotsi'u to 'elet le 'atsmam*] who will be granted the Land as their inheritance. On the other hand, one cannot easily discredit the primacy of aggadah and its constructive role in the religious imagination in a work suffused with aggadah, much of which is purveyed by a character who is a retrojection of the author. So, masterful ambiguity or writerly playfulness? I'm not sure I can determine, and I realize that that is probably where Agnon wants me.

Finally, my return to *Bilvav yamim* has taught me something about Agnon's religious Zionism. In my transactions with Agnon over the years, I have been drawn in my teaching and writing to Agnon the modernist and fabulist and to the fiction that reevokes the lost inner life of Polish Jewry. I have always been mindful, to be sure, of narratives set in Erets Israel and the deep attachment to the Land evinced in Agnon's work. Yet rereading *Bilvav yamim* has forced me to acknowledge the utter iconographic central-ity of the ideal of Zion in Agnon's imaginative enterprise. Wholeness and redemption for either the individual or the Jewish people are available—to the degree to which they are possible at all for modern man in the world after faith—only through a wholehearted identification with the ideal of Zion and a commitment to its realization. The ideal and the real, alas, remain dis-tinct throughout Agnon's work, as the narrative of *Bilvav yamim* illustrates. Nothing is more ennobling and sustaining than the belief in Zion on the part of the faithful as they leave their comfortable lives behind them and seek to raise themselves to a higher spiritual plane by their journey to the Holy Land. The way is one thing, the arrival another. In the end, nothing tries their faith more cruelly than the reality of Zion.

Turning back now to my first encounter with Agnon's text in 1966, I am astonished first by the fact that it took place in Hebrew. *Bilvav yamim* was, I am sure, the longest Hebrew text I had ever read, and the term paper I wrote about it my most sustained and serious attempt at writing expository prose in Hebrew. I state this with no sense of my having been a prodigy. When I came to New York for college from Worcester, Massachusetts, Columbia and Barnard were teeming with undergraduates who had attended the Yeshiva of Flatbush and Ramaz and spent summers at Camp Massad and for whom Hebrew was a secure attainment, even if many of them took it for granted and did little to develop it. I had gone to public schools and my Hebrew was more hard won, having been acquired in the afternoons at my synagogue school, which was connected to the Boston Hebrew Teachers College. For me, writing a college paper in Hebrew was an assertion of will that stretched my capability. Even though I no longer have the paper, I still remember specific instances of putting together awkward Hebrew equivalents for conceptual phrases I knew well in English; and I also remember Avraham Holtz's exasperated question marks in the margins. I am moved by this picture of myself at age nineteen struggling to enter into an intellectual relationship to Hebrew separate from folk songs of youth movements and the pidgin conversations at summer camp. My connection to Hebrew had no professional intimations at the time; it would not be until some seven years later, toward the end of my graduate studies in English literature, that I would seize upon the study of modern Hebrew literature as a vocation. To discover that long ago my imagination was engaged and nurtured by the mystique of Hebrew puts me in possession of a deep-running continuity in the formation of my self.

Other aspects of that self are thrown into relief by the fact that I translated my Hebrew paper into English and published it myself. Writing a student paper is one thing; setting it in print and disseminating it is quite another. From this distance I look back and wonder at the self-importance, the grandiosity, the hutzpah. There are two factors—separate from the Jewish motives, which I'll get to in a moment—that help me to understand this impulse toward self-advertisement. The first has to do with the intellectual temper of Columbia College in those days, with its hoary legacy of the Great Books and its more recent legacy of the New Criticism. As first- and second-year students, we were expected to write analyses of the great texts of western civilization—a passage from the *Iliad*, say, or a chapter from Machiavelli—without consulting criticism or scholarship or delving deeply into the historical context. It was assumed that, left alone with the text, we could come up with something to say and that our thoughts would be worth listening to. (Over the years I've had many contradictory thoughts about the encouragement given to this mystique of brilliance; and I've felt cheated more than once by teachers who dazzled me with their originality until I later discovered that their ideas had been cribbed from others without attribution. But on balance I have to admit that I am grateful for the self-confidence I feel when it comes to taking chances and making my own interpretations even before I know what other minds have already gone on record as saying.)

The other influence was a kind of crush on the world of the New York Jewish intellectuals. Lionel Trilling taught at Columbia. Norman Podhoretz, whose memoir *Making It* had just appeared, had not only gone to Columbia but had also studied at the Seminary. It was a world that was close enough to touch and at the same time beyond reach. We, by which I mean the group of us who started *Response*, had come too late to the party. The quarrel between the Communists and Anti-Communists was not our issue, and we were not part of a post-war generation that had rushed to put Jewish "particularism" aside in order to seize the mainstream of American letters. And we weren't, by and large, from New York. Yet the glitter of those passions drew us nonetheless. We wanted to stage an intellectual life for ourselves around the Jewish issues that engaged us, and we wanted to do it in print, writing as controvertialists, on the pages of intellectual journals, even if we had to create them ourselves.

In turning my term paper into a review-essay, I was, in furtherance of this goal, displaying a prescient intuition about one of the key differences between academic writing and intellectual journalism: the necessity of creating a contemporary, relevant occasion for any extended analysis of a particular work. In my *Response* essay on *Bilvav yamim*, I took this charge as a matter of great gravity rather than merely as a convention. The chief theme I identified in the novella was the tense dialectic between the individual and the community as enacted in the relationship between Hananya and the faithful. The contemporary context which I used to introduce and justify my examination of Agnon was fraught with great moment:

> The question of the relationship between the individual and the community is now so pressing because the last forty years have witnessed its almost complete disintegration in the American Jewish community. Until now, because Judaism has been misunderstood, and there have been few around to properly explain it, bright people growing up in the Jewish community have become dissassociated [*sic*] from it. They have acknowledged Jewishness but rejected Judaism, and have reserved a special key on their typewriters for this syndrome: *Alienation*. Members of the generation coming of age now, however, find their connection with the organized just as tenuous but for different reasons. They think they are on the verge of discovering the contemporary value of Judaism, but at the same time they are repulsed by the vulgarity and hostility to criticism and creativity that Judaism's organized forms display.

This analysis of the crisis of American Jewish life—which I believe represents the shared urgency behind the founding of *Response*—proceeded from a stance of conservative rebellion. We viewed the Jewish institutions around us, especially suburban synagogues and the national organizations, as corrupt entities that had betrayed the real values of Judaism. We were "on the verge" of discovering the contemporary relevance of those genuine values; it was a process we had to go alone in the absence of true teachers and in the face of the community's hostility to "criticism and creativity." The tragedy of our generation lay in the fact that most Jewish young people, seeing only the vulgar misrepresentation of Judaism, naturally lapsed into disaffection and alienation.

After establishing this context, my analysis of the text of *Bilvav yamim* offered two arguments. The first insisted on an essential distinction between Hananya and the rest of the travelers. They are householders who, despite their readiness to make serious material sacrifices, remain conventional in their attitudes and piety. This is expressed in their relegating Hananya to a lower status and accepting his humbleness as their due. Hananya, on the other hand, exists on a different plane of reality, and he shines above the faithful "as a totally free individual who exudes love and values men for their qualities, not their positions in society." His kerchief, with its magical properties, is the symbol of his irreducible individuality. The second argument is that the relationship between Hananya and the others is implied by the structure of the plot. Hananya is with the faithful during the first stage of the journey; he is absent in the middle and then rejoins them in Erets Israel. It is on the sea voyage in Hananya's absence that the entire enterprise nearly founders. Since form is content, it follows that their spiritual project prevails only because the faithful are joined with Hananya, and that in general "we can say that without the inclusion of the free individual the effort of the community cannot succeed." Leaving little doubt with which term in this binary opposition I and my comrades identify, the essay concludes:

> In the story, Hananya had love, freedom and singleness of purpose to offer the Faithful. Similarly, today there are people finishing school who have a vital and creative vision of Judaism to offer to the organized community. Whether they will try to contribute, whether the community will receive them, and whether they will have the courage to persevere in the face of disregard, all constitute questions not yet answered.

My ears burn as I read these lines aloud to myself after these many years. Could I have been that self-serious and that self-important? How could I have managed to shift the responsibility so completely away from myself and onto "the community"? How could I have so blithely epitomized myself under the sign of love, freedom and creativity? My mind crowds with all the structures and themes in the novella that I did *not* see. Many things I can be forgiven for failing to notice because of the lack of training and learning. But how could I have been oblivious to the centrality of the Zion theme? These are issues I will surely have to deal with in my own reckoning with my personal history.

More to the point, here is a different question: Does my preoccupation with the theme of individual and community contribute anything to our understanding of *Bilvav yamim*? Or, was I only catching a glimpse of myself in the mirror of the text? I say "only" because in an era of hermeneutical self-awareness we know that it is never wholly one or the other. Yet with a childlike need for assurance and a dread of its being withheld, I still need to ask whether there was something really there.

After revisiting the novella and thinking about it critically and reading what others have said about it, I am prepared to venture—with a catch in my throat and rush of relief—that, yes, there really is something there. Agnon could have spun an enchanting tale without Hananya, but he chose to include the figure and endow it with singularity. The collective really does seem collective; none of the faithful stands out in full relief. Their piety is impressive, but it comes off as stolid, passive, and even noisy when compared to Hananya's silent and graceful service and his energetic undertaking of acts of ḥesed. And the faithful company are certainly lesser and even lost without him. So, I would conclude, the insight is sound, once, that is, it has been disentangled from the self-regarding lessons I wished to learn from it. I will even go so far as to say that in some small way I feel retroactively instructed by what I saw then. For in my recent rereading of *Bilvav yamim* the tension between the individual and the community was not particularly present to me as an issue in the story. Having "gone over" to the side of the community over the course of the years, I suppose that my empathic identification with Hananya may have become attenuated. The corrective lens from the past is thus most welcome.

I also welcome, in conclusion, the chance to feel again what I must have felt when I first picked up and read Agnon as a college student. I have no certain way of knowing what attracted me to his stories then, but my recent return to *Bilvav yamim* has opened up what feels like a direct channel to those early promptings. As best I can tell the motive was this: the desire to experience the poetry of religion. I grew up in mid-century America as Jews were rushing headlong to enter the mainstream; because of certain influences on my life and certain needs of my own, I decided as an adolescent to move in the opposite direction. I became more observant of the rituals of Judaism than my parents and more knowledgeable about Jewish history and culture. Yet however much I strove to learn, I was frustrated in my desire to penetrate the authenticity of Judaism by the very embeddedness of my life in the American milieu. I caught glimpses of the pockets of European orthodoxy that survived at the time, but only from a distance; this was not and could not be my world.

Here Agnon came to my aid. Because of the great good fortune of my having had a Hebraist education, I was able to read a novella like *Bilvav yamim* in Hebrew and feel I was peering directly into the inner romance of faith and hearing its music in its original tones. Setting aside some of the story's playful and ironic wrappings, I think this is exactly the experience Agnon was trying to convey. The critique of the obscurantism and otherworldliness of Hasidism is present and accounted for in plenty of other locations in Agnon's work. But here, with clear-minded resolve, Agnon chose to create an idealization in the tradition of the naive but not the sentimental. And I was ready to listen, and grateful to be given the chance to seize through the reverie of reading what could not be given to me in life. As a proper intellectual in training I was constrained to use the novella to make a point in print about cultural and political realities of the day. But that seems, on reflection, to have been a mask for a deeper satisfaction.

## NOTES

Originally published in *Prooftexts* 21 (2001), pp. 57–70. © 2001 Alan Mintz. Reprinted with permission of Indiana University Press.

1. For a facsimile of the offering, see Martin Goldner, ed., *Die Gabe: For Franz Rosenzweig on His 40th Birthday* (New York: Leo Baeck Institute, 1985). For reflections on Agnon's contribution, see Anne Golomb Hoffman, *Between Exile and Return: S. Y.*

*Agnon and the Drama of Writing* (Albany: SUNY Press, 1991), 177–79.

2. Dan Laor, *Hayei Agnon: biografiyah* [S. Y. Agnon: A Biography] (*Jerusalem and Tel Aviv*: Schocken, 1998), 542–49.

3. Vol. 1, no. 1 (Summer 1967), 28–31.

4. Arnold J. Band, *Nostalgia and Nightmare: A Study in the Fiction of S. Y. Agnon* (Berkeley: University of California Press, 1968), 262–70.

5. Robert Alter in Alan Mintz, ed., *The Boom in Israeli Fiction* (Hanover, N.H. and London: University Press of New England, 1997), 17–34.

6. Gustav Krojanker, *Yetsirato shel Shai Agnon* [The Work of S. J. Agnon] (Jerusalem: Mossad Bialik, 1991), 125–30.

7. Shmuel Werses, *Shai Agnon kifshuto: keri'ah bikhtavav* [S. Y. Agnon Literally: Studies of His Writings] (Jerusalem: Mossad Bialik, 2000), 153–88.

# CHAPTER 5

# On "The Sense of Smell" by S. Y. Agnon

"The Sense of Smell," a beguiling short narrative, provides a revealing glimpse into the contradictions of Agnon's self-conception as a modern religious artist, or, depending on one's point of view, as a religious modern artist. On the one hand, the story's narrator presents his vocation as a writer of stories as being continuous with the creativity of the sages and sacred poets of classical and premodern times; a Levite by birth, he views the prose fiction he writes as lineally descended—despite shifts and transformations imposed by history—from the Levitical songs sung in the Jerusalem Temple. The guarantor of this vertical continuity is the Hebrew language itself, whose sacred and revealed nature imposes a discipline of faithfulness upon its belated users. On the other hand, the modernist axis of the story is manifest in the self-conscious and even playful way the author creates the persona of the narrator and goes about manipulating the discursive forms of the story. The anachronistic style of the story and the grandiosity of the narrator's self-presentation open up a space of parody and irony that qualifies in subtle ways the sincerity of the narrator's religious vocation. Whether the story overcomes these contradictions or merely contains them is a difficult determination that likely depends on the stance of the interpreter in relation to the very issues of tradition and modernity raised by the work itself.

It should be noticed at the outset that the story breaks into two distinct pieces: chapters 1 through 3 and chapters 4 through 7. It is in the second, longer part that the actual story, such as it is, is told. This is the tale of criticism the narrator received for using a word in a particular grammatical construction and the eventual vindication that came his way by both natural and supernatural means. The first part, by contrast, has little directly to do with the tale and has no narrative of its own to offer. It serves rather as a kind of expository prologue that expatiates on three subjects: the glory and sanctity of the Hebrew language; the craven shortsightedness of scholars who write in languages other than Hebrew; and the factors that sanction the narrator's vocation as a writer of prose fiction. The purposeful heterogeneity of "The Sense of Smell" as a whole, as expressed in the disproportion between these two pieces, is part of the story's playful modernity even as it mimics the style of earlier forms of writing.

One of those antique styles is already in evidence in chapter 1, "The Excellence of the Holy Tongue." (There is, to begin with, a sense of mock seriousness conveyed in the very notion of dividing a short short story into formal chapters with at times long descriptive titles.) Although the style is not immediately recognizable as belonging to a particular text or period, the rhetorical ingredients suggest the discourse typical of a pious savant. The chapter begins with an ostensibly learned distinction between the languages of the world, whose meanings are based on the conventions of human usage, and the Hebrew language, whose meaning is guaranteed by the divine revelation of the Torah. But the pretense to scholarly observation is quickly swept aside by a kind of rapturous catechism in which the narrator poses a series of rhetorical questions, all of whose answers underscore the primacy of Hebrew. Rather than presenting historical evidence for his assertions, the narrator adduces quotations from the Song of Songs and from the liturgy in a manner that amounts to a midrashic exposition. (Because the passage is not, in fact, a real midrash—although it allows the reader to experience it as such—it belongs to a category special to Agnon that Gershon Shaked calls the "pseudo-midrash.")

After describing Hebrew as the language that embodies the intimate relations between God and Israel, the narrator brings his exposition to an eschatological apotheosis that is surprising in the practicality of its logic. When the Messiah reveals himself—which will be sooner rather than later, asserts the narrator, because we live in the later generations of history—he

will of course speak Hebrew, and we shall not be able to understand him—
nor he us—unless now, in the present moment, we exert vigilance over our
use of the sacred tongue, guarding it from impurity and keeping it clear and
precise. The linkage between proper language usage and the messianic age,
while entirely taken for granted by the narrator, may not seem so manifestly
self-evident to us.

In fact, the narrowly pious and messianic temper of these arguments
is likely to make the contemporary reader more aware of what is excluded
than included. Most of the arguments for the revival of Hebrew as modern
written and spoken idiom were based on a nationalist premise: a nation
needs a language of its own as well as a land of its own, Hebrew is the
national language of the Jewish people, Hebrew bridges the gap between the
ancient people and the people reborn, and so on. For the narrator of "The
Sense of Smell," however, there remains only the single divine, revelatory,
and messianic axis.

After the loving encomium for the Hebrew language in chapter 1, the
polemical tone of the second chapter ("Against the Scholars of Our Generation...") comes as something of a surprise. The targets of the narrator's ire
are the majority of scholars who write Hebrew badly or who write in another
language altogether, in addition to those "stupid folk among the Jews" who
doubt whether a "dead" tongue like Hebrew can ever be revived as a spoken
language. Against these voices stands the narrator's conviction of the utter
self-sufficiency of Hebrew. In the chain of textual tradition stretching from
Scripture through rabbinic literature, he asserts, all the necessary linguistic
resources are to be found in abundance.

The catch, however, is that it is only God's beloved to whom "all those
treasures of the holy tongue" are revealed; without immersion in these
sacred texts, this abundance is not vouchsafed. That the narrator sees himself as included in this circle of the divinely favored is made manifest in
chapter 3. In this chapter, his religious stance is disclosed by the method of
his argumentation. Although he discourses on the scholars of his time and
their failures, the way he uses evidence is very different from the practices
of the academy. For example, to make his point that Gentiles who write in
Hebrew are to be preferred to Jews who write in other languages, the narrator adduces evidence not from history but from Scripture. Even though
Balaam, the Moabite prophet who appears in the Book of Numbers, is
held accountable for the deaths of 158,600 Israelites in the desert, he merits

having a portion of the Torah known by his name and a quotation from his prophecy placed at the beginning of the daily liturgy because of the very fact that he uttered his oracles in the Hebrew tongue. The narrator's indifference to history is similarly evident when it comes to the reasons he gives for why some of the great works of medieval Jewish thought were composed in Arabic. While any literate reader might be expected to know something of the role of Arabic in the transmission of Greek philosophy, the narrator offers an exclusively messianic explanation. Such a reader will not find it easy to accept the presumption that such a work as Maimonides's *Guide for the Perplexed* was written in Arabic solely because the Jews of the time were exhausted by the exile and needed to be pacified like children by being spoken to in "whatever language."

The distinctness of the narrator's voice, at times fervent and at times querulous, has been wholly recognizable in the declarations and judgments he has uttered so far. Yet those statements have been directed toward others, and it is not until chapter 3 that he speaks of himself; and when he does so, he takes off in a new direction rather than continuing to engage either of the subjects he has just taken up: the paean to Hebrew and the denigration of its betrayers. Instead, with no warning, he presents the reader with nothing less than a rationale for his vocation as a modern Hebrew writer. It is a moment of stunning self-revelation, although the elliptical concision with which the revelation is presented makes it fleeting and cryptic. The whole chapter is no more than fifteen lines in the Hebrew, and within that brief compass, the narrator presents a sequence of shifts and transformations whose import is heady but whose inner logic is elusive. We have to work hard to supply the connections.

The narrator begins by explaining that the reason he forgoes the pleasures of the world and devotes himself to studying the words of the sages is so that these words will be "present to his lips." There is a presumed comparison between the narrator and the so-called sages excoriated in the previous chapter, who complain about the poverty of Hebrew as a modern language. Unlike them, he experiences no such insufficiency because he immerses himself in the Hebrew texts of the tradition. But instead of a metaphor of immersion, we are given a metaphor of ingestion. The narrator stores up the words of the sages in his belly, and through an unexplained process of absorption and incorporation, the words—now his own Hebrew words?—present themselves on his lips.

Yet the ascetic life devoted to textual study, a high and virtuous calling, turns out to be distinctly second best. The narrator is a Levite—like Agnon himself, the biographically minded reader might recall—and if the Jerusalem Temple still stood, he opines, he would be singing in the Levitical choirs in the Temple precincts. In the present moment while the Temple is still destroyed (the emphasis on the "still" underscores his messianist outlook), he contents himself with study as a compensation for the stilled songs that accompanied the Temple worship. At this juncture, we are still at a distance from the enterprise of writing fiction, and the threefold sequence that leads to this end unfolds with telegraphic brevity.

First comes the sadness that arises from the realization that of the great tradition of learning there is nothing left but a memory (*zikhron devarim*). The sadness causes his heart to tremble, and it is finally this trembling that leads him to the writing of stories. The term the narrator uses for stories is *sippurei ma'asiyot*, and it would be a mistake to take it unquestioningly as a reference to modern fiction. If one is intent on reading "The Sense of Smell" as a story by Agnon about Agnon, thus conflating the author with the autobiographical narrator, then one arrives at that conclusion directly. Yet the term is, in fact, taken from the discourse of Hasidism and refers to allegorical narratives (as opposed to textual commentary and sermons) told by hasidic masters to convey esoteric religious meaning; it is closely associated with the tales told by Nahman of Bratslav. Consistent with his self-presentation so far, the narrator remains within the orbit of piety and does not identify himself with the enterprise of modern literature. Yet at the same time, he describes a trajectory of fallenness that passes from the sacred songs of the Levites through the textual erudition of the sages to the prosaics of telling tales.

As if to give us an illustration of this belated vocation, the narrator concludes with a parable; although the parable is familiar from the classical midrashim about the destruction of the Temple, it takes on new meaning in this context. In the midrash, the father's palace is the Temple itself; in exile, the Jews sit in synagogues and study houses, fallen substitutes for the Temple, and tell of the glory of the destroyed sanctuary. In the way in which the narrator is appropriating the midrash, it is the postbiblical writings of the sages (Mishnah, Talmud, etc.) that correspond to the father's house, and in the wake of the loss of that tradition the narrator sits in his hut (the impoverished house of fiction or stories, as it were) and tells (*mesapper*) of the glories that are no more.

It is the hut that serves as the thematic hinge between the story's discursive introduction and its narrative proper. The hut is, of course, nothing other than a sukkah, and in "The Sense of Smell" the notion of the sukkah is used in three senses: as a humble temporary dwelling, as a traditional epithet for the Jerusalem Temple, and as the booth that Jews erect and take their meals in during the week of the autumn Sukkot festival. Although it is in this last sense that the sukkah is understood in the remainder of the story, the echoes of the transcendent, lost sanctuary are never wholly absent. This is part of a larger fundamental duality in "The Sense of Smell" that is never overtly resolved. The narrator presents himself as embarked on a mission of high seriousness whose stakes involve nothing less than the purity and integrity of the divinely inspired Hebrew language. At the same time, techniques of parody deflate the high drama of the episode and present it as a tempest in a teapot that ultimately draws attention to the grandiosity of the narrator's self-conception.

The deflationary effect is chiefly conveyed through the story's stylistic register and outward organization. The division of this short text into fullblown chapters with cumbersome titles that importantly summarize the matter of each chapter—all this evokes the tracts and controvertialist literature of the eighteenth century in Western Europe, and later, the Haskalah in Hebrew literature. The deployment of grand rhetoric on behalf of a grammatical controversy about two words recalls such mock-epic works from an earlier period as *The Rape of the Lock* and *A Tale of the Tub*. The spat is given a mock-heroic elevation in which the conflict assumes the proportions of mortal combat. The carping grammarian lances the narrator with his pen, and the narrator swoons. "The Sense of Smell" could have been properly renamed "A Tale of Two Words." Even though the incident that gave rise to the story had taken place just before the time of the writing and within the arena of modern novels and their serialization in newspapers—a scene from Agnon's most secular novel *Sippur pashut* (A simple story) as excerpted in *Ha'aretz*—the language of the story is pointedly archaized. The figure of the narrator, moreover, resembles not the modern writer that Agnon was but a pious author from an earlier age. As Anne Golomb Hoffman has noticed, the narrator makes a point of referring to himself not as a *sofer*, a writer in the modern sense, but as a *meḥabber*, an older term for an author-compiler-redactor who has no pretensions to originality or artifice.

Chapter 4 summarizes the narrator's dilemma. He cannot dismiss the grammarian's attack because, in his eyes, the charge is far from trivial. For if he has, in fact, misused the verb in question by inventing a new grammatical construction, then he is indeed guilty of sinning against the divinely ordained properties of the Hebrew language as interpreted through the chain of tradition. The quest for vindication he now embarks upon, in fact, nearly ends in failure. The so-called experts he consults adduce opinions but no evidence, and the one obscure reference he is directed to does little to put his mind at rest. He is about to accept his guilt and recant, but at the last moment he is mysteriously rescued from the fateful act of erasure.

The first stage of the narrator's rescue revolves around the figure of Jacob of Lissa, a rabbinical scholar active in Poland at the end of the eighteenth century and the beginning of the nineteenth. While Jacob of Lissa is hardly an obscure figure, he is not one that would be immediately recognizable to the average Hebraically literate reader. The fact that his familiarity is limited to pious and scholarly circles is a further indicator of where the narrator locates himself. The qualities the narrator admires in Jacob of Lissa also tell us as much about the former as the latter. In conversation with the scholar who was carrying the prayer book of the Sage of Lissa, the narrator expatiates on Jacob's rare commitment to the ideal of utility. Even though he was a master of sophisticated and erudite talmudic scholarship, the sage took the time to compile a useful and usable compendium of laws and customs related to prayer.

When later that night, the sage appears to the narrator in a dream, holding his prayer book open in his hand, what is remarkable is not the ghostly visitation itself but the narrator's confidence in recognizing the identity of the sage, whose likeness he has never before seen. He makes the identification on the basis of the radiance of the sage's face, which, he explains, God bestows on scholars as a reward for the privation they endure in their devotion to the study of Torah. The radiance is given to he who "darkens his face over study of Torah," and this phrase, unsurprisingly, is exactly the same one that the narrator uses at the beginning of chapter 3 to describe his own self-deprivation in the service of the study of Torah and the purity of the Hebrew language. The linkage between the narrator and the Sage of Lissa is further strengthened when, upon awakening, the narrator goes to his bookcase, takes the sage's prayer book in hand, and triumphantly discovers what he has been looking for: a passage in which the verb "to smell" is used intransitively. Although the providential prompting to consult the prayer book surely comes through the dream, the exact location of the exculpatory passage is marked by a slip of paper inserted by none other than the narrator himself, who, at some time in the unremembered past, had marked—and apparently absorbed—the verb in this unusual usage. The standing of the narrator is hardly diminished by this fact. Not only do the "righteous from paradise come to the author's aid," as encapsulated in the chapter's title, but their intercession serves less as a revelation of something unknown than as a catalyst for the narrator's recovered memory of his own scholarship.

The validation offered by the Sage of Lissa and his uncle Javetz (Jacob Emden) is pleasing to the narrator, but there remains a final and more exalted level of confirmation to be granted him. It is more exalted because it issues not only from an earlier link in the chain of tradition but from the greatest authority of that earlier age. The Sage of Lissa and his uncle may be great lights of the latter authorities, the *aharonim*, but Rashi is the greatest light of the earlier authorities, the *rishonim*. The story of how the narrator is vouchsafed Rashi's approval of his intuitive use of the Hebrew language occupies the final movement of "The Sense of Smell." The earlier sections of the story concern the narrator's production of language as a writer and the responses it provokes from others. The final section concerns the consumption of the language rather than its production. We see the narrator in a private moment of communion with the text, and it is in that posture that he is given, as if by grace, the final consummation.

When the narrator awakes from his dream at the beginning of chapter 6, it is too late to go back to sleep and too early to recite the morning prayer. This time, between the states of sleeping and waking and night and day, is a liminal zone that is vulnerable to the unsettling vagaries of the imagination. The narrator takes the deliberate step of filling this interval with the recitation of psalms, a traditionally pious measure aimed at rescuing "dead" time from unwanted thoughts. The narrator frames his choice in terms of a substitution of one kind of language for another. Once the day comes with its social intercourse, one's lips will inevitably be "defiled by wicked chatter"; but now, while the "soul is still pure," he grasps the chance to infuse it with the discourse of the sacred. The posture of receptivity is the key here. Psalm saying is not "learning" in the traditional sense of an active engagement with the contradictions of a text in order to wrest new meanings from it. He is communing with the text and letting its words wash over him; he moves quickly and fluidly through dozens of psalms, pausing to consult Rashi's commentary only when he needs to.

The consummation of "The Sense of Smell" comes in the form of a textual reverie. The reverie is presented as a kind of contest between the realm of nature and the realm of the text. In the darkness before dawn, the two realms start out in sympathetic vibration; inside, the table lamp crowns every letter with light, while outside breezes and fragrances dance and waft without disturbing the quiet recitation of psalms indoors. At first light, the song of one bird is heard and then the song of a second bird; the two compete jealously at first and then join to sing in harmony "new songs, the likes of which no ear had ever heard." Although this music would ordinarily be irresistible, the narrator is at pains to point out that he had no trouble remaining absorbed in his recitation because the psalm he was reading "played itself like an instrument of many strings" and produced a "Song of Love, next to which all other songs are as nothing." The beauty of nature is thus ultimately absorbed and superseded by the greater beauty of sacred textuality in which the narrator has immersed himself. As he consults Rashi for a gloss on verse 9 of Psalm 45, he is given the ultimate gift of having his suspect deployment of a Hebrew verb vindicated by none other than the greatest of the medieval sages.

Why Psalm 45? Most modern students of the Bible read Psalm 45 as a hymn written by a court poet celebrating the marriage of a young king. In the rabbinic reading followed by Rashi—and followed in turn by the narrator—the subject of the psalm is Torah scholars as a class. The praise of the young king's military prowess is transformed by Rashi into admiration for the scholar's intense acuity in learned debates. The pen of verse 2 becomes the sword of verse 4, and vice versa. Rashi's appropriation of the trope of militancy brings us back to the polemical premise of "The Sense of Smell" as a story. (There are, in fact, an abundance of intertextual connections between the psalm and the story that a fuller analysis would profitably bring to light.) As a kind of scholar-knight militant, the narrator repulses an attack by his antagonist and is confirmed in the purity of his faithfulness to the Order of the Holy Tongue.

For the sake of a single word of this holy tongue, the ultra-short concluding chapter worshipfully tells us, a holy man bestirred himself from heaven and the narrator was guided to his psalmic revelation. Yet the attentive reader knows that this is far from the whole story. The pious naivete of the narrator's persona is progressively undercut by the self-referential nature of the narrative; it is he and no other who is decisively there as the recipient of revelation. This becomes a principled and critical self-importance when the narrator locates his belated vocation of storytelling as the last link in the great chain of authority and learning. The narrator's self-regard, it should be kept in mind, is contained within the larger authority of Agnon the author. This is a saving distinction. For in his capacity for self-ironization, Agnon reveals himself as one of the great modernists of our literature.

NOTE

Originally published in *Reading Hebrew Literature: Critical Discussions of Six Modern Texts*, ed. Alan Mintz (Waltham: Brandeis University Press, 2003), pp. 126–34.

# CHAPTER 6

# Reading *Haḥazanim*

One of the wonders of *'Ir umelo'ah* is Agnon's creation of a narrator who can curate the memory of Buczacz over a period of several centuries. The nearly 150 stories in this volume represent the most ambitious project Agnon undertook in the years between the end of World War II and his death in 1970. To provide coherence to this epic cycle of stories, Agnon fashioned a narrator-chronicler who is the reader's guide to this ancestral world. The narrator is a man of Buczacz who shares the religious norms of the society he is chronicling but stands at somewhat of a distance. His conspicuous endowment is his omniscience: He knows the intimate thoughts of a lowly shamash in the middle of the seventeenth century as well as the text of a letter of rabbinical appointment a century later. He confirms the reliability of his authority by acknowledging the small details he is not sure of, whether, for example, a traveler paid 12 or 15 coins for a particular inter-city carriage ride at the end of the eighteenth century. The temporal range of his knowledge is similarly magically comprehensive. Although he knows about the extermination of the Jews of Buczacz in World War II, he narrates the events of earlier centuries from the point of view of a close contemporary. Above all, the narrator is in charge of the executive organization of the narrative, meting out by the yard the representational coverage allotted to each character and incident, and all the while offering justifications for abbreviating the account of certain plot events and lavishing generous digressions upon others.

Fashioning this narrator required Agnon to make some significant renunciations. One of the most fertile and most familiar modes of Agnon's classic mature style is based on what Arnold Band called the "dramatized ego." A story is typically told in the voice of, or from the point of view of, a middle-aged religious writer very much like Agnon himself, or even, in the case of *Oreiaḥ natah lalun,* one who bears his name. Agnon's willingness to leverage his own persona for ironic and even parodic purposes was one of his greatest strengths as a writer. Yet these kinds of reflexive, narcissistic entanglements no longer served when it came to the task of chronicling the spiritual history of Buczacz in periods far removed from Agnon's time. For the same reason, Agnon could not have recourse to a less ironic mode of relatedness to the immediate past that had served him well in such stories as *Hamitpaḥat* and *Shnei zugot:* the sensibility of the child—again very much like the persona of the young author—who savors the grace of family love within the bosom of an enchanted religious world. In both cases the involvement with self had to be put aside in favor of a narratorial stance marked by impersonality and anonymity.

How Agnon constructs the narrator of *'Ir umelo'ah* is not merely a technical question; it goes to the essence of the master's most innovative and ambitious undertaking of his later years. During that period, which we might call "late Agnon," Agnon is busy revising earlier works, compiling thematic anthologies (*Atem re'item, Sefer, sofer, sipur*), rethinking the years of his German sojourn (*'Ad henah, Beḥanuto shel Mar Lublin*), and writing more stories in the high modernist mode of *Sefer hama'sim* (*'Edo ve'enam, 'Ad olam*). The one project that was a wholly new departure was a cycle of some 150 stories about Buczacz that were written during the 1950s and 1960s. The majority of the stories were published in *Ha'aretz* during the author's lifetime; all the stories were gathered and arranged according to Agnon's instructions by his daughter Emunah Yaron and published in a single volume in 1973 as *'Ir umelo'ah.* What was new about the project was obviously *not* the fact that its subject was Buczacz. Agnon had been writing about his hometown—often dubbed Shibbush, an inversion of Buczacz— from many different perspectives throughout his career. But the murder of the Jews of Buczacz by the Nazis and their Ukrainian helpers in the spring of 1943 marked a fateful boundary. Agnon had already anatomized the

physical decimation and spiritual decline of Buczacz in the aftermath of
World War I in *Oreiaḥ natah lalun;* the finality and totality of what occurred
during the next destruction required Agnon to undertake a fundamental
rethinking of his relationship to the ancestral world represented by Buczacz.
What of this complex, titanic, centuries-old civilization is it most important
to remember? Given his age, Agnon must have understood that this was
his last chance to answer this question. And given his self-identification
as the only real link between the classical past and the renascent world of
Israeli-Hebrew letters, he likely did not view himself as free to desist from
taking up the challenge.

The choices Agnon made are implicit in the composition of *'Ir umelo'ah.* Fundamental was the decision to avoid the modern period and focus
on the two centuries following the Khmelnytsti Massacres of 1648. This
was the period when, as the book's narrator tells us repeatedly, "Buczacz
was Buczacz," that is to say, when the town was truly a *qehilah qedoshah*
living under the sway of Jewish law and learning. The removal of the focus
from the present made another fundamental point: On Agnon's watch the
memory of East European Jewry would not become fused with catastrophe
and atrocity as had become the case with the emerging "Holocaust literature." Within this more remote timeframe, Agnon made further choices
to delimit his subject matter. From among the many aspects of a complex
society, Agnon—not unexpectedly—chose to make worship and study the
norms around which the larger world of Buczacz would be constellated. *'Ir
umelo'ah* begins with a description of the synagogues and study houses of
the town and their functionaries and then proceeds to an accounting of the
great rabbis and scholars who served the community. The stories contain
a wealth of attention to political, economic and even criminal events and
forces, but these matters are always presented in their relationship to the
privileged norms of worship and study.

The pronounced specificity of the information presented in *'Ir umelo'ah* is the sign of another critical choice: The world of Galician Jewry can
be adequately rendered only by a radical allegiance to one place. It is the
delimited anatomization of Buczacz that enables the town to stand for a
whole civilization. As Dublin was to Joyce, Bucacz was to Agnon. Another
key decision was to insist on fiction as the medium for engaging the lost
ancestral past as opposed to a spectrum of other, more documentary, modal-
ities such as yizker bikher, anthologies of historical sources, ethnographic

or folklore studies, and memoirs. *'Ir umelo'ah*, to be sure, contains a certain amount of concrete information about the customs and institutions of Buczacz. But the core of the book is a series of stunning short stories that we as modern readers unhesitatingly identify as fiction, even if the book's narrator presents them as truthful chronicles. Camouflage is in fact central to the book's enterprise, and the traditionalist conventions of the narrator's discourse have kept many readers from seeing the way in which Agnon refused to put away his modernist toolkit when he undertook this project. And finally back to the critical role of the narrator. In the enterprise of reimagining the lost ancestral world, the narrator is Agnon's gatekeeper. It is he who mediates the relationship between us, the modern readers, and Galician Jewry centuries ago and shapes the attitudes we adopt toward this remote world.

It is my hope that this general introduction to the ambitions and poetics of *'Ir umelo'ah* will help to explain why *Haḥazanim* is such a fascinating story. The placement of the story, to begin with, is important. The story comes early in Book One of *'Ir umelo'ah*; after the synagogues and study houses of Buczacz have been described, the account of the various *qelei qodesh* begins: first the ḥazanim and then the gabbaim, and later on the rabbanim. When it comes to the ḥazanim, the narrator emphasizes the dynastic continuity of the incumbents of that office. It is the many generations of the Wernick family, descendants of R. Yitzhak Wernick, who have led the congregation in prayer, delighted bridegrooms at their weddings, and enlivened circumcision ceremonies. The narrator similarly emphasizes the deep continuity in the sacred music of Buczacz, whose traditions loyally hark back to the customs of the town's founders, who came from the Rhineland Valley of Germany. Each ḥazan in this chain of tradition may have introduced some new melodic setting of his own and by which he is known; but the innovation remains an ornament in a fabric of tradition that has been carefully preserved. In chronicling these continuities, the narrator is documenting and manifesting the normative thrust of *'Ir umelo'ah*. Here is a world he is happy to show that is at one with the norms of worship and study.

Here is a world, however, that *also* contains instances of rupture and deviance, and the narrator, the responsible chronicler that he is, is not free to disregard them. Yekutiel, the eldest son of R. Yitzhak Wernick, loses his voice and cedes his office to his younger brother Eliah. Eliah's wife, Miriam Devorah, is herself a gifted composer of liturgical music and folk songs; but because she is a woman her talents are largely demeaned and disregarded, and she dies an early death from melancholy. Her children are raised by a good woman who insists that the boys become businessmen rather than professional ḥazanim so they will not be dependent on the community. Thus, by the end of the story, most of the norms cherished by the narrator—continuity, succession, individual fulfillment within the tradition—have been subverted or come to naught, along with, at the center, a kind of gruesome, prolonged suicide. It is precisely here, in the disheartening and dispirited gap between norm and deviation, that the fictive tissue of 'Ir umelo'ah is generated. Agnon's narrator is duty bound to relate these deviations and to explain them as best he can, and from this duty comes the need to imagine the characters' motives and their inner thoughts, that is, to tell a story that is more than a chronicle.

Before turning toward the story itself, there is one remaining general question to be asked: Who is the implied audience/reader for this and the other stories of 'Ir umelo'ah? Although this is a perplexing issue in Agnon's work as a whole, and one not sufficiently investigated, it has special poignancy because of the avowed purpose of the book, stated in large letters in a special declaration following the title page, to make known "to our children who will come after us that our city was a city full of Torah, wisdom, love" before its destruction. But this explicitly stated audience is not necessarily the same as the audience that is implied—projected and created, really—by the discourse of the narrator. That narrator, as we have seen, does not speak in the language of the generations to come but rather in the language of "Buczacz when it was Buczacz," that is, within the world of the tradition, even if he stands a little above and a little to the side. So although he knows about the Holocaust, he does not have accessible to him—or he does not avail himself of—modern explanatory frameworks for understanding human experience. Take the example of Miriam Devorah's marah sheḥorah in our story. Whereas we might call her illness clinical depression resulting from social and gender marginalization, the story's narrator, operating within the norms of the society he is writing about, relies on a premodern repertoire of explanations, including the evil eye, demons, and the doctrine of gilgul nefashot. We can now better understand the ironic manipulation Agnon has contrived for us. He provokes us into savoring the gap between the behaviors described by the narrator and the limitations of the traditional explanations the narrator adduces for them.

Before understanding Miriam Devorah's problem, it's important to understand her gift. The daughter of a ḥazan and the wife of a ḥazan, she outshines them on several scores. She not only has a voice that matches her father's in quality but she possesses a capacity for original musical composition that goes beyond anything attested in the region. Other ḥazanim may at best become known for the musical setting of one particular prayer, whereas others, like her brother-in-law Yekutiel, "did not change a single melody and composed no new melodies of his own" (p. 79).[1] Miriam Devorah, on the other hand, produces original compositions in several genres of sacred music, including, "new melodies for prayers and piyyutim—in particular, for the kerovah recited on the Sabbath just before the month of Nisan" (p. 80), as well as composing original folk songs in Yiddish, one of which the narrator produces from memory on pages 81–82. The provocation she presents, then, is twofold. Not only is she a woman who makes her voice heard within the male precincts of liturgy, but she presumes, abundantly, to compose original material in a way that implicitly challenges the allegiance Buczacz prides itself in to the ancient traditions brought by the founders from Ashkenaz. Her liturgical melodies, in any case, are not performed because "it was said that a woman's voice could be discerned in them" (p. 81). As a halakhic concept, *qol eshah*, of course refers only to the performance of music by a woman and not to its composition by a woman. But in their zeal—and, we would say, their misogyny—the men of Buczacz take the injunction to an unmandated further step.

Miriam Devorah's gift is disruptive in two additional ways. Because of her early death, her sons are raised by a stepmother who steers them away from depending on the community for their livelihood as impedes the business of chronicling the succession of the town's religious professionals, professional ḥazanim; and so the generations-long hold of the Wernick family on the office of ḥazan is broken. On the level of the narrator's mission within *'Ir umelo'ah* as a whole, Miriam Devorah's case an account in which women would seem to play no part, until, of course, they do. Her story is thus a necessary diversion from the main road, or to put it in the terms used above, a deviation from the norm.

I count five different explanations offered to account for Miriam Devorah's affliction.[2] Their order of occurrence in the story is significant, as is the matter of who presents them. The first is offered by her own father R. Nissan, who travels from a neighboring village where he serves as ḥazan in order to dispel her melancholy. To amuse her and lift her out of her funk, he uses his uncanny vocal skills to imitate the voices of familiar village characters. But when he sees that his efforts provide only a fleeting distraction, he changes his tone entirely and speaks to her with the utmost gravity. He surmises that the root of her sadness is a harsh disappointment with the world. Her asks her, "Did you think that the world was created for rejoicing?" and then concludes, "Now that you see that there is no happiness in the world, you are distraught at your mistake" (p. 82). After unexpectedly throwing this glass of existential cold water in her face, he boasts that he himself had never made the same error, or if he had, he would never let anyone catch him at it. Behind this rebuke would seem to be the assumption that his daughter's malaise is due to her failure to adjust her expectations to the realities of adulthood. (We find out later that she is the only surviving child of her parents' many children, and, married at a young age, she had found it difficult to attach herself to her husband; but this is information we do not have at this point.) R. Nissin does not endeavor to investigate the sources of her unhappiness, and he curtly tells her, as we would say today, "Get over it!" or "Snap out of it!"

The second diagnosis is teased out by the narrator from an enigmatic statement made by R. Mikhl, the buffoonish wonder-working *ba'al hashem* summoned to cure Miriam Devorah. The story of R. Mikhl and his extravagant beard, a comic gem in itself, is the longest narrative subunit in the story, and it comes complete with the narrator's over-wrought apologies for the digression and the order in which it is told, with the phrase, "I will pause now from this story" (p. 84). The digression is set in the decades before one *ba'al shem* would come down from the hills and found a revivalist movement that would conquer this part of the known Jewish world. In the meantime, we are shown the farcical self-importance of one such specimen through the normative rabbinic eyes of the narrator. This is a perspective shared by Miriam Devorah herself, who has no compunctions about ridiculing him to his face and predicts that R. Mikhl's beard will be burned off in a mock-epic battle with bed bugs. Her cheeky disrespect would seem to express a sense of hurt and outrage at the idea that her affliction, in all its tangled pain, could be comprehended, much less treated, by an imbecile like R. Mikhl. Nonetheless, the narrator takes pains to decipher the diagnosis that is encoded in R. Mikhl's riposte to her taunt, and he shows himself surprisingly adept in parsing the nuances of the demonology that the *ba'al shem* traffics in. The upshot is this: Because Miriam Devorah inverted the proper order of gender relations, since, as the narrator explains, ". . . it is accepted that a man courts a woman, and it is not generally accepted that a woman does the courting" (p. 86), she has been set upon by female evils spirits, which are known to be crueler and more unrelenting than male spirits.

R. Manele, the next healer consulted, is another story entirely. He lives in a workers' quarter across the Strypa River in Buczacz itself, and the narrator has a good time ventriloquizing the hectoring voice of Miriam Devorah's mother Pua as she berates her husband and son-in-law for not taking advantage of a resource to be found right under their noses. As vain and silly as is R. Mikhl, R. Manele is ascetic and humble. The narrator treats us to an extended description of R. Manele's daily spiritual exercises, which begin with a complex sequence of early-morning immersions in the river, summer and winter, configured differently each day according to esoteric kabbalistic principles. (The way in which the narrator imitates the discourse of each of the distinct religious circles in the story deserves more attention. In a truly Bakhtinian sense, the narrator orchestrates and circulates these different discourses while maintaining control of the story as a whole.) R. Manele is a *sofer stam* who purposefully produces only a small number of tefillin and *mezuzot* because he will sell them only to Jews of true piety and because he, who is comfortable with material privation, does not want to adversely affect the livelihood of the other scribes of the town, who do not so easily embrace the ascetic life.

R. Manele also writes amulets for the afflicted, but not until after investigating the cause of the affliction and matching it to the proper esoteric formulas. When approached by Miriam Devorah's parents, the holy man tells them that rather than writing an amulet he will give them advice. Based on his clairvoyant understanding of Miriam Devorah's situation, he identifies the source of her melancholy. He explains:

> I examined the causes and saw that everything that happened to her was because of the evil eye that was put upon her. Because of our great sins, there are women who look askance at their neighbors and set the evil eye upon them. The woman on whose behalf you have come to me has had the evil eye placed upon her because of her voice, a gift that God gave her (p. 89).

The sure remedy for her malady, R. Manele confidently advises, lies not in writing an amulet but in taking a piece of a fish fin and hanging it around her neck. Why? Because the numerical value of the Hebrew word for "fin" (*snapir*) as well as the expression for "evil eye" (*ayin har'a*) is 400, and this will allow the former to neutralize the latter. For the reader, the revelation that fish fin therapy is the best R. Manele has to offer bursts the balloon that has been inflated by the narrator with his careful and admiring description of the holy man's self-abnegating piety and his solicitude toward those who appeal to him for help. In the final analysis, this austere kabbalist has no more to offer than the foolish *ba'al shem*, and, diagnostically, there is more common ground between them than we might have expected. R. Mikhl too locates the origins of her trouble in female-to-female hostility. He at least acknowledges her voice as a divine gift and views her as a victim rather than a party responsible for provoking others. Given the norms of the period, it would not be surprising for men to assign the blame for female hysteria or melancholy to the catty and envious essence of women's nature if it were not for the abundant evidence provided earlier in the story. Miriam Devorah is in fact described as being much beloved and sought after by the women of Buczacz. And if her musical compositions for the synagogue service are rejected by the male religious leaders, her Yiddish folk songs gladden the hearts of women when they gather together to do their chores:

> ... women, while working or sitting and plucking feathers or sewing and weaving, would sweeten their labor with her songs (p. 81).

The fourth interpreter of Miriam Devorah's condition is Miriam Devorah herself. The narrator has it on the authority of the *tsadeket* Leah Rahel, who was confided in by Miriam Devorah at an early point in her illness that her depression was the result of a dream she had one Yom Kippur evening. She dreamt that she was dressed in a kittel and talit and leading a large congregation in prayer. The sequence of her responses to the dream is significant. At first she was suffused with joy; but then she began to interpret the dream in one direction and then in another. Finally she concludes that the dream was a means of informing her that in a previous *gilgul* she was a man and not a woman. Thus began a project of self-examination in which she reviewed all the actions she had taken in her life with a view to identifying the sin or shortcoming that had been responsible for her being returned to the world as a woman. Once begun, the process of self-scrutiny could not be arrested. As the narrator explains, "She became melancholy and wandered about despondently until she came to the gates of death" (p. 90).

Note that there was nothing predetermined about the meaning of the dream. Miriam Devorah felt joyful in its aftermath and could have easily taken it as a heavenly confirmation of her gift rather as evidence of hidden sin. But in the end she is as much a creature of the spiritual universe she lives in as are the men of her generation, and that universe had had imprinted upon it the theological doctrines of Lurianic Kabbalah that had begun to be transmitted to Polish Jewry in the seventeenth century. (Miriam Devorah's husband becomes dangerously immersed in Sefer Hemdat Yamim, one of the links in that transmission.) Transmigration of souls, *gilgul*, is one of those new doctrines, and, to the tragic detriment to her mental health, she adopts it as the interpretive template to explain her dream.

The last perspective on the origins of Miriam Devorah's illness is offered by the narrator himself, but only by implication. In the voice of the responsible chronicler who is tying up loose ends, the narrator reports on the basis of the epitaph on her tombstone that Miriam Devorah left behind six children who had been born in quick succession. We further learn that some of the children were quite young when she died and that her husband was so overwhelmed by taking care of them that he had to take a year's leave from his cantorate. In describing the long span of R. Elia's career, the narrator mentions, almost in passing, that he and Miriam Devorah were married for a number of years before they had children. By way of explanation, the narrator informs us that Miriam Devorah was still a *qetanah* at the time of her marriage, a minor below the age of 12 or 13, and that for a number of years she was so attached to her parents that she would leap on any carriage that was traveling from Buczacz to return to her village. Eventually she reconciled herself to her fate and to her role as a wife and a mother and returned to her husband: "After several years, she reconciled herself to the fact that a woman was meant to be with her husband. She returned to R. Elya and did not leave him, giving birth to daughters and sons" (p. 91).

Although the narrator draws no interpretive conclusions from these observations, after placing them before us modern readers, the facts speak for themselves and produce a commonsense psychological explanation of Miriam Devorah's depression. The lone surviving child among many, she was forcibly separated from her parents as a girl and expected to become a wife and a mother before she was developmentally ready to assume those sexual and reproductive roles. (It remains unexplained why, under the customary *kest* system, the young couple did not board with her parents in her village rather than her being installed in the town of her in-laws.) The fact that after a number of years she found it possible to do her duty does not mean that the earlier trauma did not leave a lasting impact.

Taking all of these interpretations together, it is crucial to note that the order in which they are presented in the narrative, which I have preserved in my listing above, is not identical to the order in which they occur in the events of the story. This is the famous gap between *fabula* and *sujet;* I prefer to use the terms proposed by Shlomit Rimon-Kenan: *story,* which denotes the "raw" chronological sequence of events within the work's fictional world, and *text,* the order in which these events are narrated or released into the knowledge of the reader. In our story, the two orders are almost entirely opposed to one another. Leaving aside R. Nisan's visit to his daughter, the interventions on the part of R. Mikhl and R. Manele come at the end of Miriam Devorah's illness. (A delay of several days in putting R. Manele's fish fin therapy into practice is purportedly the cause of her death.) Miriam Devorah's dream, as the initiating event of her three-year illness, long preceded the consultations with the healers. Earliest of all (yet the last to be presented) is the trauma of parental separation and premature marriage.

This deliberately inverted structure, to begin with, should disabuse us of any notions about the telling of this story, or of any of the stories in *'Ir umelo'ah* for that matter, as being merely a chronicling of events. The executive control of the narrator is demonstrated again and again. But in the particular story at hand what is the strategic purpose behind the calculated, delayed release of information to the reader? The argument I wish to make to account for this structure is based on assumptions presented earlier concerning the composite nature both of the story's narrator and of its implied audience. The narrator is at one and the same time—or perhaps he actualizes different aspects of his identity at different times—a man of Buczacz who shares the normative views of its townspeople in its heyday as well as being a man who has a foot in the modern world. Correspondingly, the implied audience is made up of listeners or readers who are similarly allied to the values of the traditional world—ranging, perhaps, over several centuries—as well as readers who inhabit the post-Enlightenment world of modernity, contemporaneous to the mid-twentieth century when the story was written and published. In the text of *Hahazanim*—as opposed to its story—the order of presentation moves from the traditional to the modern. The reality of demons and the malevolent effects of the evil eye belong to the inventory of medical wisdom of early modern Polish Jewry, though they seem most distant from post-Enlightenment readers. This is the case as well for the misogynist attitudes toward the incursion of women into the realm of liturgy and public worship. The implied traditional audience would find credible the etiologies based on esoteric lore offered by R. Mikhl and R. Manele, while the implied modern audience would understand how these very attitudes toward female spirituality contributed materially to Miriam Devorah's fatal melancholy. The buffoonery of one figure and the fish-fin remedy of the other are an obvious satirical treat for latter-day readers.

As the text moves toward the belated disclosure of Miriam Devora's dream, her situation comes into clearer and more sympathetic focus for the modern reader. We are allowed access to her own thoughts through the mediation of a female confidant (the *tsadeket* Leah Rahel). She is thereby extricated from the perceptual grid of male society and becomes a subject unto herself. The tragedy of her situation is that she cannot own that subjectivity and, simply, as it were, endure as woman with a gift for religious creativity in a culture that forecloses that possibility. New currents of kabbalistic piety, engaging men and women alike, prompt her to explain her anomalous nature as the result of a much darker transaction, which, in turn, makes her gender a punishment for an indeterminate sin. Miriam Devorah is what today we would call a transgender figure. Agnon's contemporary readers might not have been likely to embrace the cultural assumptions that accompany this term, but they surely would have been aware of the mix-match of sex and gender as a widely-discussed phenomenon in modern psychology as well as far-ranging debates about the role of women in positions of leadership in modern Jewish life. When this enlightened sensibility is added to the account of Miriam Devorah's ordeal as a child bride, the sum total of her situation paints the portrait of a martyr to her gift if not to her gender.

Yet despite the fact that her ordeal has been humanized, Miriam Devorah remains a problem for the narrator. If her existence is not a scandal, it is certainly an irritant, and it is an obstacle to the narrator's original mission to chronicle the history of the hazanim of Buczacz. Out of a debt to truth, the anomalousness of her divine gift has required him to pause and embark on a long digression. And now, after Miriam Devorah's death, the narrator seeks to repair the rupture and bring the world of Buczacz back into alignment under the banner of authority and transmission. The result is the story of Rivka Henya, which completes and recoups the tragic tale of the hazan's daughter. Rivka Henya is burdened with no special gift aside, that is, from a resourceful capacity to be the kind of mother Miriam Devorah could not be. She takes charge of the household and raises the many children of her melded family with loving impartiality; and she does all of this with little apparent help from her husband, who is absorbed in the otherworldly mysteries of Sefer Hemdat Hayamim.

Even though *Hahazanim* is a short story, its last two pages inform us of the destinies of the next generation in a way that resembles the epilogue to a great novel like *Middlemarch*. The fates of Miriam Devorah's children, as shaped by Rivka Henya's strong hand, contain elements of both comedy and tragedy. Order and happiness have been restored, but at the price of costly renunciations. One the one hand, all of the children either themselves become great merchants or are married to them. (The narrator does not know how many were girls and how many boys.) They were so distinguished and trustworthy that they were relied upon in business matters by the gentile authorities, a position that allowed them to intercede on behalf of their brethren. On the other hand, Rivka Henya does not allow them to succeed their father and uncle in the professional cantorate; she does not want them to be beholden to or dependent on the whims of the community. Thus, the hazanic dynasty of the Wernick family in Buczacz comes to an end. And even though the narrator has much more information to share with us about the children and their descendents, he is constrained by his own taxonomic principles to bring his story to a halt. As the narrator explains: ". . . since I intended only to report on the hazanim of our town, and since they [their children and descendants] were not hazanim, I will leave them behind and continue only with the stories of hazanim" (p. 97). Family history and institutional history must go their separate ways; and the narrator's ultimate allegiance is to recouping Buczacz under the banner of Torah and worship.

But the story does not leave us without offering some mediation between the terms of this inexorable either/or: a sacred musical vocation dependent on the community *or* the life of a pious and civic-minded *ba'al habayit*. Miriam Devorah's gift survives her in a minor yet significant way. The Torah *trop* she taught her sons is in turn disseminated by them to the next generations of boys in the town, and thus her style of cantillation becomes the general norm in Buczacz, although ironically its female origin is forgotten. And then there is her youngest son Elchanan, who has about him the touch of a poet. It is he who inherits his mother's gift for composition. A dreamy artist who becomes lost in creative meditation—at times, to the consternation of others—he languishes in his assigned job as a shopkeeper who relies on the indulgence of customers who forgive his abstractedness when he does not respond to their requests. Perhaps in the figure of Elchanan we glimpse a foreshadowing of a later Buczacz shopkeeper named Hirschl or even of another dreamy type named Shmuel Yosef, who managed to escape the shopkeeper's life altogether.

## NOTES

Originally published in *Ayin Gimel* 2 (2012), pp. 93–107.

1. All citations of *Haḥazanim* are taken from the translation by Saul Zaritt in *A City in its Fullness*, eds. Alan Mintz and Jeffrey Saks (Connecticut: Toby Press, 2016), 78–97.

2. The story is replete with references to how the catastrophic effects of 1648 have imprinted themselves on the souls of all the characters, including Miriam Devorah and her songs. The massacres are not a direct reason for her melancholy, but they seem to be a contributory factor.

# CHAPTER 7

# Writing About Ourselves

## *Jewish Autobiography, Modern and Premodern*

We live in an age of self-writing. It is barely conceivable that any high public official, successful business leader, or celebrity from any area of entertainment or the arts should pass up the chance to tell his or her story to the reading public. Genuine self-knowledge is the goal of few of these efforts, which attempt, instead, to advance careers, stir up scandal, create spin, secure a "legacy," or, in the best of cases, to bear witness to historical events. "Autobiography," as a phenomenon studied by literary scholars, is something else entirely. It is a historically defined genre that was initiated by Rousseau's *Confessions* in the eighteenth century and then branched out into the literatures of Europe, developing differently according to different norms and cultural pressures. The hallmark of this "classic" autobiography is a reticulated and sophisticated sense of introspection. The autobiographer attempts to account for who he or she has become at the present time of the writing by recalling and examining the succession of earlier selves, with emphasis, *pace* Rousseau, on the importance of childhood, the candid confession of shortcomings and shameful acts, and the formation of sentiments as well as ideas. The autobiographical writings of Goethe, John Stuart Mill, Henry Adams, Cardinal Newman, Osip Mandelstam, Michel Leiris, Simone de Beauvoir, Vladimir Nabokov, and many others made a strong case for the existence of a unique mode of writing, neither novel nor historical treatise, that demanded to be read on its own terms. It was not until the 1970s with the work of Philippe Lejeune in France and James Olney in America that an adequate theoretical framework for describing the poetics of autobiography was developed.

Autobiography as an object of study, however, has refused to remain stable. In the past fifty years the genre has exploded in all directions. It is not a matter of high culture versus popular culture; for it seems as if all serious writers in every field, *especially* academic scholars, are writing about themselves. The issue is that they are often doing so, very unhelpfully for literary critics, in wanton disregard for the canons of the Rousseauean paradigm. The explosion has been retrojected as well. The problem is not just new writing but an ever-expanding conception of what constitutes autobiography in the past. Slave narratives, oral testimonies, diaries, and confessional texts of all sorts composed by subjects who never heard of Rousseau have stretched the category of autobiography to the point of meaninglessness. Racing to catch up, theorists of autobiography have essentially thrown in the towel and agreed to speak of autobiography not as a distinct genre but as a vast map upon which a specific work can be located according to a variety of coordinates.

The strongest challenge to the coherence of autobiography as a genre concerns the expectation of truthfulness. In what remains, to my mind, the most durable definition of the genre, Philippe Lejeune argued that a text is autobiographical not so much for what is in it as for the expectations that readers bring to the reading of it. Fundamental to the reading of an autobiography, he proposed, is the existence of an implicit compact according to whose terms the autobiographer presents his or her work as a truthful presentation of experience and the readers agree to approach it as such. Although as readers we do not expect a novel to be factually loyal to the experience of a specific individual, this is exactly what we expect from an autobiography. Yet time after time we encounter autobiographies by prominent writers and intellectuals that have been exposed as containing mistruths, whether small or large, and we feel that the "autobiographical compact" has been abused in these cases and placed under suspicion generally. It was wickedly amusing when Mary McCarthy famously said that everything Lillian Hellman wrote about herself in her several auto-biographies was a lie, including "and" and "the." Yet it had the effect of underscoring the fact that autobiographical truth is under dispute and in play and unsusceptible to simple disproof or confirmation. The source of this instability may in fact come not so much from mendacity and fabrication as from the vagaries of memory itself. From research in neuroscience we have learned that, despite the will to truth and the conviction of truth, memory works in ways that are not always accountable.[1] This burgeoning instability has not left Jewish literature unaffected. Take, for example, two recent strong works of Israeli literature, both of which are set in the same neighborhoods of mid-twentieth-century Jerusalem. Amos Oz's *Sipur 'al ahavah veḥoshekh* (A Tale of Love and Darkness), a first-person account of the novelist's boyhood and adolescence in the shadow of his mother's suicide, has won a large and enthusiastic audience—and critical accolades as well—both in Hebrew and in translation.[2] It was in the power of this autobiographical work to return Oz to greatness after a long string of mediocre domestic novels. Haim Be'er's *Ḥavalim* (A Pure Element of Time), which was critically well received but deserves to be much more widely known, is an account of the novelist's upbringing within an Orthodox family and his first steps as a writer.[3] The narrative includes an intense evocation of an ultra-Orthodox grandmother and the pious stories she told her grandson as well as a depiction of his parents' difficult marriage. According to conventional definitions, both of these works are autobiographies because, to put it very simply, the authors of the books and the subjects of the books are the same. True, each author fashions an autobiographical narrative persona who describes the evolution of his earlier selves; nevertheless, the entire premise of each book is rooted in the "autobiographical compact," which stipulates that all of these are versions of Amos Oz or Haim Be'er. We further believe that the authors are striving to tell us the truth about their lives, and if the existence of a major distortion of the factual record were proven to us, we would undoubtedly feel violated. Oz's novella *Har ha'etsah hara'ah* (The Hill of Evil Counsel) describes a family situation—a beautiful, romantic woman married to a timid, bookish man—not dissimilar from the narrator's family in *A Tale of Love and Darkness*; at the end of the novella, the narrator's mother runs off with a British officer and abandons the family. Many contemporary readers of the novella knew that Oz's mother had committed suicide, and they understood that in refashioning a representation of the end of his mother's life Oz was exercising the creative freedom accorded him by writing fiction. Yet if in *A Tale of Love and Darkness*, which is presented to us as autobiography, Oz had conveyed his mother's fate as anything other than a suicide, we as readers would feel violated, and we would be led to impugn the integrity of the entire project.

At the same time, the great power of both of these works as literature derives, paradoxically, from the very fact that they read more like novels than classic autobiographies. We are persuaded of the profound truth of these works precisely because of the novelistic techniques they employ so skillfully rather than their loyalty to the factuality of their subjects' lives. The fictionality of these works is flagrant. Oz, for example, offers richly imagined scenes—including dialogue—from the lives of his uncles, aunts, grandparents, and parents in Vilna and Odessa that are unapologetically invented or "re-imagined" on the basis of family stories, historical research, and novelistic intuition. The same phenomenon of novelistic invention—which is never acknowledged as such but always presented as if things simply happened as described—applies to the mature narrator's imagining of the fraught exchanges between his parents based on what he remembers as a young boy. Now, even though Oz has "made up" scenes and conversations he could never have been witness to, if we have entered into the autobiographical compact, we will be inclined to accept, even rejoice in, his novelistic "inventions" as a legitimate means of deepening the work's autobiographical truth by dramatizing it more vividly. If, on the other hand, we resist entering into the autobiographical compact and view the book as an autobiographical *novel* based on Oz's life experience, we would employ a very different set of criteria in reading and judging the work. Yet why be bothered, one might ask, by restrictive definitions to begin with? Why not call *A Tale of Love and Darkness* a *cross* between an autobiography and a novel and simply enjoy it as a strong narrative? I would respond: Yes, indeed; let's do that! But at the same time those of us who are students of literature must acknowledge that this kind of hybridity represents new critical territory for which we have not yet developed adequate maps. (Why it is in fact important to have such maps is another discussion.) This is exactly what is so exciting and so frustrating and so challenging about autobiographical writing. As it crosses boundaries and propagates polymorphously, we, the theorists of literature, are left to play catch-up. Which is exactly as it should be.

By far the most dynamic strain of Jewish self-writing in our time is Holocaust memoirs. What began as a small trickle of survivor accounts has become an entire library, especially if one adds to written memoirs the vast archive of video testimony. Memoirs, to be sure, are different from what we think of as proper, classic autobiographies because they focus on historical events rather than on the inner life of an individual and the artistry of his or her self-explorations. It is just this, the complexity of the autobiographer's craft, which we tend to privilege as modern readers, whereas we regard memoirs as something lesser, as a form of literature valuable mainly as a historical source. The negative transcendence of the Holocaust has stood this ratio on its head. The reticulations of individual self-consciousness fade in importance in the shadow of a fate that is at once brutally collective and at the same time experienced in numerous individual variations. The hundreds upon hundreds of written survivor memoirs—and the tens of thousands of video testimonies—many of which are uncouth in their narrative presentation, become dear to us not only as windows upon the tremendum but as moving instances of personal testimony. Their value lies not just in the historical knowledge we can mine from them but precisely in this personal dimension, which of necessity involves the act of first-person narration in a context in which utter truthfulness is taken for granted.

Now, what role should theory play in reading the corpus of survivor memoirs? Many would argue that it is obscene to apply critical rubrics to these uncalculated acts of witness to unspeakable horror. I believe this position is mistaken even if the sentiments behind it are thoroughly understandable. We do a disservice to Holocaust memoirs if we draw a cordon of piety around them and fail to read them with at least the same intelligence we bring to bear on the reading of "serious" literature, which is often about less important subjects. Each of these memoirs, for example, is a narrative act that inevitably makes use of borrowed tropes, type scenes, and master narratives to tell its story. Each narrative, furthermore, has to do its work within a specific language—English, French, Yiddish, Hebrew, and dozens of others—each of which is its own cultural system with its particular norms of expression, and often this language is a language learned after the war. The radical difference between the Yiddish version of Wiesel's *Night* and the French version that succeeded it is a good illustration. Which of these memoirs stresses the continuity of identity in the teller before and after the Holocaust, and which presents a narrative of brokenness and survival as death-in-life? To open up these issues and explore them would add a great deal to our knowledge as well as honor the victims and the survivors. Yet this is a job of work, necessarily informed by the study of autobiography, which literary theory has not yet taken up.

Our ability to meet these challenges would be greatly enhanced if we were in possession of a clearer picture of the history of Jewish autobiography until now. The picture in fact once *was* clearer. Before the discovery of a number of illuminating premodern autobiographies, it was possible to say with some confidence that autobiography is a modern phenomenon made possible by new notions of the individual self and modeled on Rousseau's unprecedented confessional narrative. The diffusion of this Rouseauean ethos into Haskalah and modern Yiddish and Hebrew literature was easy enough to trace, although surprisingly little of this critical work has actually been done.[4] The picture blurred considerably when scholars pointed to such works as Abraham Yagel's *Ge ḥizayon* (Valley of Vision), Judah Modena's *Ḥaye Yehudah* (Life of Judah), Jacob Emden's *Megilat sefer* (not meaningfully translatable), various first-person family histories written in the form of Lamentation scrolls, and even Gluckel of Hameln's *Zikhroynes* (Memoirs) and claimed that these works should be thought of as instances of autobiographical writing in Jewish literature that either preceded Rousseau or knew nothing of him. With this big-tent approach to autobiography, the category became fungible and threatened to lose its utility as a critical term.

A signal contribution to sorting out this vexed question is made by Marcus Moseley's major study *Being for Myself Alone: Origins of Jewish Autobiography*.[5] Moseley brings to this task a formidable erudition in the Yiddish and Hebrew Haskalah as well as a solid knowledge of European literature and contemporary literary theory bearing on autobiography. He writes with great clarity and analytic wit and avoids temptations to preening despite his considerable learning. The enormous authority that the volume exudes results from Moseley's remarkable scholarly monomania. Beginning with his doctoral work at Oxford in the late 1980s, Moseley has devoted himself with rare focus to the phenomenon of Jewish autobiography and has read every relevant primary text and critical utterance. The strengths and weaknesses of this volume flow directly from this extraordinary single-mindedness. The book is rife with acute insights. Useful and fundamental terms and categories in the study of Jewish autobiography have been clarified. The extensive endnotes and bibliography constitute in themselves a rich resource. And there is no doubt that our understanding of the phenomenon of autobiography in Yiddish and Hebrew is greatly advanced. Yet there is a very real sense in which Moseley has lost his way within the many branching corridors of the edifice he has constructed.

His professed goal is to trace the emergence of what he regards as genuine modern autobiography in the Haskalah. But before approaching this task, he is drawn into a long and ever-ramifying examination of the many pre-modern and contemporary nineteenth-century instances of self-writing in order to distinguish them from his true object. Yet as the prolegomena keep multiplying and mushrooming, his goal keeps receding. When Moseley finally arrives at true autobiographical writing in the Haskalah and Tehiyah periods, he spends an enormous amount of time discussing why Micah Yosef Berdichevsky, the great polymath writer, scholar, and anthologist, never managed to realize his intention of writing an autobiography. When it comes to Mordecai Aaron Ginzburg's *Avi'ezer*, a wonderfully revealing maskilic Hebrew autobiography from the first half of the nineteenth century, Moseley has finally lassoed his real prey, and he does an exemplary job of analyzing and contextualizing this important work. But by then the book is exhausted, and the great and widely influential autobiographical masterpiece of the late Haskalah, Lilienblum's *Hata'ot ne'urim* (Sins of Youth), as well as the significant autobiographically based Hebrew fiction of the Tehiyah period, remains a bare afterthought.

That there exists a recoverable autobiographical tradition within pre-modern Jewish literature is an idea that has forcefully been put forward by recent historians, and it is the interrogation of this idea that occupies much of Moseley's attention. The traditional model begins with selections from the prophets, Josephus's *Life*, Maimonides's epistles, the Renaissance and early-modern confessions by Yagel and Modena, Yom Tov Lippmann Heller's *Megilat evah* (Scroll of Enmity) and Gluckel's memoirs in the seventeenth century, Jacob Emden's *Megilat sefer* in the eighteenth, and then connecting to Solomon Maimon and modern writers influenced by Rousseau. Moseley argues persuasively that for several reasons it is not meaningful, and perhaps even misleading, to speak of an autobiographical tradition. The key fact is the authors of these works by and large had no awareness of previous acts of self-writing because they existed only in manuscript and were hardly known beyond the family circle. A hard look at the publication data, Moseley contends, simply puts the question to rest. Yet this still doesn't allow us to account for how particular instances, each of them more fascinating than the next, came to be. To do so Moseley takes each of these works and points to models of influence that come from some place other than an autobiographical tradition. Modena's *Life of Judah*, for example, is shaped by contemporary Renaissance confessional narratives that stress the central role of chance in human affairs. Heller's *Megilat sefer* is modeled on the Scrolls of Esther and Lamentations. Gluckel's memoirs, Moseley writes, are a "mosaic of established Jewish genres and sub-genres of Gluckel's period," such as the *tsava'ah*, the *tekhines*, the *sefer musar*, the family scroll, and the *mayse bukh*.

To his credit, Moseley is less interested in scolding those who would make a tradition out of these works than in understanding the temptation to do so. The temptation arose from the fascination with all things autobiographical that came in the wake of Rousseau.

> The notion of a "tradition" of pre-Rousseauian autobiographical writing thus only arises—indeed, only arises—once an autobiographical field of discourse has come into being; the tradition itself is, inevitably and to a large degree, a symptom of the process that it seeks to explain. Pre-Rousseauian texts bearing some affinity with post-Rousseauian autobiography are, in Western Europe, subsumed within this generic category only in the nineteenth and twentieth centuries, even though they were originally neither written nor read as such. (p. 76)

Autobiography as a genre, in other words, does not exist until the modern period; but once it does, readers tend to view all earlier acts of first-person narration through an autobiographical lens. Again, this tendency is as much a testament to the indelibility of autobiographical consciousness as a hallmark of modernity as it is a sign of misreading or lapsed historical perspective.

Moseley's clarification is undeniably useful. It has the tonic force of clearing away a lot of terminological debris the better to prepare the way for a direct engagement with true Jewish autobiography, beginning with Maimon's *Lebensgeschichte* and moving forward. The problem is that accomplishing this clarity requires of Moseley over 150 pages of text and 695 endnotes (chapters 3 and 5). This is a job of work that should have been carried out in review essays in scholarly journals and then summarized in a methodological introduction, a kind of review-of-the-literature/state-of-the-field overview, in preparation for the monograph's main object. Nothing Moseley has to say is uninsightful. Quite the contrary: there is something to learn on every page. Yet his unwillingness to leave anything out or to shape his work more purposefully remains a serious flaw.

*Being for Myself Alone* is the work of a scholar so creatively preoccupied with the question of autobiography that he is given to prolonged absorption in investigations that are tangential or propaedeutic or parallel to his main object. Moseley's long chapter (90 pages, 402 endnotes) on Micah Yosef Berdichevsky is a case in point. Berdichevsky was fascinated by premodern and modern autobiographical materials and wrote one of his first articles on the subject. Having passed through many stages of rebellion and apostasy in his intellectual journey, he was acutely aware of what he called the *ker'a shebalev*, the spiritual tear in the heart between the inherited collective culture of Judaism and the anguished needs of the individual. Such tension is the very generative condition of autobiography, and Moseley sets himself to track Berdichevsky's search for an adequate literary vehicle for this impulse toward self-representation. We are taken on a journey that covers the span of Berdichevsky's career as Moseley delves into his journals and correspondence to adduce the numerous times the author framed plans for various autobiographical projects. Moseley presents the interesting suggestion that the prodigious anthological activity of Berdichevsky's later years may have been a displacement of the autobiographical impulse as well as a strategy to reconcile the individual with the collective. The tear in the heart, the badge of the new generation, is retrojected into the history of Judaism, which is now understood as a constant play between normative and repressed forces. All the while Moseley navigates the complexity of Berdichevsky's vast and variegated corpus with an erudition and aplomb surpassed only by Avner Holtzman.

But what does it all come to in the end? Moseley is forced to admit that Berdichevsky never came close to writing the "well-ordered, all-embracing, and ingenuously candid autobiography [he] had promised to deliver in 1899." "In place of this," Moseley avers, "we have an autobiographical dissemination, an almost oceanic diffusion of self throughout the entire oeuvre; the *Collected Works* [. . .] may be read as a monument to a lifetime of autobiographical endeavor." This is a weak justification for so lengthy an investigation; for there are so many other Hebrew writers of the period about whom the same, or close to it, could be said. Bialik's entire corpus can usefully be thought of as permeated with the struggles of the autobiographical self, and this is exactly what Dan Miron did in his study of Bialik, *Hapreidah min haani he'ani* (Taking Leave of the Impoverished Self). (Moseley mentions but does not discuss Bialik's key autobiographical text *Safiah* [Aftergrowth].)

The point is that when we are trafficking in dispersions, displacements, and diffusions, meaningful generic boundaries can be finessed too easily. There is something weirdly unbalanced in Moseley's discussion of Berdichevsky. Berdichevsky did in fact write an extraordinary series of autobiographically based stories—"Maḥanayim" (Two Camps), "Urva paraḥ" (A Raven Flies), and "Me'ever lenahar" (Across the River) are among them—but, although these texts are patently modeled on the author's student years, they do not figure in Moseley's discussion of a literary career marked by the "oceanic diffusion of self." The reason for the exclusion, one surmises, is that as works of fiction they fall on the far side of a frontier whose integrity Moseley is zealous to preserve. I too believe that the autobiography/fiction boundary is a meaningful, if porous, distinction. Yet if Moseley's whole approach to Berdichevsky is to take his essays on Hasidism, his philological investigations, and his anthological activity as "diffused" expressions of a will toward autobiography, then what justifies excluding forms of writing that are so much more obviously rooted in life experience?

These confusions of purpose disappear in the penultimate chapter of the book on Guenzberg's *Avi'ezer*, which, in every sense, is a true arrival. Here Moseley has finally found his quarry: the first autobiography in Hebrew or Yiddish modeled on Maimon and Rousseau. The long *via negativa* Moseley has followed in sorting through all the texts that are not genuinely autobiographical has positioned him to offer a rich analysis of the real thing. Guenzberg was a Lithuanian maskil (1795–1846) who wrote a number of successful Hebrew popularizations of modern European history. Beginning around 1828—the publication history is complicated and not certain— Guenzberg worked on an autobiography that focused on his childhood and adolescence that was published in full only seventeen years after his death. *Avi'ezer* is a fascinating text that is strung between the opposing poles of a personal confession and an educational treatise. A prodigy married off at a very young age, as was the custom in Lithuania, Guenzberg was transferred from the control of benighted melamdim to the household of his in-laws, where, during the first years of his marriage, he remained incapable of consummating the union. Impotence, a theme that figured in Rousseau and Maimon, is "domesticated" via Guenzberg into the Hebrew literature of Eastern Europe. The young husband is eventually cured of his sexual dysfunction by the ministrations of a shadowy figure in the person of an old heretic, with possible Sabbatean connections, who also cures Guenzberg of a similarly debilitating crisis concerning his faith in the immortality of the soul. These intimate woes, however, are not allowed to stand alone as the foundation for an autobiography. Guenzberg is very much of a maskil in his desire to make the personal into the exemplary; and so the afflictions related to the various stages of development—being swaddled as a baby or abused by teachers as a child or rendered impotent as a young adult—are each made the basis of a programmatic critique of Jewish social and educational practices, with the ruinous regime of the *ḥeder* and the commercialization of marriage in the shiddukh system coming under the severest attack. What bridges between the personal confession and the social critique is the theme of power and powerlessness. Guenzberg, the boy and the young man, is forcibly inducted "into a Foucault-like entanglement of power-relations" in which impotence, in all its aspects, is the all-but-inevitable outcome. With this attack on endemic passivity, Guenzberg's *Avi'ezer* legitimately deserves to be called a proto-Zionist text.

Yet no matter how fascinating *Avi'ezer* may seem to us today, it left little echo at the time it appeared. Moseley reports that he has not found a single contemporary review of the book. What measure of notice the book achieved came only vicariously through the strong gesture made in its direction by Moshe Leib Lilienblum in his autobiography *Hat'ot ne'urim* (Sins of Youth, 1873). In describing his path from the Orthodoxy of his childhood to Haskalah and then to nihilistic resignation, he begs the reader's pardon for not dealing in depth with the *ḥeder* years, for doing so, he asserts, would be unnecessary. "Of the manner of my education, I have nothing special to relate. The education that M. A. Guenzberg received, and that he described in detail in his wonderful book *Avi'ezer*, was that received by the majority of the Jews of my part of the world, myself included among them" (as translated by Moseley). *Sins of Youth* became an extraordinary success and Lilienblum's story the model for numerous novels. Hitched to this star, Guenzberg's story entered the firmament of Jewish literature.

It is for this very reason that the absence of Lilienblum's autobiography from Moseley's study is so surprising. *Sins of Youth* is the great Haskalah autobiography par excellence, clear in its generic intentions and confirmed in its Rousseauean provenance, which radiated out in all directions. It was formative in shaping the Zionist consciousness of an entire generation; its author became the model of contemporary Hebrew novels such as Reuven Asher Braudes's *Hadat vehaḥayim* (Religion and Life), and its form the model for later modernist fiction such as Y. H. Brenner's *Baḥoref* (In Winter). While it would ordinarily be carping to criticize a book for what it does not contain, Moseley's declining to take up the analysis of Lilienblum confuses and frustrates us. What by it own lights should be the book's culmination is simply not there.[6]

Instead, Moseley ends *Being for Myself Alone* with a series of reflections on post-Haskalah literature that raises provocative questions both about the centrality of autobiography in Jewish literature as well as its sovereignty as a literary category. Moseley portrays the beginning of the twentieth century as a singular moment of heightened autobiographical awareness in Hebrew and Yiddish literature in which all major writers were urged by critics and readers to preserve their letters and their documents and to write autobiographies. Some of these autobiographical projects were realized and others were not. But with the exception of Mendele's *Shloyme reb khayims* (Of Bygone Days) and Bialik's *Safiaḥ* (Aftergrowth), those that were written tended to be merely memoiristic capstones to a fulsome literary career. It is difficult to point to autobiographies that stand on their own and demand to be read as major literary or intellectual documents in the way that Cardinal Newman's *Apologia Pro Vita Sua* functions in British literature or Lilienblum's *Sins of Youth* does in Hebrew.

What happened, then, to the autobiographical impulse? The answer depends on a lot of speculative thinking about which there can be no easy agreement. But I would offer two answers. The first has to do with the constraints of ideology. Far apart from one another but closer in other ways than one might think, Hebrew and Yiddish intellectuals worked within literary cultures that promoted the collective and denigrated the prerogatives of interiority and "affective individualism" so crucial to autobiography. The reticulated inner workings of the "I" were not encouraged. It is quite striking to note, as Moseley does, that in all of twentieth-century Hebrew literature—before Oz and Be'er, that is—there are only two significant autobiographical works: E. E. Lisitzky's *Eleh toldot adam* (In the Grip of Cross-Currents) and Pinchas Sadeh's *Ḥayim kemashal* (Life as a Parable), both of which were written from positions remote from the mainstream. The second reason is that the autobiographical impulse disappeared into fiction, where it found a more flexible and resourceful home. Just as Moseley sees Berdichevsky's autobiographical struggles as "diffused" within his total output, the same is true of the key writers of the age, especially Bialik,

Brenner, and Gnessin. Many of their works, though fictional, *rely* on the expectation of autobiographical confession and play with those conventions. In such manipulations there is no greater rascal than Agnon himself, many of whose best works are written in the first person and feature a narrative persona remarkably like Agnon himself. For example, *Oreiaḥ natah lalun* (A Guest for the Night), his great novel about the decline of Jewish life in Galicia after World War I, is set in his own home town of Buczacz and goes so far as to be narrated by one Shmuel Yosef. Yet despite all the enticements to confuse the generic borders and despite the considerable insight provided into Agnon's inner life, the novel resolutely remains a novel.

Let us now return to the question posed at the outset. Does knowing more about the origins of Jewish autobiography help us to make sense of contemporary expressions of the genre? In the case of Amos Oz's and Haim Be'er's major autobiographical narratives, the answer is at best mixed. To be sure, these works are illuminated by a series of issues that come straight out of the study of autobiography: the presumption of truthfulness and the shaping of experience, the selection and exclusion of life events and the narrative resources devoted to them, the uneven workings of memory, the situation of the mature narrator reflecting on his or her earlier selves and being affected by the act of telling. At the same time, there is so much in a book like Oz's *A Tale of Love and Darkness* that cannot be accounted for by the machinery of autobiography. The portraits of the parents and grand-parents, the imaginative reconstruction of their life in Europe, climactic scenes such as the count of the UN votes in 1947, and the epic architecture of the book as a whole, as well as the semantic richness of a style that goes far beyond reporting—much that is most impressive in the book, in short, comes from the work of the novel and requires analysis with tools appropriate to the sophisticated imaginative license of the novel. This is not to say that *A Tale of Love and Darkness* should be reclassified as a novel; it remains an autobiography because of its fundamental allegiance to the autobiographical compact: it represents to its readers that it is the true story of the author's life. Yet despite that fact, what we have learned from the historical study of autobiography will only get us part of the way.

When it comes to the second contemporary example of autobiographical activity in Jewish writing, the extraordinary outpouring of Holocaust memoirs, the lessons learned from Moseley's work promise a more enduring yield. A sort of analogue to this production can be taken from Moseley's description of the hundreds of essays sent to the YIVO in Vilna in the 1930s in response to an invitation to young people to submit their autobiographies. This is a remarkable episode that has been brought to life in Jeffrey Shandler's *Awakening Lives: Autobiographies of Jewish Youth in Poland before the Holocaust*, a selection and translation of these texts, which includes an essay by Moseley on the historical context of the competition and its results.[7] The response was astounding. Many, many hundreds of young people submitted autobiographies, which averaged sixty pages, with many running to hundreds of pages. Now, to be sure, these documents and the memoirs written or recorded by survivors are vastly different. Yet there remain crucial commonalities. The principal stipulations laid down by YIVO were honesty, accuracy, and all-inclusiveness, values which, as Moseley hastens to point out, "have their ultimate source in the criteria established for autobiographical writing by Rousseau's *Confessions*." It is not far from the truth to say that, under greatly grimmer conditions, these are the same norms and intentions that govern the first-person narratives told by survivors. Like the YIVO contestants, furthermore, they are ordinary people swept up by the winds of history who tell their stories without writerly artifice, although many are unwittingly forced by the crucible of their ordeals to discover the craft of writing as they go.

In short, the fusion of searing historical experience with the exigent need to bear witness has renewed the genre of autobiography in unexpected ways. It may be—but who can predict?—that grand autobiography, by which I mean the artfully composed and designed confession and self-exploration of supremely self-conscious individuals, is over in the sense that it has been absorbed into the practices of the novel, or at least into a common tissue of high narrative in which the real self and the written self are mingled in an act of artistic miscegenation that is not easy to disentangle. The raw energy reinvigorating serious autobiography may indeed now and in the future come from people who, although they may have never read Rousseau, have imbibed his imperative and seek to tell the truth in their own voice about how history has caught them up in its grasp.

## NOTES

Originally published in *Jewish Quarterly Review* 98, no. 2 (2008), pp. 272–85.

1. Michael Stanislawski's *Autobiographical Jews: Essays in Jewish Self-Fashioning* (Seattle

Wash., 2004) is one of the first works on this subject in Jewish studies to take this factor into consideration.

2. Amos Oz, *Sipur 'al ahavah vehoshekh* (Jerusalem, 2002); (trans. Nicholas de Lange; *A Tale of Love and Darkness* [London, 2004]).

3. Haim Be'er, *Ḥavalim* (Tel Aviv, 1998); (trans. Barbara Harshav, *A Pure Element of Time* [Hanover, N.H., 2003]).

4. I have contributed to this endeavor in my book, *Banished from Their Father's Table: Loss of Faith and Hebrew Autobiography* (Bloomington, Ind., 1989). My purpose in that study was to explore how the breakthroughs of Hebrew modernism in the Tehiyah period, especially in the works of Feierberg, Brenner, and Berdichevsky, were enabled by creative and ironic use of Haskalah autobiography. Moseley has criticized my work rather harshly for straying from the bounds of autobiography proper, which remains his exclusive professional preoccupation. In so doing, he has misunderstood the trajectory and intent of my study.

5. Marcus Moseley. *Being for Myself Alone: Origins of Jewish Autobiography*. Stanford Studies in Jewish History and Culture. Stanford, Calif.: Stanford University Press, 2006.

6. Still, there are many incidental riches to be grateful for toward the end of the volume, especially the sections on Nathan of Nemerov's *Yeme moharnat* and Barukh Halevy Epstein's *Mekor barukh*.

7. New Haven, Conn., 2002.

# CHAPTER 8

# Ahad Ha-Am and the Essay

*The Vicissitudes of Reason*

When the history of the Hebrew essay is eventually written, we shall likely come to a better understanding of Ahad Ha-Am's achievement. As a literary innovator, he combined the imaginative freedom of the Russian-Hebrew *feuilleton* with the polemical earnestness of the programmatic article—a mode developed by Moses Leib Lilienblum and Peretz Smolenskin—and under the influence of such Western masters as Montaigne and Emerson, fashioned what became the norm for the classic Hebrew essay in the high style. As a norm that perhaps Ahad Ha-Am alone was able to realize, this classic form exerted a harsh authority over subsequent Hebrew writing— the shadow of Milton in English poetry comes to mind—such that those who imitated him were doomed to be derivative and those who sought to avoid that fate had to evade the austerities of the high essay form. Add to these inhibiting factors the ascendancy, closer to our own times, of more "scientific" modes of writing about literature, philosophy, and society, and it is clear why essays of the sort Ahad Ha-Am wrote have by and large dropped from sight.

My purpose is neither to proceed with a history of the Hebrew essay nor even to offer a full accounting of Ahad Ha-Am's transactions with that form. I limit my discussion to the essays written in the early 1890s, which were included in the first edition (1895) of *'Al parashat derakhim* (At the Crossroads); and among these I exclude the overtly political essays. What we are left with is about a dozen essays, the best known and most frequently anthologized and, I believe, the most influential. They include "Ḥeshbon hanefesh" (Reckoning of the soul); "Letoledot haḥiyyuv vehashelilah" (On the history of affirmation and negation); "Mukdam ume'uḥar baḥayyim" (Early and late in life); "'Avar ve'atid" (Past and future); "Shetei reshuyot" (Two domains); "Ḥikkui vehitbolelut" (Imitation and assimilation); "Kohen venavi" (Priest and prophet) and others. These pieces, I shall argue, evince a remarkable kinship in the structures of consciousness and argument that lie beneath the surface of their changing themes and subjects. As a way of understanding what Ahad Ha-Am was about in these essays and the powerful norm they subsequently established, I will attempt a description of these structures.

Before doing so, I am obliged to define some terms. This is not easy. We all know an essay when we see one; yet if we were required to supply a definition of the form, we would likely appear either evasive or simpleminded. Like the poem, the essay is protean and virtually unregulated. Without undertaking the larger task of definition then, I wish to isolate two general properties of the essay that bear on the particular case of Ahad Ha-Am. These two properties I call *totality* and *authority*. By totality I mean a quality that signifies the opposite of a fragment. In an essay a writer "takes on" a subject that is large and consequential; he assumes the responsibility for a conclusive statement on the subject, so that when the reader finishes the essay, he feels that the last word on the subject has been spoken, that what needs to be said has indeed been said. The dynamics of the reading process involve this expectation on the reader's part, regarding the successful production of totality. The essay is a gamble, literally an *essai* (an attempt) in which the stakes rise in proportion to the ambitiousness of the subject and in which the chief drama lies in whether the player, having broached great issues, will or will not succeed in bringing them to closure. The second relevant property of the essay is authority or personal voice. Voice and authority come into play because in the essay conventional ways of validating statements—logical proofs, documentation, quotations from authorities, historical precedents, statistics—are, by and large, suspended. The essayist is allowed to go about building his argument by laying out his assumptions as truths; our willingness to assent to the argument depends,

in the absence of conventional means of validation, on the authority of
the writer and the ability of his voice to win our trust. Authority is linked
to voice because the essay, unlike narrative, disallows the manipulation of
*personae*; the essay depends on the absolute identification of the voice of
the discourse with the author. When a writer is well known, this authority
accrues to him without effort; when he is starting out, as Ahad Ha-Am was
in the early nineties, it has to be won. Having considered these two terms
of totality and authority, I shall now put them aside and return to them later
in judging the overall achievement of the Ahad Ha-Am essay.

The Ahad Ha-Am essay—I want to reiterate that we are speaking only
of the philosophical, nonpolitical essays of the early nineties—bears a three-
part structure. The thesis opens with a striking and subversive truth about
human nature and history, presented in the form of a dialectic between two
terms. In the second part of the essay, the development or exposition, these
terms are elaborated by applying them either to various historical periods or
across different realms of human activity. The essay concludes with a brief
application of what has been said to some issue in Jewish life. The middle
section, the development of the argument, is largely predictable; but the
beginning and concluding sections are each remarkable in different ways.

Unsparing, even brutal, are Ahad Ha-Am's efforts at the opening of
his essays to undermine and deconstruct our ordinary sense of reality. We
go about the world comfortably assuming that what we see is what there
is, that the arrangements of personality, institutions, and society came into
being to perform certain functions and fulfill certain needs and that they
go about their business doing so. The degree to which this is not the case is
best stated in the opening of "Letoledot haḥiyyuv vehashelilah."

Even in times of peace in the world there is neither rest nor repose
for its inhabitants. In the depths of life, underneath the veil of
peace, all things, from worm to man, fight for their lives, pursuing
and overthrowing each other without cease, each side triumphing
only at the expense of the defeat of the other. In spite of this we still
make a distinction between times of war and times of peace; we
reserve the term war for the times when the struggle between the
two camps becomes manifest, and at these rare moments we observe
and examine the causes and effects from first to last. Yet the smaller
wars that are waged universally and endlessly on all sides, the wars

of whose existence we know, but whose details and consequences
are beyond our comprehension—these we call peace, because such
is the normal state of things in the world.[1]

Time and again, in variations, Ahad Ha-Am opens his essays by revealing
this scene of strife and spoilation, this Darwinian rampage of tooth and claw
which rages just below the surface of things and which, because it forms
part of the nonrational and unconscious, we by definition can know nothing
about. In several essays what is exploded is the cherished illusion of human
freedom. In "Shetei reshuyot," Ahad Ha-Am adduces the recent discovery
of hypnotism as a special case of the general fact that our behavior is determined by suggestions both from within and without the self, commands of
which we have no awareness and over which we have no control. In "Ḥikkui
vehitbolelut," our pretense to be self-motivated and self-guided is given the
lie by a deeper desire and need to imitate others. In "Kohen venavi," the
harmony of temperament and the integration of parts that make up the
ideal character of liberal man are exposed as surface phenomena that, like
vectors, are the median results of a clash of opposing and hardly harmonious
forces. In two other essays, there is a kind of double fault. Instead of harmony
what appears on the surface of society is a swarm of conflicting institutions
and practices; and beneath this apparent chaos lies a force which, though
it confers a rationale to what goes on above, is itself nonrational. In "Ḥeshbon ha-nefesh," the force is the instinct for survival, which cares nothing
for good or evil; in "Mukdam ume'uḥar baḥayyim," it is the imponderable
changes in the Zeitgeist. Even for us as readers today—used to the unsettling
literature of the twentieth century—having our knowledge and control so
suddenly and violently undermined is hardly an easy experience. These
essays appeared in publications in Odessa in the early nineties; and if we
consider the sensibilities of readers then, their commitment to the values
of reason, freedom, and will central to the intellectual inheritance of the
Haskalah, it is not difficult to appreciate the full destructiveness of the essay's
opening move. The opening move establishes the authority of Ahad Ha-Am
as essayist. Having been disabused of our certainties about the world, we are
in his hands. It is in a classic sense a coup in which the old order is suddenly
overthrown and we are thrust into the hands of the new regime.

Not for long are we left at a loss, gaping inside this void. After having
taken our certainty away and shaken us up, Ahad Ha-Am restores some

of our ease by explaining that although we are oblivious to the chaotic forces that range beneath the surface of our lives, it is just as well, because the destructiveness of those forces is neutralized by mutual conflict; the outcome is the equilibrium, even the progress, that forms the basis of our lives. What appears to be the reign of chaotic impulse, he argues, is in reality not chaos but the interaction of two forces in conflict. The interrelations between these two forces are the major theme of the main portion of the Ahad Ha-Am essay. These are the terms highlighted in the actual titles of the essays: reason and imagination, justice and affirmation, past and present, competitive emulation and self-effacement, absolute advocacy and defensive conservatism. The thesis laid down in the essays is that there exists or existed a privileged point, either in nature or in primitive history, when these two terms were vigorous in their force, pure in their substance, and locked in a balance whose creative tension produced the greatest artifacts of humanity and the pillars of the natural world.

There can be no more graphic and paradigmatic example of this than the opening of the essay "Kohen venavi," which describes the operation of a vector. The impact of two forces moving in different directions, each of which is unaware of the other and refuses to turn from its course even a hair's breadth, will "produce an intermediate movement, which takes a direction not identical to either of the two."[2] In the case of astronomy, the opposing gravitational pulls of the sun and the other planets force the earth into its elliptical orbit; if for a moment one of these forces became dominant, the tension would snap and catastrophe would ensue. In the light of the discoveries of mechanics, we moderns know that the earth's orbit remains stable because each force fiercely refuses to accommodate itself to the other; ancient man, however, understood the intermediate movement as the result of a compromise and thought he was hearing the music of the spheres for what were in reality the shrill sounds of stubborn resistance.

Tracing the career of the two terms laid out in the thesis is the business of the middle section of the essay, the exposition or development. This is perhaps the least problematic part, but it is interesting in what it reveals about Ahad Ha-Am's cognitive processes. The argument at each state bears the marks of a neoclassical orderliness: first an abstract generalization and then an illustration from a specific area of natural or human activity. The larger movement in the exposition proceeds from step to step along two, usually distinguishable, tracks. In such essays as "Ḥeshbon hanefesh" and

"Middat hadin vemiddat haraḥamim" (Justice and mercy), the movement
is entirely along historical-evolutionary lines, demonstrating the changing
fortunes of a set of terms such as "reason" and "imagination" from primitive
times through antiquity and the Middle Ages to modern times. In other
essays the movement is less historical than categorical, in the sense that
Ahad Ha-Am does not demonstrate the truth of his thesis through historical
development but in area after area of reality. The precedence and hierarchy of
categories are quite clear. Ahad Ha-Am begins in the world of science with
a fact about nature that has been proved empirically. The presence of this
phenomenon in the individual, demonstrated by the science of psychology,
will often be the next stage. From there the jump is from the individual
to the nature of societies as a whole and sometimes, as a final step, to the
relations of societies to one another. One would think that with his references to natural science, psychology, and sociology, Ahad Ha-Am would
be dealing throughout in the hard currency of rules of behavior, individual
and collective; but in the middle or expository section of the essays, the
nature of the subject invariably shifts from the material to the ideational,
from matter to spirit, whether imperceptibly or by an announced transition.
It seems that Ahad Ha-Am is interested in the natural and social sciences for
two reasons: to produce an aura of authority and legitimation by appealing
to what is rationally, empirically, and universally known about the world,
in contrast to the customary Jewish starting point from within a body of
received beliefs and myths; and secondly, to provide a structure, a dialectic
of two terms, that can be used to discuss ideas. The two larger tracks I have
been describing, the historical and the categorical, are followed separately
in some essays; in others, the two are mixed. The essay "Shetei reshuyot,"
for example, begins on the plane of science, with data about hypnotism as
applied to the individual and then to societies as a whole, whereupon the
argument shifts to two ideational terms, past and present, and follows the
historical course of their relations from a state of equilibrium in antiquity
to a dangerous destabilization in recent times.

To understand what happens toward the end of the exposition, I will
dwell for a moment on this essay, "Shetei reshuyot." The domains in the title,
as so often is the case, are progress and tradition in the moral evolution of
culture; and at times of social change these two forces can make bitterly
conflicting claims. Under ordinary conditions the contest is waged beneath
the surface of social consciousness; we are aware only of the results, the

gradual, definite success of innovation, not the violent conflict below. This is the paradigmatic privileged moment we spoke of earlier: the gradual moral betterment produced by the unconscious, unmitigated clash of principles and interests. When men interfere with this self-regulating mechanism and force it to consciousness, trouble sets in. When in revolutionary times the radical partisans of either the old or the new force the conflict to the surface and artificially attempt to coerce the process in their direction, they wreck the equilibrium of moral change and produce results opposite to what they intended. This is an important moment; the model Ahad Ha-Am has built becomes destabilized. Somehow the rigid symmetries are weakened, the pristine dialectical oppositions muddied. This occurs in "Heshbon hanefesh," when the dialectic between reason and imagination breaks down and bifurcates into otherworldliness on the one hand and sophism on the other. In "Kohen venavi" it is the moment when the priests falter in their custodial function and allow the pure idea to pass from their hands. In "Hikkui vehitbolelut," it comes when a failure of integrity and self-identity allows creative imitation to lapse into self-effacement; in "Heshbon hanefesh," when the spirit of universal forgiveness fosters expediency and self-justification. In two essays, "Mukdam ume'uhar bahayyim" and "Letoledot hahiyyuv vehashelilah," the mechanism does remain intact; yet Ahad Ha-Am stresses how fragile it is and how close it can come to breaking down.

With the dialectic unstrung and its forces unleashed, the expository section ends. What comes next, in the last quarter or fifth of the essay, is the Jewish section, the application of what has been described so far, to Jewish history and to the contemporary Jewish situation. This movement does not prolong the development because nothing further is really developed. No new structures are presented, elaborated, or refined; rather, all that has already been shown to be true about nature and man is now transferred and applied to the Jewish sphere. The shift from the general to the Jewish is one of the most conspicuous moments in the Ahad Ha-Am essay. Although this may or may not be a manifestation of Ahad Ha-Am's epistemology, it is indubitably an indication of his rhetorical strategy. To understand the persuasive power of this move, we must again imagine the late nineteenth century reader of the Hebrew periodical press and his respectful, even adulatory, attitude to the natural and human sciences of Western learning. When Ahad Ha-Am finally turns to the analysis of the Jewish world, it is with the full weight of Western truth behind him.

Though this last section may be the most important in that it brings home the point of the essay, in literary terms, within the larger economy of the text, it is the most problematic for several reasons. The neoclassical method of argumentation—generalization, example, summary, with generalizations and summaries rendered in balanced, epigrammatic formulas, and the whole set out with explicit step-by-step clarity—this entire complex is gone. In its place is a style that is compressed, elided, cursive, as it flies over the whole of Jewish history in a few paragraphs. Equipped with concepts and categories from the preceding sections of the essay, we should expect to be able easily to apply them to the corresponding terms of Jewish history. But it is not always easy to do so. The elliptical quality of the Jewish section highlights the disproportion between it and the earlier, non-Jewish expository sections. The moral of the essay—or the message relevant to contemporary events, as distinct from the themes expressed in the larger issues—is reached only in the last sentence or so of the composition. The actualities referred to here—antisemitism, Reform Judaism, *Wissenschaft des Judentums*, and of course the tensions between Hibbat Zion and political Zionism—are in certain cases merely pointed to in a manner that if described as "sketchy," might grant too much. What is put into question by the problematic nature of the Jewish section and its closing gesture to reality is the unity of the essay, its totality. We are prompted to ask whether in order to make the points that are made, the grand exposition of science and history is in the end truly necessary.

I wish to put forward a speculative proposal to explain why the Ahad Ha-Am essay is shaped the way it is. Is it not possible that the generic model for the texts of Ahad Ha-Am is not one but two, not just the essay form of modern European and Hebrew literature but also an older, more traditional form: the *derashah*, the classical homily or sermon? The threefold function of the *derashah*—to instruct, to exhort, and to entertain—explains some of the anomalies of the essays. The situation in which the *derashah* is delivered elucidates the context of communication in the essays. The message of the *derashah* is pronounced to recipients already committed to the truth of the message; a sermon is preached to the faithful, who are, quite literally, there to hear it, just in the way that Ahad Ha-Am's readers were most likely already sworn to the cause of Hibbat Zion. To the faithful the faith does not have to be explained; the faithful have only to be urged to maintain the faith and be given support and uplift for that task. That is why the essays can end so sketchily and why the tone at the end is one of inevitability and exhortation. The audience for the *derashah* expects, in addition, to be taught something, some *ḥiddushei torah* (novel insights into the law), and this is why Ahad Ha-Am supplied such copious quantities of the latest discoveries of Western knowledge, regarded by him as a kind of new *Torah*. Finally, the question of entertainment. The *darshan* must find a bridge between the lesson of the day's text and some broader context (*me'ein hame'ora*), and the spectacle of his virtuosity in constructing this bridge, is part of the audience's expectations. Ahad Ha-Am's model, conscious or unconscious, was one of the oldest forms of the *derashah*: the *petiḥta* or proem. In the *petiḥta* the *darshan* begins with a difficult verse from the Prophets or Writings that at first blush bears no relation whatsoever to the day's scriptural reading. Knowing from the outset where he must eventually touch down, the audience savors the *darshan's* ingenuity as he "homes in" from the remote to the familiar. So, I submit, Ahad Ha-Am's readers, the faithful of Hibbat Zion, knew that the essay must culminate in an affirmation of the truth of their cause relative to the other nostrums of the century. And they looked on with some amazement and much delight and a firm expectation of learning and uplift as Ahad Ha-Am began with ideas coming from seemingly rampantly unrelated directions—hypnosis, anthropology, law, mechanics—and then, through a masterful set of manipulations, brought the point home to the National Home.

I wish to conclude by recalling to mind the two properties of the essay, totality and authority, with which I began. These are useful categories because they help us locate the special achievement of the Ahad Ha-Am essay. It should be evident from our discussion that the rhetorical resourcefulness of these texts is impressive—the wrenching of the reader's complacency and his deliverance into the hands of the essayist; the insistent development of the two dialectical terms along historical and categorical tracks; the legitimating movement from the empirical, secular, individual to the ideational, collective, Jewish; and the final arrival at the familiar truth. On the score of authority, the ability of the essayist's voice to establish a disposition to belief and acceptance, the Ahad Ha-Am essay merits very high marks. On the question of totality, however, I believe the evaluation must be different. The forces of unreason unleashed at the beginning of the essay, after our naiveté has been exploded, are not in the end brought under control. Intellectually, the essays open up more than they can account for;

there is a cognitive confusion betokened by the wobbly compression of the essays at their conclusion and by the resort to the *derashah* form.


Ahad Ha-Am does not manage to close the circle and produce totality, though the authority of his rhetoric covers up this failure impressively. Should we be surprised? If, in the face of the conditions of Jewish existence in the 1890s, Ahad Ha-Am had indeed seen his way to producing an easy totality, we should probably not be investigating his works now and discovering that fact.


## NOTES

Originally published in *At the Crossroads: Essays on Ahad Ha-am*, ed. Jacques Kornberg (Albany: State University of New York Press, 1983), pp. 3–11.

1. *Kol kitvei Ahad Ha-'Am* (Tel Aviv and Jerusalem, 1962), 75.
2. Ibid., 90.

# CHAPTER 9

# Sefer Ha'aggadah

## Triumph or Tragedy?

The enormous success of *Sefer ha'aggadah* seems to have been matched by the enormous pleasure it brought Bialik over the many years he worked on it. The project began modestly shortly after the turn of the century as a kind of updated *Ein Ya'akov*, the medieval anthology of talmudic aggadah. But after Bialik's return to Odessa from his sojourn in Warsaw early in 1905, the project grew considerably in its ambitions and in the claims it made upon the poet's attention. Bialik became increasingly devoted to the daily working sessions with his collaborator Y. H. Ravnitzky, and even the anti-Jewish pogroms and the revolutionary unrest that roiled Odessa at this time did not distract him from the desire to hasten the project along. The enormous satisfaction the project gave Bialik was punctuated, Ravnitzky relates, by frequent cries of childlike delight when some hitherto unfamiliar aggadic gem came across their work table.[1] Bialik lavished particular attention on the typographic design of the final product. Ravnitzky was dispatched to the printing firm of Josef Fischer in Krakow to have trial pages set in different fonts—with distinctions insisted upon among notes, sources, and the main text—and then sent to Odessa for Bialik's inspection, with the result that in the end an altogether new set of type was specially ordered from Vienna. When book 1 of *Sefer ha'aggadah* was finally completed and set in type, its arrival in Odessa in the winter of 1908 elicited a degree of emotion that Ravnitzky can describe only by recourse to an epic rabbinic topos: "He who did not see Bialik's joy when the completed volume arrived from Krakow has never seen joy in his life."[2] There were three more books planned for *Sefer ha'aggadah* at the time, and Bialik looked forward with gusto to continued work on the project. Indeed, with all the supplements, addenda, and vocalized editions to come, Bialik's involvement with *Sefer ha'aggadah* would cease only with his death.

When the main burden of the work had been discharged, Bialik paused in the summer of 1910 to write "Lifnei aron hasefarim" ("Before the Book-case"), a 105-line poem that reflects upon the many years devoted to the "ingathering" of the aggadah. The black despair of the poem is utterly astonishing. Even if we discount Ravnitzky's enthusiastic descriptions, keeping in mind his adoration of Bialik and the thirty intervening years, nothing prepares us for the terms in which the poem's speaker describes his condition after years of toiling on the aggadah. He compares himself to a thief and a grave robber who, without benefit of lamp or candle, has been rooting around in the dust heap of culture and now, dispirited and exhausted, has nothing to show for it.

> Emerging again into the domain of night / after digging in the nation's graves and the desolation of its spirit, / I have nothing to show and have saved nothing / except for this trowel that sticks to my hand and the dust of the ancients on my fingers. / I am even emptier and poorer than when I started out (lines 85–90).[3]

There is no indirection here and no oblique persona. For contemporary readers, the poem's speaker could be taken for no one other than the poet Bialik, and the subject of his despair was unavoidably understood as the long years of investment in *Sefer ha'aggadah*.

The contradiction is fierce and profound, and no amount of dialectical acumen can explain it away. In 1910, at a major point along the way to the completion of *Sefer ha'aggadah*, Bialik experienced his many years of intense work on the project as both a source of sustaining pleasure and a soul-destroying waste of time. This is a contradiction that should be respected, I would submit, rather than being made the object of attempts at resolution. It is the meaning of this contradiction in Bialik's creative life and in the life of the Hebrew Revival in general that I wish to explore in the brief compass of this essay. To do so I adduce the two major documents that were not part of *Sefer ha'aggadah* proper but reflect on the project: the poem "Lifnei aron hasefarim" and the essay "Lekhinnusah shel ha'aggadah" ("On Anthologizing the Aggadah"), which Bialik eventually used as an introduction to the final project. The poem and the essay each tell a different story about a search for something that was carried out through the work on *Sefer ha'aggadah*. One search was successful, the other a failure.

The happier story is told in the essay, which is dated Sivan 5668 (= 1908) and written soon after book 1 had been printed and the work on the subsequent books was in full swing. No less than Bialik's other great essays, "Lekhinnusah shel ha'aggadah" deserves full attention for its metaphoric intensity and complexity. The first few lines shed light on one of the chief objects of the project as a whole. Against a variety of implied criticisms of the aggadah (it is inferior to the halakhah; it is fanciful and unphilosophical; it is unsystematic; it is antiquated), Bialik asserts that for many centuries the aggadah was the central literary embodiment of the Jewish people, that it remains the classical body of national creativity, and that altogether it constitutes "one of the great manifestations of the national spirit."[4] The national spirit Bialik refers to is the *ruah ha'umah*, the term that Ahad Ha-Am, borrowing from the contemporary discourse of romantic nationalism, had coined to designate a distinctive and integral national genius that is embodied in Hebrew and inheres in the unfolding of Jewish civilization in different historical expressions. Bialik's contribution lay not so much in the theoretical elaboration of this notion as in his practical determination to recover and re-present one of the great classical sources of *the ruah ha'umah*. It is the search for the *ruah ha'umah*, in the face of all the detractors and trivializers of the aggadah, that is the theme of Bialik's essay.

Although the goal was clear, its realization was beset by many challenges. The aggadah as Bialik found it was intelligible only to expert religious readers, who had little interest in it per se, and inaccessible to modern readers of Hebrew, who might make use of it in the revival of Jewish culture. The individual aggadic passages, the aggadot themselves, were scattered over a thousand-year period throughout the vast reaches of the Babylonian and Palestinian Talmuds as well as among dozens of other rabbinic collections, some obscure, out of print, or extant only in manuscript. The same aggadot often existed in numerous incomplete variants and parallel passages, and the intermixture of Aramaic with antique Hebrew increased the difficulty.

Within this dispersed galaxy of texts, moreover, there were those aggadot that had enduring spiritual value and those that belonged only to their far-away time and place. Once choices were made, the key challenge was to make them available. In the "rough," aggadot were arranged by no thematic principle; one has to know the whole to make use of the parts. Bialik set himself the great task of arranging the best of the aggadah according to master rubrics (the history of the nation, its major figures, key concepts) that would make it possible for literate outsiders to rabbinic literature to find what they needed when they needed it.

In envisioning the form these arrangements might take, Bialik's thinking in "Lekhinnusah shel ha'aggadah" turns around the axis of a central architectural metaphor. Bialik knows what the edifice of the aggadah once was and what it should not be; what it is now and what it should be are implied but less clear.

> The beautiful palace that the aggadah built and refined through its creative power over the course of several generations was not in the eyes of the people a museum of antiquities that one enters for an hour, takes in the exhibits, and then leaves. The palace of aggadah, rather, functioned like a permanent dwelling for the nation's spirit and soul. The plan of the palace, its layout and configuration were the very vistas of the nation's spiritual life, the arrangements of its inner world, the sights and sentiments of all it thought and did. (2:255)

In the high bourgeois culture of late nineteenth-century Western Europe, the idea of the museum was the master trope for the appreciation of the treasures of the classical past. But the aestheticized distance of the visitor's appreciative gaze—and the forbidding impersonality of the monumental surroundings—was not what Bialik was after. Although modernity had made it impossible and even undesirable to reinhabit the aggadah, the memories of living on intimate and familiar terms *inside* the palace were too recent to settle for the mere ceremony of the cultural *hommage*. What the new edifice of the aggadah might look like is never spelled out, although the reader who has caught the drift of the essay's architectural thinking can extrapolate as he or she wishes. I see in my mind's eye a large, stately—dare one say, palatial?—and user-friendly neighborhood lending library with a classification system that allows you to get what you need for specific purposes. It is not where you live, but you're always jumping in and out of it.

Yet beneath the surface of this homely and constructive image of beneficent institution building lurks something else: an act of systematic violence, and one that Bialik's essay—to use his own phrase from a later essay—is much better at concealing than revealing. If the essay contains an implied architectural image of the *current* state of the aggadah (as opposed to what it once was and might be), it is that of the palace in ruins, its debris misshapen and randomly scattered. Bialik presents himself as gathering, selecting, dusting off, and putting into a new order, but never tampering with the essential integrity of, the materials themselves. Yet anyone who has ever studied rabbinic literature knows that there is more to it than that. Virtually every aggadah in the galaxy of talmudic and midrashic collections is connected to a verse from Scripture. The verse serves either as the stimulus and irritant for the creation of the aggadah or as the peg upon which its homiletical ideas are hung. The connection is more like an umbilicus than a lifeless tether, and to lop it off is to do some essential violence to the aggadah. Yet Bialik knew that unless the aggadot could be cut loose from their scriptural anchors he could never move them from their remote and serendipitous locations and arrange them into tight conceptual and thematic alignments that would make *Sefer ha'aggadah* the useable work he wanted it to be. This necessary violence does not seem to have caused Bialik much anguish; the exegetical embeddedness of the aggadah in Scripture smacked to him of the casuistry of the *beit midrash*, and he went about "liberating" the narrative core without compunction. It presented itself to his mind in Berdichevskian terms as an act of destroying for the sake of building. All this is obscured in the atmosphere of curatorial benevolence in "Lekhinnusah shel ha'aggadah." It is worth bringing it to light in order to appreciate the strength of will, even the ruthlessness, Bialik brought to bear in pursuing his goal of revealing the *ruah ha'umah* in the aggadah and pressing it into service of the national revival.[5]

Like the essay, the poem records the pursuit of a prized goal, but it is one that is easy to miss the first time around. "Lifnei aron hasefarim" is a classic instance of the self-subverting Bialik poem described by Menahem Perry, which sets up expectations and undercuts them, thereby compelling the reader to adopt a revisionary second reading.[6] At the outset of "Lifnei aron hasefarim," the speaker stands before the bookcase of rabbinic classics and addresses them in a manner that evokes one of the earlier great odes of the genre: "Al saf beit hamidrash" ("On the Doorstep of the Study House,"

1894). The poem, we assume, is going to deal with the problem of tradition and perhaps explore the possibility of some reconciliation between the grown poet and the talmudic culture that nurtured him as a child and was rejected by him as a young man. The assumption is strengthened by the retrospective account of a childhood in the lap of learning and the dark night of religious crisis dramatized so effectively by the blood-curdling storm. Yet at the midpoint of the poem, when the speaker returns to the present time of his life, it becomes abundantly clear that there is not now, and has never been, a chance for reconciliation and that the content of the books remains for him, literally, a dead letter.

The true object of his revisiting of the ancient books has been a quest for something else.

> My eye, exhausted, gropes between the lines, / searching silently among the crowns of the letters, / and struggling to catch a glimpse there of the tracks left by my soul / and to find a path to its first stirrings / in the place where it was born and began in life (lines 53–57).

The quest turns out to be a kind of Wordsworthian project of recovering the origins of the self in childhood by returning to the scene of the most formative early experiences. (It is young adulthood that is being referred to rather than childhood, whose memories are reimagined in other works.) What the poet seeks from the years spent studying Talmud in the *beit midrash*, then, is not an intimation of his lost religious beliefs and the world of Torah he once inhabited. He seeks, rather, the tracks that his soul left (*'iqvot nafshi*) among the pages of the folios. He returns to the *beit midrash* not because of what the books have to say but because they constitute the setting, literally the birthplace, in which his self first stirred to life and began to take shape.

Although the true object of his search is not put before the reader until the middle of the poem, when we go back to the beginning we realize that it was there all along. In addressing the books, the poet declares that these tomes have been the sole companions of his youth and have served as his playground during the heat of the day and his pillow in the cold of night. Furthermore, and this is the giveaway, he says:

> I learned to roll up in your scrolls the deposit of my soul / and to interleave among your lines my most sacred dreams (lines 12–13).

"Deposit of my soul" is an admittedly awkward rendering of *piqdon ruḥi*. A *piqadon* is an object of value placed with a trusted person for temporary safekeeping. The inchoate soul of the poet did not emerge from the books nor did it merge with them. It is a separate entity that was only *stored* there, and now the mature poet, having journeyed far and endured much, returns if not to retrieve it from among the books then at least to catch a glimpse of it and locate the path of its first stirrings.

If the religious-cultural project of reconnection is out of the question, might not this more modest and personal romantic quest have some chance for success? Alas, no. The reason for the failure has to do with issues of communication and intelligibility that now emerge as the main theme of the poem. In order to extricate the thread of his youthful self from among the books, he must at the very least reestablish some rapport with them. He stands before the books and stares at them, yet he experiences a total failure of recognition. He cannot make sense out of these old tomes or even pick up the faintest murmur from their grave; and they for their part do not stare back, as they once did, into the depths of his soul. Who is to blame for this breakdown? The poem is curiously insistent on assigning responsibility here, because, after a different failure at the end of the poem, the account will be settled differently. "Is it my eye that has dimmed and my ear that has grown deaf?" the speaker asks, "Or are you, the forever dead, rife with rot / and bereft of the least trace of life?" (lines 69–71). The subsequent lines, describing the utter waste and futility of years spent digging around in these rotting graves, leave no room for mistaking where the fault lies.

Fault, however, is not the same as explanation. Beyond the speaker's angry despair, we are also offered a penetrating image of what went wrong.

Like a necklace of black pearls whose string has snapped / your lines are to me; your pages have been widowed / and each and every letter has become an orphan (lines 66–68).

The simile is simple and unambiguous, yet throughout the whole literature of the Hebrew Revival I know of no image that captures the breakdown of a culture with more insight and greater economy. The crisis the image dramatizes is not about untenable religious beliefs or outmoded ideas; it is, rather, a crisis of coherence. The beliefs and ideas may in themselves be credible and, like pearls, valuable; but when the overarching system of plausibility that holds them in place is destroyed, they scatter into unintelligible fragments. The reason why the string has snapped is not explained; it is a given, it is what happened. It is the result that rivets our attention: the sudden devolution of the family into widowhood and orphanhood.

Surely there can be no more pointed contrast to this image of breakdown than the enthusiastic construction plans rehearsed over and over again in the essay on anthologizing the aggadah. The central difficulty presented by the aggadah, in Bialik's analysis, begins exactly at the point where the image of the unstrung pearls of the poem ends: the problem of *pizzur*, scatter. The materials of the aggadah are chaotically dispersed throughout all the many collections of rabbinic literature like "blasted stone fragments" among the "ruins of an ancient temple" (2:238). The rub is that there *never was* any ancient temple; even in its own classical age the aggadah was ever and always scattered. So it falls to Bialik not to rebuild a destroyed structure but to construct one that never existed before.

> The shards of stone will be joined into bricks, the bricks into walls, and the walls into a palace in which all who enter will find everything in its proper place, each matter *in its entirety* in the location assigned to it (2:258; emphasis original).

In his essay, Bialik pledges himself to the making of meaning and the conferring of order; in his poem, he bears witness to the foundering of coherence and the collapse of classical culture into unintelligibility.

Surprisingly, it is not this breakdown that is the real trauma dramatized in "Lifnei aron hasefarim." The speaker surveys the scattered letters and the desiccated books with complete detachment: "[M]y heart is still and there is no trembling tear on my eyelid" (lines 58–59). He regrets only the stupidity of the years wasted searching for his youthful soul in precisely the wrong place. The real blow comes when, after emerging from his underground futility and appealing to the night to gather him in and give him rest, the nighttime firmament stares back with blank indifference. This ending of the poem has long created problems for readers. Because the advertised theme of the poem is the belated encounter with the books, the abandonment of this subject in the final phase of the poem is perplexing. Attempting to stay within the given terms of the poem, many readers have taken the appeal to night as a sign of the poet's exhaustion unto death, even suicidal impulse, after the futile ordeal of the books. Yet this approach, which makes the night simply into a site of last resort, fails to explain the depths of the speaker's disappointment when he receives no answering gesture from the darkened heavens.

Dan Miron has demonstrated that the appeal to night can in fact be understood only by going beyond the bounds of the individual poem into Bialik's larger poetic career.[7] By pointing to the crucial 1898 poem "Razei laylah" ("Night Secrets"), Miron shows how night became—in the crucible of Bialik's late-romantic, early-symbolist art—the powerful symbol for the forces of the cosmos that reveal themselves to the artist's imagination. It was to this source of inspiration the poet turned—and was successful in finding sustenance—long after the world of the *beit midrash* had ceased to speak to him. Although one must indeed go outside the poem to appreciate fully the devastating force of the ending, the unanswered appeal to the night remains bound to the poem through a deliberately framed structural analogy. This turns, again, on the question of communication and intelligibility. When the speaker attempts to account for the failed reconnection with the books, it will be remembered, he asks first whether it is his fault and then whether it is the fault of the books. It turns out to be the second; it is not because he is incapable of deciphering their message but because their inherent intelligibility has broken down. Now, in the poem's concluding lines, when he asks why the stars make no reply to his entreaties, the order is reversed, as is the apportionment of responsibility.

> Do your golden eyebrows indeed have nothing for me, / not even the slightest hint to tell me and my heart? / Or do they perhaps have much to say, but I have forgotten your tongue / and will never again hear your language, the language of secret things? / Answer me, mighty stars, for I am wretched (lines 101–5).

In contrast to the books, the stars still possess untold reservoirs of meaning, but this time it is the poet who has lost the key, and, as the forlorn last utterance of the poem implies, he will never find it again.

I have, I believe, made good on my promise to sharpen the contradictions between the two important literary statements that Bialik made concerning the work of *Sefer ha'aggadah*. In doing so I have been impelled by no deconstructive pleasure in demonstrating the existence of a deep cleavage within the imaginative world of a great writer. Rather, my motive has been to call attention to a structure that is significant not only for Bialik's larger career but for the career of the Hebrew Revival altogether: the gap between personal salvation and collective salvation. With many fits and starts and crises, the Hebrew Revival, as a literary-cultural project, slowly established itself and eventually took part in the burgeoning society of the Yishuv. Yet for many of the young men and women whose creative endeavors made the revival possible, this sense of fulfillment and consolidation was always beyond reach. Deprived first of the nurturance of religious tradition and then of the nurturance of the natural world, they fell unprotected into the harsh void of modernity, and the personal pain of their fall could not be softened by the forward-looking march of national institutions. It is a plight from which we have never entirely escaped.

## NOTES

Originally published in *History and Literature: New Readings of Jewish Texts in Honor of Arnold J. Band,* ed. William Cutter and David C. Jacobson (Providence, RI: Brown University, 2002), pp. 17–26.

1. Y. H. Ravnitzky, "H. N. Bialik and *Sefer ha'aggadah*" [Hebrew], *Keneset* (1936): 312.

2. The reference is to Mishnah Sukkot 5:1: "He who did not see *simḥat beit hasho'evah* never saw joy in his life."

3. Dan Miron, ed., *Hayyim Nahman Bialik: Shirim* (Tel Aviv: Dvir, 1990), 281–84. Translations of passages by Bialik quoted in this essay are mine.

4. *Kitvei H. N. Bialik* (Tel Aviv: Dvir, 1935), 2:253.

5. For an excellent overview of the relationship of *Sefer ha'aggadah* to rabbinic literature, especially on the issue of the excision of the exegetical connection, see David Stern's introduction to the English translation of the work. Hayyim Nahman Bialik and Yehoshua Hana Ravnitzky, eds., *The Book of Legends, Sefer haaggadah: Legends from the Talmud and Midrash,* trans. William G. Braude (New York: Schocken, 1992), xvii–xxii.

6. Menahem Perry, *Hamivneh hasimanti shel shirei Bialik* (Tel Aviv: The Porter Institute for Poetics and Semiotics, Tel Aviv University, 1977).

7. Dan Miron, *Bo'ah laylah: 'iyyunim bytsirot H. N. Bialik ve M. Y. Berdichevski* (Tel Aviv: Dvir, 1987).

# CHAPTER 10

# Israeli Literature in the Minds of American Readers

The past twenty-five years have been a heady time to be an observer of cultural developments in Israel. In the 1960s the literary scene began to explode, especially in fiction. Poetry had long been at the center of the action with fiction playing a secondary role. Agnon's eminence, rooted in a different place and a different time, persisted while the native-born writers who began to produce stories and novels after 1948 never seemed able to carry their efforts much beyond the struggles and controversies of the hour. But then suddenly there were the short stories of Amos Oz, A. B. Yehoshua, Aharon Appelfeld, and Amalia Kahana-Carmon and then their first and second novels. They were joined by Shulamith Hareven, Yehoshua Kenaz, Yaakov Shabtai, and David Grossman. Into the eighties and nineties the debuts of good new writers became more frequent and the productivity of by-now established ones only intensified. What was different about this new literature was the quality and inventiveness of its fictional techniques and its ability to explore universal issues through the milieu of Israeli society. There was also a new audience for this literature; children of immigrants had become sophisticated Hebrew readers. Many of the best books became not only critical successes but best sellers as well.[1]

Was this a party to which outsiders were invited? Very few American Jews knew Hebrew well enough to read a serious modern Hebrew book, so even if they were aware of the celebration, they could not hear the music. But soon English translations began to appear: Yehoshua's short-story collection *Three Days and a Child* (*Shlosha yamim veyeled*) in 1970 and his novel *The Lover* (*Hame'ahev*) in 1978, Oz's *My Michael* (*Michael sheli*) in 1972, Appelfeld's *Badenheim 1939* (*Badenheim 'ir nofesh*) in 1980, Shabtai's *Past Continuous* (*Zikhron devarim*) in 1985, and Grossman's *See Under: Love* (*'Ayien 'erekh: Ahavah*) in 1989, with many others between and after. The translations were generally of high quality and were published by good houses and they mostly received enthusiastic and discerning notices in major critical venues such as the *New York Times Book Review* and the *New York Review of Books*.

This was a special moment for someone like myself who was devoted to modern Hebrew literature as a teacher and a scholar. That literature had reached its first great flowering in Eastern Europe at the turn of the twentieth century in the works of Mendele, Bialik, Brenner, and Berdichevsky; it had attained another high point with Agnon and Uri Zvi Greenberg in Palestine between the two world wars. In this early phase of the Zionist revolution, it was often literature that led politics. Long before the Yishuv (the new Zionist settlement in Palestine) prospered, sophisticated masterworks in modern Hebrew were being written and read. With the establishment of the State of Israel, the roles were reversed, and it took time for the impressive social, political, and military accomplishments of the new enterprise to be matched by the same resourceful innovation on the literary imagination front. When the two finally came together, as happened in the seventies and eighties, the combination was very powerful. One had the feeling of living through a moment of immense creativity in the life of the Jewish people. Never since the time of the Bible and the ancient liturgical poets had *so* much that *was so good* been written *in* Hebrew. When, after a while, the English translations began to appear, a unique opportunity presented itself. Those who had been following these developments in Hebrew could finally turn to their students, their readers, and their friends, put something in their hands, and say, "Look here! This is what we've been talking about; this is what has been so exciting!"

The response, to put it mildly, was underwhelming; the excitement turned out not to be infectious. Now, it might be said that those who were advocates and special pleaders for Israeli literature to begin with were bound to be disappointed by the absence of an answering enthusiasm. Yet even judged by more objective measures, it is difficult to argue that Israeli literature has enjoyed anything more than a very limited success in America. Despite very favorable notices, Israeli novels in translation have not sold very well.[2] A few have done respectably and gone into paperback, but many of the key texts are out of print entirely, as anyone who tries to put together a syllabus for a college course in the field soon discovers. Even if commercial criteria are put aside, the record remains equivocal at best. When it comes to the generality of committed Jewish laypeople who are affiliated with Jewish institutions and are involved with the life of the community, it is difficult to find much recognition of the names of Israeli writers, not to mention experience reading their works. In the elite of the community—the rabbis, the educators, the lay and professional leaders of organizations and federations—the name recognition may be there, but familiarity may extend only to the political views of the writers, say those of Oz or Grossman, and not to their main literary works. Even university teachers of Jewish Studies tend to regard Hebrew literature not as a source of current cultural creativity that makes claims upon them as intellectuals but as one area of academic specialization among many others. In the end, however, the muted reception of Israeli writing in America is less a reflection of the absolute number of its "users" than a sign of a failure of these writings to become part of the intellectual discourse of the American Jewish community and its cultural repertoire.

Should one be surprised? Is this not just another expression of a pervasive strain of anti-intellectualism in American Jewish life? This is not the case, I argue. One might have reasonably hoped for more, especially because of the relationship of involved American Jews to Israel. The Zionization of American Jewish life has been one of the most remarked upon developments since World War II.[3] Although only a small number of American Jews are Zionists in the classical ideological sense of the term, a substantial majority are pro-Israel in their attitudes, and a significant number are attached to Israel in a variety of ways. Moreover, American Jews buy books. A greater proportion of Jews buy fiction and works of general interest than do the general public and other ethnic groups, and they buy many more books of Jewish interest than they used to, judging from the explosion of titles relating to Jewish life and the Holocaust in recent years. It is, also, not as if the Israeli novels under discussion are unapproachable or unenjoyable. Quite the contrary. That it is by no means a punishment to read them is indicated by their enormous sales in Israel. Sales of forty to fifty thousand, which are not uncommon for a successful novel in Israel, a country of some five million, would still be counted a substantial success in America; given the tiny proportion of readers in Israel to readers in America, the numbers are astounding.

That there is, in fact, something to wonder about in the American situation is supported by a look at the reception of Israeli literature in Europe. Since the early 1990s, the sales of Israeli literary works (these occasionally include volumes of poetry in addition to novels) translated into European languages have been steadily increasing. Again, the exact sales figures are difficult to come by, but the number of new titles translated each year gives some indication. In Italy, for example, during the seventies and eighties only two or three titles appeared on average; beginning in 1989, the number began to climb in increments to twelve in 1994. In Germany, five or six titles appeared yearly until 1988 when the number began to climb dramatically to twenty-seven in 1994. In America, by contrast, translations reached their height in 1989 when twenty-seven were published, but then dropped to fewer than twenty in 1994.[4] It is rather startling to contemplate the fact that in Germany, a country with a tiny Jewish population, the same number of translations of Israeli literature is appearing as in America. After Germany comes France in number of titles translated, and then Italy, Spain, and Holland with a scattering of titles in Polish, Swedish, Portuguese, Arabic, Greek, and Chinese.

More important, perhaps, than the quantitative dimension is the fact— to me the ironic fact—that important new writers in Israel can become familiar to European readers while American readers, especially American Jewish readers, have no inkling of their existence. Orly Castel-Bloom, for example, is regarded as the most brilliant practitioner of an audacious, postmodernist sensibility in Israeli writing. French, Dutch, and German readers can sample four of her titles; none of her books have appeared in English. Itamar Levy's *Otiot hashemesh, Otiot Hayareaḥ* (Letters of the sun, letters of the moon) is the most important recent contribution in Israeli letters to the representation of the inner experience of the Arab; it will soon appear in Italian, French, German, and Spanish along with two other books of Levy's. Savyon Leibrecht is an accomplished short-story writer who is central to the rise of women's writing in Israel. She is being translated not only into Italian and German but also into Chinese. Until very recently none of Leibrecht's books have appeared in English, and Levy's work still awaits translation. There are many other examples.

The European comparison helps to bring a question to the forefront: Why is it that when Hebrew literature has come of age and finds itself in the midst of its greatest boom that American Jewish readers, so cultured and so committed to Israel, should have so little use for it? This is a question to which I believe there are answers, some obvious, some less so. The answers have to do, in part, with the differences in the reading habits of Americans and Europeans, with the general fate of the audience for serious fiction in America, and with the deep ambivalence American Jews feel at the prospect of encountering the realities of Israeli society. These are explanatory conjectures that are worth probing and developing with care. I defer that task to the end of this chapter to concentrate first on the substance of the record of the reception of Israeli literature in the United States so far. To sharpen and define the issue, I have emphasized the failure of Israeli literature to secure a broad audience in America. But that is only one dimension of the "career" of these books on these shores. These Hebrew novels are acquired and translated and published by prestigious commercial houses without subsidy; they are reviewed thoughtfully in respected journals; they make their way into bookstores and public, synagogue, and university libraries and onto the lists of book clubs and reading circles and the syllabi of college courses and adult education offerings. And, of course, they are purchased and actually read by thousands of people. So even though the impact of Israeli literature has been circumscribed, the substance of what that impact has been—what these books have meant to whom in which circles—is the first order of business. One is likely to form better conjectures about force and volume if one understands more about the trajectory so far.

Taking that measurement turns out to be a deceptively difficult thing to do. In the interplay of forces and mediations, the reception of a work of art is an enormously complex process, no less so than, say, the ways in which foreign policy is shaped in government or certain ideas become central to a society's discourse. In the limited compass of this introduction I aim to accomplish two goals. My first objective is to sketch an account of the reception process as it applies to Israeli literature in America. How does a piece of writing written in Hebrew and produced in Israel get translated, published, reviewed, distributed, read, and discussed in America? What are the constraints and mediations that favor some works over others? My second objective is to see what can be learned from a closer look at a number of case studies. I have chosen ten books by six writers (Oz, Yehoshua, Shabtai, Hareven, Appelfeld, and Grossman), which generally represent the first publication of the authors' works in English, and I have analyzed the reviews written about them in national journals. What I have looked for is not so much the evaluations given by the reviewers ("Is this a good novel?") although these judgments are obviously not unimportant. Rather, I have focused on the reviewers' encounters with the books as works of Israeli literature. What are the reviewers' implicit assumptions about Israeli society? What awareness is shown in the reviews about the existence of Hebrew literature and its institutions, and what expectations are placed upon that literature? What themes are brought to the forefront, and in what way do they express the concerns of American and American Jewish readers?

## THE DYNAMICS OF RECEPTION

One of the consequences of living in an advanced consumer society is that one has little sense of either the prehistory of the commodities one consumes before one acquires them or of the forces that tend to determine one's choice of one object over another. When one purchases a car or a computer or a suit of clothes, one is unlikely to be fully conscious of the stages of research, design, engineering, manufacture, marketing, and distribution that took place under highly competitive conditions, eliminating many possibilities and advancing a limited set of others, with the result that one chooses from the several models made available. That final choice, in turn, is shaped by advertising and consumer journalism (reports and reviews of products). The commodity one finally acquires has undergone what Marxian theorists call a process of reification; the object has become a thing stripped of the labor invested by many hands in producing it.

When one reads a newly published book, whether bought or borrowed, one tends to be similarly innocent of the Darwinian provenance of the object held, unless, perhaps, one is involved in the business of writing or publishing. This is particularly true of a translated book, which has an imposing hurdle to clear before it comes into the world altogether. In the case, then, of the English translation of an Israeli novel, one is dealing with a book that is, in a sense, doubly a survivor. The book first has to be published in Israel before it becomes a candidate for the exceedingly smaller ranks of books published in a foreign language. How it joins these ranks and is reviewed and read abroad is the story that is of interest here, but one should not be unmindful of how the publishing scene in Israel has changed over the years.

During the first decades of Israel's existence, the key players were large publishing houses established by the political parties and the kibbutz movements: Sifriyat Po'alim, Hakibbutz Hame'uhad, 'Am 'Oved, and others. Beginning in the seventies, these institutionally backed publishers were made to share the market with commercial houses such as Keter and Zemora-Beitan, which conducted themselves much more like their American counterparts. This shift, which echoed the larger retreat from ideology and the move to an open-market economy, produced complicated consequences. On the one hand, it made it easier for women and Oriental Jews and other marginalized groups to get their voices heard in the literary marketplace and to connect with new audiences for literature. On the other hand, quality writing had to pay its own way and could no longer depend as much on institutional subsidies. The publishing scene became more driven by the search for bestsellers, whose appearances were attended by intensive public relations campaigns.

How then are writers' works chosen for translation once they have achieved some success in Israel? It is easier for some writers than for others, of course. Established writers such as Oz and Yehoshua and, by now, Grossman have long-term contracts with publishing houses that have become their "homes" in America: Oz with Harcourt Brace Jovanovich, Yehoshua with Doubleday, and Grossman with Farrar Straus and Giroux. Anything major that they write will almost automatically appear in English. (The justice of this arrangement is another matter; many critics think that the last several novels that Oz has written are inferior to the work of several younger writers who remain untranslated. But his arrangement appears to be a general state of affairs that is not special to the case of translation.) Another factor is genre. Short stories have always been difficult to sell in translation although Israeli publishers and readers are more sympathetic to first books of stories than are their American counterparts. Often, as was the case with Oz's *Where Jackals Howl and Other Stories* (Artsot hatan), the stories that were written and published at the outset of the writer's career have to wait until there is a successful novel (Oz's second novel *My Michael* was his debut work in English) before a publisher agrees to bring out the earlier stories. Although the "serious" novel has long reigned as the genre of choice in translation, mysteries and thrillers are now mounting a challenge. Until recently, Israeli readers have been able to satisfy their appetite for detective novels and *romans policiers* by recourse to the many translations into Hebrew from English and French, two languages in which this genre of writing has reached high levels of sophistication and variety. Now accomplished Hebrew writers such as Yoram Kaniuk, Shulamit Lapid, and Batya Gur have been turning out mysteries rooted in the particularities of Israeli life. In the tradition of Ruth Rendell and P. D. James, they aspire for these works to be something much more than entertainment. The success of Batya Gur's recent detective series, including *The Saturday Morning Murder*, *The Literary Murder*, and *Murder on a Kibbutz*, is a case in point.

Then there are works that resist translation and writers who resist having them translated. Amalia Kahana-Carmon is one of the key figures in the New Wave that reshaped Israeli fiction in the sixties and seventies and the most import precursor of the current boom in women's writing; she is usually grouped with Oz, Yehoshua, and Appelfeld and is spoken about with the same high regard. Yet whereas interested readers of English are familiar with the work of the latter, Kahana-Carmon is locked away in a secret garden. It is a concealment of her own making, in part. It is said that she has never permitted her work to be rendered into English because she believes it is untranslatable.[5] Although her stance is idiosyncratic, it is not entirely a conceit. Her classic work explores the imaginative and fantasy life of female protagonists; the highly lyrical and figurative language used to represent these inner states is indeed difficult, although, to my mind, not that much more so than the style of Oz's early stories. What has kept her from being translated—beyond her own reported unwillingness—has more to do with the fact that the lives lived by Kahana-Carmon's women seem unconnected to the Zionist master plot (the struggles with the aftermath of ideology and collective purpose) that animates much of the other writing of her generation.

Sometimes the size and subject matter of a book may simply be too imposing. Even if the translation is paid for by the author or is subsidized by a foundation or is aided by some other kind of subvention and comes free of charge, as it were, a publisher is likely to balk when presented with a project that has little prospect of selling. By most accounts, S. Yizhar's

*Yemei Ziqlag* (The days of ziklag) (1958) is the best Hebrew novel of the fifties, the first important native Israeli novel, and the only work of the Palmah-generation writers to transcend the strictures of socialist-positivist aesthetic. Yet despite the importance of the work, it runs to some 1,143 pages in Hebrew (Hebrew usually translates up to one-third longer in English), and although the story is set during the War of Independence and follows a fighting unit in the southern campaign, there is no conventional plot and no stirring battle scenes. The enormity of the novel consists almost entirely of the internal monologues of the young soldiers and the elaborate nature description of the northern Negev. *The Days of Ziklag* has never been translated into English although the German rights have been bought by Suhrkamp in Frankfurt. Another example is Haim Be'er's '*Et hazamir* (The time of trimming) (1987), a long novel (560 pages) that examines the boundaries between Orthodox and ultra-Orthodox Judaism by focusing on a small army unit staffed by religious Jews and charged with burying soldiers who die in action or in training accidents. Be'er is one of the best of a small group of writers who probe the religious world of Israeli society using novelistic tools. His first (and shorter) novel *Notsot* (Feathers) (1980) is set in the ultra-Orthodox Jerusalem neighborhood of Geula during the fractious controversy about accepting German reparations monies in the fifties. (Hillel Halkin's translation of *Feathers* exists in manuscript, but it has never been published.) Although centering a long novel such as *The Time of Trimming* on the business of an army burial unit may work well with Israeli readers—the book was, in fact, quite successful—it simply may not translate in a way to engage American readers. Or, at least, it has not done so up to now. Some years ago I was contacted by a junior editor at a major New York house who could read Hebrew and was enthusiastic about the novel. In the hope of persuading her bosses to bring out the novel, she asked me to write a reader's report. I was happy to do so; I, too, was enthusiastic if less hopeful. That was the last I heard of it.

Personal relations, personal contacts, and personal presence should not be underestimated as factors that help to get a book translated. There are literary agents who represent Israeli writers, and the Institute for the Translation of Hebrew Literature in Tel Aviv acts as an agent on behalf of individual writers to promote and negotiate contracts for publication abroad, more in Europe than in America. Many of the deals are done at the industry's great trade show, the Frankfurt Book Fair. But the exertions of authors in their own behalf remain important. Yoram Kaniuk, a writer of comic grotesque fictions, lived in New York for many years in the fifties and sixties and was involved with the Israeli bohemian scene there. He is one of the best published Israeli writers in America with six or seven books from *The Acrophile* (Hayored lemala) in 1961 to the more recent *His Daughter* (Bitoh) (1989) appearing here. I know little about the people he met and the contacts he made during those years, but I would be surprised if his long sojourn in New York did not make it easier for him to get his work published here. He is an important writer, but his hefty representation in English is out of proportion to the standing he is accorded by most critics and readers in Israel. Yehoshua Kenaz and Yeshayahu Koren, by contrast, are two very highly reputed writers who have been writing for as long as Kaniuk but who have just very recently seen some of their work appear in English: Kenaz's *After the Holidays* (Aharei hahagim) (1987) and *The Way to the Cats* (Baderekh lahatulim) (1994) and Koren's *Funeral at Noon* (Levaya batsohorayim) (1996). How their work came to be translated makes a related point. Both authors have been published in America by Alan Lelchuk's Steerforth Press, a small quality house located in Hanover, New Hampshire. (*After the Holidays* was published by Harcourt Brace Jovanovich.) Lelchuk is an American writer who for a long time has taken an interest in Israeli writing; together with Gershon Shaked he edited the important collection *Eight Great Short Hebrew Novels* (1983). Lelchuk's familiarity with the literary scene in Israel—and the flexibility afforded by a small press—have drawn him to some very fine writers who have been overlooked by the industry giants. Ted Solataroff, who for many years was Yehuda Amichai's editor at Harper Collins, is another example of a powerful editor within the publishing world whose commitment to Israeli writing has been an important fact in establishing careers and advancing reputations.

Authors also have to be lucky in their translators, and I think that Israeli writers by and large have been. S. Y. Agnon and Haim Hazaz, from an earlier generation, were less well served. Although he is regarded by many as the greatest Hebrew prose writer, Agnon wrote in a learned pseudonaive style that laid many traps for translators; two of his great novels, *The Bridal Canopy* (Hakhnasat kalah) (1937) and *A Guest for the Night* (*Oreiah natah lalun*) (1968), do not come across as particularly magisterial in English.[6] The native writers discussed here write in styles that are more recognizably novelistic and are laden with fewer allusions to classical texts. Therefore, with some of the exceptions noted above, their work does not throw up obstacles to good translations. The standard has generally been very high. The life of a professional translator, as is well known, is a very difficult one on many scores, and this is particularly the case for a "minor" language such as modern Hebrew in which there is vastly more translation *into* Hebrew from Western languages than there is from Hebrew into Western languages. It is a hugely unequal balance of trade in which export is by far the weaker side. In the corps of translators into English are two preeminent figures. Dalya Bilu is a translator of enormous energy and scope who has worked with most contemporary Israeli writers; born in South Africa, her translations have a slight Anglo rather than American hue. Hillel Halkin, who is American, has also worked with a wide spectrum of current writers although he has devoted considerable time to translating the classics of modern Hebrew and Yiddish literature, including the works of Mendele, Shalom Aleichem, Feierberg, Brenner, and Agnon. Another group of translators are principally associated with single writers: Nicholas De Lange with Amos Oz, Betsy Rosenberg with David Grossman, and, recently, Jeffrey Green with Appelfeld. In each of these cases, a writer (and his publisher, one supposes) has found a translator who has a special affinity for his or her work and who can be relied upon to provide a continuity of voice from work to work. Other accomplished translators include Zeva Shapiro, Seymour Simckes, Richard Flantz, Philip Simpson, and Barbara Harshav. Whatever problems Israeli literature has had in connecting to the American audience, in sum, cannot be attributed in any extensive sense to the quality of translation into English.

GETTING NOTICED

Once a Hebrew book is translated into English and published in the United States, it embarks upon the uncertain journey of dissemination. One can usefully speak of a book proceeding along two tracks. One is a commercial track, involving marketing, advertising, shipments to booksellers, and sales. The other track involves the growth of the book's critical reputation as formed by published reviews, word-of-mouth comment, and standing within the academy. The two sometimes go together, and sometimes they do not. As noted previously, it has often happened that an Israeli novel has enjoyed a considerable succès d'estime here but has simply not sold well. Of course, certain publishing projects can be born into more privileged circumstances than others and be given better chances before they enter the world. An enthusiastic editor can build momentum for a book by exciting the sales people about it, and their interest makes a great deal of difference when it comes to convincing the large chains such as Barnes and Noble, in whose hands book selling has been increasingly concentrated, to carry the book and display it prominently. An advertising budget certainly helps, as does a budget for a book tour. If the author can present him- or herself respectably in English, then personal appearances at bookfairs, talk shows, campus and bookstore readings, and consulate-arranged parties can make a difference.

There is no denying that published reviews play a role in the commercial dissemination of a book. A glowing notice in the *New York Times* is good business. Not to be underestimated also are the low-profile but influential services that preview new books for libraries and book stores such as *Publishers Weekly*, the *Kirkus Report*, and *Library Journal*. Book reviews, like movie and restaurant reviews, certainly function on one level as consumer reports read to decide whether a given book may be worth acquiring. Yet on another level reviews have a life of their own in the making of reputations and the general circulation of ideas that is quite separate from commercial success or failure. For the curious literate person, the ritual of sitting down, bagel in hand, of a Sunday morning to read through the *New York Times Book Review* is not an activity whose goal is to locate a desired commodity in a catalog; it is an opportunity to eavesdrop on culture and to find out what people are talking about in the world of ideas. The old saw that people read book reviews nowadays rather than read the books is true on many levels.

This truth gets truer the more thoughtful the review is. The book supplements and daily reviews of the *New York Times*, the *Washington Post*, the *Los Angeles Times*, and the *Chicago Tribune* probably have the most impact on sales. But in intellectual and literary circles they carry little weight compared to a number of smaller journals that, to begin with, usually publish their reviews too late to have an effect on the crucial initial sales of a book. Reviews in the *New York Review of Books*, *Commentary*, the *New Republic*, the *Nation*, the *New Leader*, and *Midstream* tend to be longer and more nuanced and more ambitious in seeking to relate the book at hand to larger complexes of ideas and cultural phenomena. Sometimes the book under review serves more as a pretext for airing broader issues. In these intellectually influential journals the main challenge is getting noticed. Only a small number of the serious books published in a given season are chosen to become the subjects

of these deeper and more extensive essays. Israeli literature has been moder-
ately successful in competing for this scarce intellectual air time. It has been
aided by the fortuitous fact that some editors are not only familiar with the
Israeli cultural scene but also read Hebrew. Neal Kozodoy at *Commentary*
and Leon Weiseltier at the *New Republic* are two cases in point. It has also
helped that figures of immense intellectual authority are actively concerned
with Hebrew literature. Chief among them is Robert Alter, whose interest
in Hebrew literature is particularly persuasive because of his distinguished
contributions to many other areas of the humanities. The late Irving Howe,
who also was an enormous presence in so many areas, developed a strong
interest in Israeli literature in the seventies and eighties; although Howe
could not read in the original language (Yiddish yes, but Hebrew no), his
third wife, Ilana, is an Israeli with interests in literature.

Insiders such as Howe and Alter call attention to the role of reviewers
and reviews as mediators between cultures. Translation is surely the great
step in the process by which a work of literature written in one language
and culture reveals itself to another language and culture. But reviews serve
as the forward stations that first receive and process the messages sent by a
foreign culture. It makes a significant difference, to my mind, if these stations
are manned by "insiders," who are conversant with the cultural discourse of
the foreign society, or by "outsiders," for whom the foreign culture remains
foreign. In reality, of course, there is a continuum between the two, and in
no sense is this an evaluative distinction that privileges the perceptions
of one over the other. Nevertheless, being an insider is different because
it brings with it a special burden of judgment. Knowing not just the work
itself that one is asked to review but the societal and cultural formations
from which it emerged forecloses a kind of innocence and opens another
set of responsibilities.

At least, I know this to be true of myself. Although I do not presume
to probe the motives of others, I pause to take advantage of my own status
as an insider reviewer to turn myself into a kind of "native informant" and
to reflect on the experience of at least one practitioner in the field. Most
often, to begin with, I already know a fair amount about the book and the
public discussion it engendered. Because of the gap between the Hebrew
publication and the appearance of the translation, I usually have had a chance
to read the original before I read it in English. (My reading, incidentally, is
often not solitary; for many years I have participated in a Hebrew reading

group made up of other English speakers, almost all of whom have no academic or professional involvement in the subject. My first responses to a book are affected by the group discussion.) There are some books whose reception in the Israeli press is difficult not to notice. Israel has a lively culture of weekend literary supplements and passionate, feisty readers. When a novel such as Grossman's *See Under: Love* or Yehoshua's *Mr. Mani* (Mar Manni) or Orly Castel-Bloom's *Dolly City* (1992) provokes noisy controversy, it does not take much to catch the reverberations. Best-sellers such as Meir Shalev's *Blue Mountain* (Roman rusi), although less provocative, call attention to themselves through their conspicuous success. The quieter waves made by important books by newer authors such as Itamar Levy or Leah Aini usually become known through word-of-mouth consultations with colleagues and friends or in the pages of *Modern Hebrew Literature*, an English-language journal edited by Gershon Shaked and published by the Tel Aviv-based Institute for the Translation of Hebrew Literature, which publishes reviews of new poetry and fiction and excerpts from them. Because my discretionary time for reading, like that of most people, is circumscribed and because it takes me longer to read in Hebrew than in English, I limit the Hebrew books I can read in a given year to those that are truly significant and put me in touch with the best products of Israeli culture. I may not in retrospect have chosen wisely in a given season, but I remain impatient to get it right next time.

If I find a particular book exciting, if it has been an "important" event in Israeli culture, and if it is being translated into English, then I consider writing about it. Most of the substantive review essays I have written have been initiated by me rather than solicited from me. I have phoned an editor and made a case for a book to be given attention if such attention is not self-evident, and I have asked to have the book assigned to me if no one else is doing it. What this means is that I am already a partisan before I embark upon the task of assessing the book. This does not mean that I will not be critical, but the criticisms I have will be presented within a space of cultural importance that has already been cleared for the book in my mind. Not having the responsibilities of a regular critic has also made it possible for me to avoid writing about books that are disappointing. This selectiveness, I think, does not stem from an arrogant insistence that only certain books are prestigious enough for me to devote time to them. It comes, rather, from a kind of necessary ruthlessness imposed by the constraints of time. In my university job, I am paid to teach and conduct research; reviewing is an elective adjunct, something done "on the side." The time given to reviewing must, therefore, be justified by the inherent interest of a project and by what I can learn by undertaking it.

Once the arrangements for the assignment have been made, I become supremely aware of the dimension of audience. This is determined in some measure by the profile of the publication in which the review is to appear. The differences between writing for the *New York Times Book Review* and *Commentary* and the *New Republic* have to do with a great deal more than great disproportions in the size of readership. The smaller journals have well-known political and cultural differences, as well as distinct editorial cultures, although the "back of the book," the cultural reviews, are often more weakly linked to the journals' political stances. A reviewer perforce becomes a participant in the kind of invisible community determined by the journal; the way in which an argument is framed, however unconsciously and however slightly, is likely to be affected by the signature constellation of conventions and expectations associated with the journal. The "Jewishness" of the imagined community is also a key fact, yet a very elusive one. If one is writing for *Hadassah Monthly* or the *Jerusalem Report*, on the one hand, or for *Commonweal*, on the other (as I have done at various times for all three), then the identity of the audience is more in focus. In other instances it is more blurry. Even though *Commentary* is published under the auspices of the American Jewish Committee and regularly includes comments on developments in Jewish culture, the editors are more insistent on avoiding insider references and allusions than are those at the *New Republic*, which, despite the Jewish identity of its owner, has no communal affiliation and has historically been more focused on the political affairs of the republic.

Apart from these differences of milieu, I have found myself over the years remarkably consistent in the audience I imagine myself addressing. That audience is modest and almost always a small subset of a journal's broader subscription base. These diminished expectations derive from a skepticism about the very possibility of a large general audience in America for serious Israeli literature or, for that matter, for serious Jewish scholarship, thought, and criticism. Although I am persuaded as much as anyone that Jewish culture is a wonderful thing and has much to say to the world, I believe that it will speak most eloquently to those who already hold some brief for its importance. Writing about Israeli literature in national journals brings a number of secondary gains. It keeps the discussion from becoming parochial, and it forces connections to be made to general literature and currents of ideas. It enhances respect for the subject and legitimizes its inclusion in the discourse of American culture. And there is always the hope that, having found the matter of a review intriguing, readers with no previous associations with Israeli literature will pick up the book, read it, and take an interest in the subject.

My primary imagined audience, however, remains circumscribed. In my mind's eye I see friends and colleagues and, by extension, other involved participants in the American Jewish community who regard my subject, Israeli literature, as surely legitimate and, perhaps, even important but largely irrelevant and unread. My goal is to interest them, to get them to pay attention, and to persuade them that Israeli literature has something to say to them and that they should be open to the intellectual claims it makes upon their lives.

But this role of advocate—perhaps even cheerleader—has another side to it. To the degree that I represent Israeli literature to American Jewish readers, I also represent diaspora Jewry to Israeli culture. I read the novel before me with the eyes of the American Jew that I am—although granted, not the typical American Jew. I know a great deal about the cultural milieu out of which the work emerged, and I have "gone native" in my partisanship of this foreign literature. Yet in the end I speak from here rather than from over there. Two examples illustrate how "situated" is my understanding of this material. I greeted the publication of David Grossman's *See Under: Love* as a major event and as the most important exploration of the Holocaust in the generation after Appelfeld.[7] At the same time, for all of the many conspicuous influences on Grossman's writing from Bruno Schultz to Gabriel García Márquez to postmodernist fabulists, I was struck by the utter failure to make use of any of the rich imaginative resources contained in the responses to catastrophe in Jewish tradition. Similarly, in writing about A. B. Yehoshua's *Open Heart* (Hashiva mehodu), a novel that describes the turning toward Eastern mysticism by a group of young Israelis who are disaffected from the growing consumerism of Israeli society, I remarked on the sense of déjà vu this provoked in American readers. In rejecting the materialism of American life, I pointed out, Jews who had once looked eastward were more recently turning toward the resources of their own spiritual traditions, whereas the characters in Yehoshua's novel do not give that inheritance a second look.

Observations such as these locate the act of reading Israeli literature in English translation as part of the rough-and-tumble dialectic between Israel and American Jewry. It is part of that dialectic which is, to my mind, irreplaceable. Reading Israeli fiction and poetry provides one of the only ways possible to probe beneath the political emergencies, the newspaper stories, and the organizational pronouncements to get at the existential core of Israeli experience. That most American Jews are deeply ambivalent about wanting to probe so deeply and to see so clearly helps to explain, incidentally, the muted reception of Israeli literature here. For those who do welcome the engagement, then reaction, response, and criticism become integral parts of the process of "active knowing" that the literature enables. In my reviews I try to model this kind of engagement by mixing an empathic presentation of the subject in the context of its own milieu together with a response that is shaped by the very different reality lived here.

What turns out to be the reality of *there* is often not very handsome, and despite myself I often feel apologetically mobilized by this fact. The scenes of Israeli life and the adventures of its psyche as depicted in contemporary Hebrew fiction are not inspiring: Oz's ideological monsters and enfeebled sons, Yehoshua's alienated intellectuals who wound others in trying to confirm themselves, Appelfeld's seedy and emotionally arrested survivors, and, above all, that great epic of folly and dissipation, Shabtai's *Past Continuous*. The much-discussed double standard that is routinely applied to Israel's political behavior operates on the literary front as well. Readers of contemporary American fiction have been socialized into maintaining a certain separation between art and life and abandoning expectations that serious literature should provide exemplary models of family life. If one finds murder or adultery in a novel by Joyce Carol Oates or Philip Roth, one does not take it as a description of American society as a whole. Seasoned readers are equipped with various procedures for "recuperating" the violence and venality found in works of art by understanding them as part of the artist's vision and technique in a tradition that goes back to the theatrical blood Shakespeare freely spilled on the stage of the Globe Theater. These decoding procedures sometimes are suspended when American readers approach Israeli literature, or, at least, I fear they do. I then feel called upon to try to do for the readers the work that they might naturally do on their own when reading on native grounds. I point to the long tradition of social criticism in Hebrew literature going back to the critique of the shtetl. I demonstrate how the comic and the grotesque are used to create ironic distance. I speak of how the perfection of artistic form can yield a sense of transcendence even when the subject matter is repugnant. And I extol the virtues of a society that is self-aware and willing to tell itself hard truths.

Am I being an apologist? Perhaps I am, but I do not believe my stance is inappropriate. Israeli literature is not written for export. It is composed in Hebrew as an internal communication among readers who share a similar exposure to risk and a similar burden of citizenship. Although most Israeli writers are happy to be translated into foreign languages, the audience they are addressing resides at home. Reading literature in translation is, therefore, a kind of eavesdropping. My job as reviewer is to supply the rules of the game for the conversation being overheard. It is not to pretty up what is being said but to explain the context in which the dialogue is taking place.

## TEN BOOKS / SIX AUTHORS

I have selected ten books by six authors and read what has been written about them in prominent journals to generalize about the reception of Israeli literature in translation in this country. As I do this I am well aware that reviews of this sort represent only a segment of a reception process that unfolds on many levels and never approaches closure. There are, I know, other measures and other places to look. It would be revealing to check the acquisitions of libraries (university, city, Jewish community, and, especially, synagogue) and the borrowing patterns of their users. Many groups, especially synagogue sisterhoods and Hadassah chapters, have book circles or periodic programs in which reviews are given. It would be informative to know how often Israeli literature is discussed and the kinds of reactions to it that are voiced. Examining published reviews in local Jewish community newspapers would represent a different level of search, but one that, unfortunately, is beyond the resources of the present study. There are dozens of community papers; many carry notices by local reviewers and others carry syndicated columns. I speculate that only certain works of Israeli literature in translation are selected for attention at this level, and it would be telling to find out which are and which are not, not to mention what is said about them. Is the unromantic presentation of Israel in these works more vexatious here, closer to the streets and neighborhoods of Jewish life, than in national publications? In the end the individual reader is the smallest but most important unit in the reception process. I would pay dearly to observe focus groups of ordinary readers reacting to novels such as Yehoshua's *Mr. Mani* or Grossman's *The Book of Intimate Grammar* (Sefer hadikduk hapnimi).

In the meantime, the reviews at hand have not a little to tell. The fact that they are taken from elite publications is a strength and a limitation. The discussions that take place in the venues and settings I have just listed (community papers, synagogue libraries, etc.) are more likely than not to be internal to the Jewish community. But when a review appears in the *New York Times* or the *New York Review of Books* or the *New Republic*, then, even if it is written by an insider, it enters a discursive space that is at once national and ecumenical. This is even true for a reviewer like myself who admits to directing his words to a subset of that ideally broad audience. It is a conversation all can listen to even if I believe only the few are interested, and I must conduct myself with that in mind.

The following are the works I have chosen to track. I have listed the Hebrew publication date first, and then I have listed the American publisher and the date of publication in translation.

Appelfeld, Aharon. *Badenheim 1939.* 1979. Translated by Dalya Bilu. Boston: David R. Godine, 1980.

Grossman, David. *See Under: Love.* 1986. Translated by Betsy Rosenberg. New York: Farrar Straus and Giroux, 1989.

Hareven, Shulamith. *City of Many Days.* 1972. Translated by Hillel Halkin. New York: Doubleday, 1977.

Oz, Amos. *Elsewhere, Perhaps.* 1966. Translated by Nicholas De Lange. New York: Harcourt Brace Jovanovich, 1973.

Oz, Amos. *My Michael.* 1968. Translated by Nicholas De Lange. New York: Alfred A. Knopf, 1972.

Oz, Amos. *Where Jackals Howl and Other Stories.* 1975. Translated by Nicholas De Lange. New York: Harcourt Brace Jovanovich, 1981.

Shabtai, Yaakov. *Past Continuous.* 1977. Translated by Dalya Bilu. Philadelphia: Jewish Publication Society, 1985.

Yehoshua, A. B. *Early in the Summer of 1970.* 1972. Translated by Miriam Arad. New York: Doubleday, 1977.

Yehoshua, A. B. *The Lover.* 1977. Translated by Philip Simpson. New York: Doubleday, 1978.

Yehoshua, A. B. *Three Days and a Child.* 1962. Translated by Miriam Arad. New York: Doubleday, 1970.

I picked these particular books because they generally represent the first appearances of these important writers in English; they afford readers an opportunity to see the beginnings of their American careers and the initial reactions to their works. The periodicals I have surveyed are those tracked by two standard references: the *Book Review Index* and the *Index to Jewish Periodicals*. These guides cover major national and Jewish journals; they do not, however, index most newspapers except for the *New York Times*. In a more comprehensive treatment one would have liked to canvas as well the book supplements and columns of the *Washington Post*, the *Chicago Tribune*, and the *Los Angeles Times*. My goal has not been to document reception case histories of individual works but to look for patterns of response to these works as parts of the larger phenomenon of Israeli literature. So if there is some subjectivity in my choice of books or lack of exhaustiveness in the coverage of periodicals, the general patterns, nevertheless, remain quite noticeable. These organized themselves under four general headings.[8]

### The Status of Israeli Literature as Literature

Whether Israeli literature should be taken as a reflection of the embroiled and besieged nature of Israeli society or as a more removed literary artifact is an issue for reviewers encountering these materials for the first time, especially when the first important translations came out in the seventies. Richard Locke's enthusiastic review in the daily *New York Times* (May 25, 1972) of *My Michael*, Oz's first work to be translated into English, begins with an admission of astonishment.

> [A]dvance rumors hardly prepare one for this first translation of his major work. "My Michael" is anything but a provincial achievement; it has nothing to do with noble kibbutzim, Sten guns and sabras, nor with the Talmudic dryness of Israel's Nobel Prize-winner, the late S. Y. Agnon. It's quite the last kind of book one expects from a young writer living in the midst of a melodramatic political situation, for "My Michael" is an extremely self-conscious and serious psychological novel, slow, thoughtful, self-assured and highly sophisticated, full of the most skillful modulations of tone and texture.

One wonders what Israeli writing, suffused with sabras and Sten guns, the *Times's* reviewer had been reading up to now to make his surprise so stunning. Alan Lelchuk makes a similar point in reviewing Shabtai's

*Past Continuous* in the *New York Times Book Review* (Apr. 21, 1985): "No kibbutz utopias here, no Jerusalem mystique, no Zionist uplift, no sabra heroics—in other words, no magical society." A variation on this theme is the offhand comment in the *Times Literary Supplement* brief review (by "A. D.," Dec. 7, 1979) of Yehoshua's *The Lover*: "[T]he translation . . . suggests some—though less than usual—of that prickly-pear quality so often found in Israeli writing."[9] In a review of the same novel in another British publication, the *Spectator* (Aug. 25, 1979), Paul Abelman utters a sentiment that I suspect is more widely shared then one might realize. After complimenting Yehoshua on not "loading every incident with epic significance," he opines, "[a]ctually . . . a touch more of the heroic mode might not have been inappropriate. At the other end of the spectrum, I felt positive nostalgia for good old ghetto humor and the Jewish joke." How unfortunate, he seems to think, that Israeli literature cannot serve up the comic routines of the Borscht Belt or the East End.

This was certainly not the tenor of Israeli literature before the debut of Oz and the other writers discussed here. For all the shortcomings of the Palmah-generation writers, glamorizing kibbutz life or military exploits was not one of them, not to mention their general unavailability in translation. (Aharon Megged's novel *Living on the Dead* (Haḥai 'al hamet), for example, which appeared in English the year before *My Michael*, made a point of deflating these myths.) It is much more likely that these impressions of "Israeli writing" derive not from actual writings by Israelis but from writing about Israel by Americans. There is no exaggerating the impact of popular novels like Leon Uris's *Exodus*—and their Hollywood versions—in forming the literary image of Israel in the American mind. American Jewish organizations labored very hard, and with impressive success, during the first decades of Israel's existence to project an image of Israel as a country that, although beleaguered and vulnerable, was populated by a resilient collection of idealistic soldier-farmers. This, however, is not the world according to Israeli fiction, for as Faiga Levine remarked in reviewing Oz's kibbutz narratives in *Where Jackals Howl and Other Stories* for *Book World* (May 31, 1981), "[t]heir characters are not the joyous prototype kibbutzniks of the United Jewish Appeal posters." So whatever the source of the previous conceptions of Israeli reality and its literary representation, the encounter with genuine Israeli Hebrew literature in translation, experienced as sophisticated and nuanced literary art, comes with the force of a revelation.

Its artistic refinement acknowledged, the new literature was often welcomed for its truth-telling capacity. In writing about Oz's *Where Jackals Howl* in the *Times Literary Supplement* (Sept. 25, 1981), Judith Chernaik states that [Oz's] "fiction is indispensable reading for anyone who wishes to understand the contradictions of life in Israel, the ideology that sustains it, and the passions that drive its people." She concludes her review with the claim that the "reader coming to Oz for the first time is likely to find his perception of Israel permanently altered and shaped by these tales." Implied in these words is an actively inquisitive but perplexed reader who acknowledges the complexity of Israeli society but who can penetrate it only with the help of Israeli literature. This sense of Israeli literature as a key that unlocks a mystery or as a projectile that penetrates layers of misperception is especially strong for "insiders," that is, reviewers in Jewish publications who are sensitive to the ostensibly negative and even scandalous portrayal of Israeli life in these works. As the longtime director of education and cultural affairs for B'nai Brith, Lily Edelman was a quintessential insider. Reviewing Yehoshua's *Early in the Summer of 1970* (Bithilat kaiyts 1970) in the organization's journal, the *National Jewish Monthly* (Apr. 1977), Edelman remarks that "[o]n the eve of the annual celebration of [Israeli] statehood, there is little to make the heart dance, even less to make the spirit soar." To understand "the malaise, the despair, the somber reckoning of the soul that constitutes the stuff of the contemporary Israeli nightmare," one has only the "key" offered by the stories of A. B. Yehoshua. Although she finds the translation of his stories flawed, they remain "indispensable for any reader desirous of touching truth about contemporary Israeli mood and situation."

More ambitious still are the claims made for the truth-telling function of Israeli literature by James S. Diamond in the pages of *Conservative Judaism*, the journal of the conservative rabbinical organization. Both a rabbi and a scholar of Hebrew literature—he was director of Hillel then at Washington University and now at Princeton—Diamond speaks to his fellow rabbis in an attempt to get them to take Israeli literature as something more important than "just" literature. His text is Yehoshua's recently translated *The Lover*; and after describing the plot with all its admitted deviance and family dysfunctionality, he abjures his readers that it would be a "grave misreading" of the book to regard it "as a pulp novel best serialized in a women's magazine." After a serious critical discussion of the novel, Diamond concludes:

> What I . . . wish to claim is that [*The Lover*] offers as revealing an
> insight into post–Yom Kippur War Israel as any political, economic
> or sociological tract of the last two or three years. The novel was
> written during the months preceding the May 1977 election and
> can be read as a fictive presentation of the context in which the
> Labor-led coalition was repudiated. By exposing the immoralities
> and the emptiness of much of life in Israel today, Yehoshua is tacitly
> reaffirming a rational Zionism of humanism and moral development.
> It is antithetical to the mythic Zionism that celebrates Jewish power,
> blood, and soil.[10]

Diamond's stance, one to which I myself have a close affinity, is that of an
American Jewish reader of current Hebrew literature who is striving to
convince his fellows, in this case busy rabbis in search of sermon material,
that they are ignoring a valuable resource. His claim is actually two claims.
The first is that a novel such as *The Lover* provides a window onto the
Israeli situation in the sense that it delivers information about the internal
operations of that society besides doing something much more. Like a psy-
choanalyst or psychotherapist, Israeli literature initiates a process whereby a
people gains insight about its obsessions and neuroses and, perhaps, release
from them, too. This is a process that can be observed by American Jewish
readers who care to pay attention. The second claim I would categorize as
an effort at moral recoupment. Diamond argues that the desperate, alienated, and sordid behaviors described in the novel can be seen as exposing a
fallen Zionism and dialectically affirming a rational and humanistic one.[11]
Diamond is invoking an element in the explicit self-conception of Hebrew
literature from a time long before the State of Israel was ever thought of:
social critique as part of the duties of being what Ezekiel called a *tsofeh leveit
Yisrael*, a watchman for the house of Israel.

   Separate from this prophetic horizon, some reviewers discern in Israeli
literature a collective dimension that sets it apart in its very conception from
American literature. These are arguments that arise largely in discussions
of Shabtai's *Past Continuous* and Appelfeld's *Badenheim 1939* but which are
generalized to make a statement about the difference of Israeli literature
as a whole. For all the vast differences of scale and technique, both novels
have a large cast of characters whose actions are returned to over and
over again and are narrated from an impersonal distance that renounces

inferiority. In reviewing *Badenheim 1939* in *Partisan Review* (vol. 49, winter 1982), William Phillips, the editor of the journal, makes the extraordinary statement that "[i]t is the weight of the *Badenheim* theme that forces one to reexamine the ideas about fiction that we have inherited from both the modernist and avant-garde traditions." Those traditions give priority to the reticulations of individual consciousness and to the self-conscious and mythmaking properties of language. Writing at a time when there was much talk influenced by structuralism about the "disappearance of the subject" of literature, Phillips sees in Appelfeld's work the centrality of historical events as they are experienced by a people or a society as a whole. At the heart of the fiction are historical and social forces, not individual psyches.

From a different frame of reference, Irving Howe makes a similar claim in his review of *Past Continuous* in the *New York Review of Books* (Oct. 10, 1985). In writing of the dozens of characters who are "glimpsed rather than developed," Howe writes that despite the sparse physical description of them one soon comes to feel that one "knows" a good many of them, for [Shabtai's] is an art of the representative, an art of the group. A community is releasing its experience, a generation is sliding toward extinction: the community, the generation of "labor Israel," socialist Zionism, which was central in the creation of the young country but has by now—say, the late 1970s—succumbed to old age and debility. If there can be such a thing as a collective novel, then *Past Continuous* is one.

Similarly, in the *New Republic* (May 27, 1985) Sven Birkerts speaks of the way in which Shabtai turns the stream-of-consciousness mode of writing, which is "by definition a subjectively centered idiom," "into a means for expressing the collective life of an extended human network." "Identities, and the problematic particulars of time and place, are diffused within the larger life of the clan." Shabtai's and Appelfeld's works are surely distinctive in this regard, yet throughout the critical responses to Israeli literature in translation, even in the adumbrations of the most recent postmodernist and "post-Zionist" narrative to come from Israel, one hears the echoes of a similar perception: this enterprise, despite individual realizations, is about the nation as a whole.

## What Is the Subject of Israeli Literature?

As learned long ago, people do not read a work of literature—or encounter any new phenomenon—without bringing some preexisting interpretive framework to the task. That framework may, indeed, be revised by contact with a strong work of art, but the interpretation that ensues has its point of departure in some foundational set of assumptions. Of the reception of Israeli literature in America, it is fair to say that every reviewer reports on a new work in translation from within some previous concept of what the enterprise is about. Readers "realize" the meaning of the work according to what is most relevant to their individual concerns. These concepts, as they are shared in communities of interpretation, are variously called by literary theorists "master plots" or "metanarratives." So for reviewers to state what they believe is the main theme of a novel is not simply to offer informed subjective opinions nor to render accounts of rigorous objective analyses. Whatever else it does, such a statement also discloses something of the framework of interpretation the reviewers bring to the task and within which they work individually to domesticate the foreignness of the artifact laid out for inspection.

In reading through the many reviews of many books, I have tried to look for patterns in how the subject of Israeli literature is construed. (I am deferring the subject of the Holocaust until later and dealing with it on its own terms.) The gross events in a given work, of course, prompt discussions in certain directions; I have attempted to look for points in which the directions taken are not so obvious or in conflict with other readings of the same material. It goes without saying that for many reviewers the overarching story is life in Israel under the conditions of war. Anatole Broyard said it very systematically in the opening paragraph to his review of Oz's *Where Jackals Howl* in *Books of the Times* (vol. 4, Aug. 1981): "What is it like, the emotional life of people who exist in a constant state of crisis? Does the political cheat, or does it intensify, the personal? Do deeply felt causes constrict or expand character?" (The answer, by the way, is that they constrict; Broyard finds Oz's writing powerful but his characters lifeless and controlled by principles and fixed ideas.) This is a very widely applied grid. It expresses a sympathetic understanding of the constraints under which Israelis live their lives, it identifies those constraints (and the unremitting and tragic conflicts that produce them) as the basic truth or dominant fact of Israeli existence, and it expresses a detached inquisitiveness about the nature of behavior under these conditions.

That the "Arab question" should be prominent in the minds of reviewers would seem to be most natural if it were not for the fact the subject has had a rather slight presence in the literature being reviewed. With the exception of some stories by Tammuz and Yizhar, Israeli literature had largely construed Israeli reality internally; the tense constraints under which Israelis live may be the result of Arab enmity, but Arabs were largely excluded from the Israeli literary imagination. With the arrival of Oz and Yehoshua on the scene, the issue was reopened, yet still in sporadic and partial ways.[12] For example, although Oz's *Where Jackals Howl* contains only one story in which an Arab character is portrayed ("Nomad and Viper"), the reviewer for the *New York Times Book Review* (Apr. 26, 1981), A. G. Mojtabai, observes that the "most haunting issue raised" in the book "[i]s that of exclusion, dispossession—the question of Isaac and Ishmael, why one son is favored and the other not." Praising the book as "strong, beautiful, disturbing," Mojtabai locates its distinction in grappling with "a dimension of the Israeli experience not often discussed, of the specter of the other brother, of a haunting, an unhealed wound."

Time magazine is a venue in which very few works of Israeli literature have been noticed. In reviewing Oz's *My Michael* (Jul. 3, 1972) A. T. Baker points to the Arab twins who appear in Hannah Gonen's dreams as an explanation for the novel's "smashing success" in Israel. "The passion that animated the early founders of Zion has cooled. The new passionate people are the Arab fedayeen, and in some small dark recess of the national psyche, the Israelis are jealous." This, of course, reveals much more about the mentality of *Time* magazine than it does about Oz's novel, but it remains significant that this is what gets said in this rare moment of attention given to Israeli literature. Robert Alter, the great "insider" reviewer of Israeli fiction in America, must have been aware of how widely the novel was being read along these lines when he reviewed the book in the *New York Times Book Review* (May 21, 1972) two months earlier. His review is polemically focused on counteracting a political reading of the novel. "Any consideration . . . of a Palestinian Question is irrelevant to [Hannah's] conjuring with the Arab twins, who represent an alluring, threatening *dédoublement* of the male principle, an image of suppressed desire to submit to brutal sexual forces." Between these two poles Alfred Kazin offers something of a mediating position in his remarks on *The Lover*, a novel in which the Arab theme is indeed conspicuous if not central, in the *New York Review of Books* (Dec. 21, 1978). After admiring the portrayal of Naim, the fifteen-year-old Arab boy who works in a Jewish-owned garage, Kazin offers, "What I value most in *The*

*Lover*, and never get from discourse about Israel, is a gift for equidistance—between characters, even between the feelings on both sides—that reveals the strain of keeping in balance so many necessary contradictions." What I think he means when he says "discourse about Israel" is *political* discourse about Israel, the embroiled and polarized assertions and counterassertions that constitute discussion of the Arab-Israeli conflict. The "gift for equidistance" that Kazin finds in Yehoshua's work characterizes a different kind of discourse, an imaginative or novelistic discourse, in which the impacted conflicts are not resolved but allowed to be observed with varying degrees of sympathetic distance. Kazin's is an argument for Hebrew literature as a different mode of knowing the reality in which Israel is enmeshed, and he touches upon a true, extraliterary potentiality of the enterprise as a whole.

Other efforts to identify an essential "subject" of Israeli literature concentrate—to my mind, more appropriately—on the internal changes within Israeli society, especially the transition from what Amos Elon has called the founders to the sons. Although this is the central preoccupation of Amos Oz's excellent early work, the theme is not picked up by most reviewers until Shabtai's magisterial *Past Continuous* placed it unavoidably between the cross hairs of critical focus. That novel begins and ends with both the death of one of the members of the founding generation (Goldman's father) and the suicide of his son (Goldman). In his extraordinarily perceptive review of *Past Continuous* in the *New York Review of Books* (Oct. 10, 1985), Irving Howe argues that the novel takes off from one of the conventions of Western literature—"a myth of historical and moral decline." Stirred in their youth by a "whiff of the absolute," the generation of Goldman's father was seized by "a tremendous yearning for social and moral transfiguration, a leap through history, a remaking of souls" in the struggle to establish a Jewish state. In the aftermath of that state-making enterprise, they have now slumped "into an irritable mixture of rectitude and cynicism" while, in the absence of privation and challenge, their children wander in and out of despair and dissipation. The plight of these belated offspring of socialist Zionism is seen in the largest possible perspective by Sven Birkerts in the *New Republic* (May 27, 1985): "The transformations that other nations have undergone over centuries have in Israel been compressed into decades. The elders were faced with clear obstacles and did what had to be done. Goldman and Israel and Caesar have had no such luck. To them has fallen the task of defining the values of the culture, and they do not know where to begin."

The velocity of that transformation and the violence of the compression that ensued have produced as by-products both nostalgia and a desire to escape history. These are trends I noticed in surveying a broad sampling of Israeli writing from the 1970s (*Commentary*, Jan. 1978). I found many works, especially Shulamith Hareven's *City of Many Days* ('Ir yamim rabim), that gave expression to a yearning for the Mandate Period as a time when the cleavages between Jews and Arabs and among Jews themselves had not hardened and the possibilities of individual identity, even for women, had not yet been overwhelmed by historical necessity.

Between the individual and society stands the family, and for some observers the disintegration of the family is one of the major stories told in Israeli literature. Again, it is Shabtai's key work that draws attention to this theme, for in addition to being "about" the disintegration of families, *Past Continuous* is structured—and held together—at its very core by an interlocking network of family relations. Highly dysfunctional families populate Yehoshua's fiction throughout the long course of his career from his earliest stories such as "Three Days and a Child" to the more recent novels *Mr. Mani* and *Open Heart*. Encountering the stories collected in *Early in the Summer of 1970* leads Nicholas Shrimpton, the reviewer for the *New Statesman* (Feb. 1, 1980), to remark: "Marriages are made in Heaven. The families which spring from them, by contrast, appear to be the product of some wholly owned subsidiary of Hell. . . . Even Israeli fiction, which might seem to have grander subjects under its hand, shares the tendency to turn from the workplace and battlefield to the dolorous events of the life of the hearth." For others, the focus on the family scarcely represents a fall from "grander" themes. Writing of *The Lover* (*New York Review of Books*, Dec. 21, 1978), Alfred Kazin places the vivid dysfunctionality of the family described in the novel within a weighty perspective indeed. The family is "the traditional 'center' of Jewish existence," and in Yehoshua's work it is a center that dramatically does not hold.

Societies undergo transformations and families fall apart for a variety of political and historical reasons. Yet the pain that is experienced by individuals in the wake of these collective events knows little of history and politics. When they are not caught up in the "grand" theme of "the conflict," reviewers have been able to discern in many Israeli writers a fidelity to the fundamental contours of human experience. The persistence of the nonrational, the crushing of sons by fathers, the corrosive effects of isolation and repression—these are some of the themes that have been noted by readers in Amos Oz's early work. Yehoshua's early work invites an even greater concentration on the universal. The stories in *Three Days and a Child* conspicuously eschew markers of time and place and present protagonists whose troubles come across as archetypal exercises in deracination and bad faith. As Yehoshua moves from these early stories to *Early in the Summer of 1970* and *The Lover*, the embroiled particularities of Israeli society come into sharper focus and the contours of political allegory become visible around the edges. This shift, however, does not signal a discounting of the universal-existential but its incorporation into a larger vision in which it is situated within the horizon of history and politics. In writing of *Early in the Summer of 1970* (*National Jewish Monthly*, Apr. 1977) Lily Edelman caught this dynamic synthesis between the particular and the universal very acutely. "[I]n a masterly mix of realistic detail and bemused perception, Yehoshua raises the particular to the universal. War of husband vs. wife, Arab vs. Jew and national vs. nation is transformed into man's battle against himself, against his ideas, his goals and purposes, man's eternal, unrelenting struggle against nature, society and God Himself."

### The Critique of Israeli Literature from the Standpoint of the Diaspora

Although Israeli literature has been generously received by the reviewers, a sign that it is taken seriously is the fact that it is also routinely criticized on literary grounds. *Elsewhere, Perhaps* is overly melodramatic toward the end. *The Lover* does, in fact, bog down in overplotting. The Bruno section of *See Under: Love* makes unfair demands on the reader. If anything, Israeli literature has been handled delicately and given a free ride in comparison to the rough-and-tumble of literary reviewing in Israel. Another kind of criticism, however, arises from an awareness of the differences between Israel and America and from an acknowledgment of the fact that a work of literature may be read very differently in different communities.

This difference is presented with much prescience by Richard Locke in his review of *My Michael*, the same review in which he expresses his surprise to discover serious writing amid the political melodrama of Israeli life (*New York Times*, May 25, 1972). Aware that the novel was an enormous success in Israel, Locke attempts to offer a differential explanation for its reception here and there. As for Israel, he points out that "Amos Oz is suggesting that in her heart Israel is going mad dreaming of Arabs, while on the surface emotionally stunted 'new Israelis' are going about their nation's business cut off from self and history. It's hardly surprising that the book caused controversy and was a bestseller in Israel." What might stir the blood of Israeli readers is something very different from the qualities that might capture the hearts of their American counterparts. "For American readers, though, *My Michael* is distinguished by its warmth, its lyricism and remarkable technical control, its fluent pattern of repetitions—threads of words and associations that weave and interweave a vast underwater net."

American Jews are diaspora Jews, and the way in which the Diaspora is represented in Israeli fiction—which is, for better or worse not very frequent—can generate strong responses on the part of readers who have firsthand experience of the subject. Oz's first novel, *Elsewhere, Perhaps* (Makom aḥer; published in translation after his second, *My Michael*), describes the threats posed to a kibbutz by both the irrationality of the human heart and the hostility of the Arab nations. But by far the greatest threat comes from the Diaspora in the character of Siegfried Berger, who seems to embody a kind of radical evil that is unlike the nature of any of the other figures in the novel. In *Commentary* (July 1974) David Stern finds Berger's character to be "embellished by Oz with all the grotesque flourishes that once marked the typical anti-Semitic caricature of the Jew." Stern goes on to declare that "Israeli literature, if it is ever to mature, will undoubtedly have to confront the critical issue of the relationship of Diaspora Jewry to Israel and the relation of Israel to Diaspora Jewry, in all its troubled complexity. . . . The novel fails precisely where the imagination might have offered insight into the nexus of Zion and Diaspora." Although Stern's tone ("if it is ever to mature") strikes a note of impatient condescension, the issue he points to is a real one—in 1974 and now. The imagination of the Diaspora in Israeli literature has never been nuanced or deeply probing. Although infrequently demonized as it was in Oz's first novel, the Diaspora is more often a kind of "elsewhere" that merely serves as a foil or an escape.

The unheroic and unromantic nature of the Israeli reality represented in the literature is experienced by some diaspora readers as disquietingly subversive. Jerome Greenfield's review of Yehoshua's early stories in the *Jewish Frontier* (Dec. 1970), the magazine of the Labor Zionist movement in America, records the difficulty in squaring the existential despair reflected in the stories with a constructive and uplifting vision of Israel. Greenfield's sense of disorientation is worth quoting at length because it expressed what must have been a sincerely felt dilemma for many readers.

> In the space of some half century [Israel] has succeeded in creating a new type of society, a new type of man. Granted that the image one gets of this new society and man is often polished over by public-relations efforts of various Zionist organizations or ideology-blinded observers. Yet there is, by common agreement, an irreducible core of truth to this image, attested to not only by the objective achievements of Israel and Israelis in peace and war but also by the thousands of outsiders who have been visiting the country every year over the past decades and come away invariably entranced by the open vigor of its life style, the uncomplicated patriotism of its people, the direct affinity they feel for their natural environment, their simple, unself-conscious ease in the general social milieu—which often stir American Jews so deeply, beset as they are with the many complexities of their own intricate, hyphenated existence in the U.S. And the problem that Yehoshua poses is how we are to relate his unrelenting morbidity, the invariable isolation of his protagonists, their destructive self-negation, their total unadjustment to their forests, their deserts, their climate and cities to this other image we have of Israeli life and, indeed, that Israelis have of themselves.

Aware of the respect Yehoshua's work has been accorded in Israel, Greenfield knows that the contradiction cannot be "rationalized away" by taking the stories as "sickly atypical." Instead, he works toward the difficult realization that one's understanding of Israel needs to be enlarged to accommodate what is learned from Yehoshua's writing about the "persistence of human irrationality and destructiveness and the need of such feelings for outlet at the expense of civilized, constructive rationality." This is a learning that is courageously arrived at but scarcely celebrated. Although the reviewer has learned something about how Israelis "deal with their inner lives," the conclusion of the review leaves some question about whether the native admiration of American Jews for Israel can remain unaffected by the unwished for sights thrust upon them by Israeli literature.[13]

Then there are issues that figure importantly in the minds of American Jews and find little resonance in Israeli literature. Feminism is surely one of them. Israeli literature of the 1970s is not rife with portrayals of self-actualizing women, yet this is the lens through which Gloria Gold-reich, writing in *Hadassah Monthly* (May 1972), sees Hannah Gonen, the troubled heroine of Oz's *My Michael*. For Goldreich, Hannah is a "woman, programmed into women's work—marriage and motherhood—struggling to free herself and become her own person." Another issue is baldly stated by the unnamed reviewer in *Choice* (April 1979), who, after generally prais-ing *The Lover*, opines—with an enormous reserve of naiveté—that the only weakness in the book "is its rather shallow treatment of Judaism and its religious values." As mentioned earlier, I expressed similar disappoint-ment—less naively, I hope—with Grossman's failure to draw upon the enormous and various repertoire of responses to catastrophe in classical Hebrew sources.

Finally, political values can be used as a position from which to inter-pret Israeli literature, although this happens less frequently than one might imagine. It goes without saying that political convictions about Zionism as a whole, the Arab-Israeli conflict, and Israel's domestic and foreign policies inform a journal's likelihood to pay attention to an Israeli work of literature and a reviewer's proximity to or distance from the material. Yet I did not find many instances in reviews in which these values came into play explicitly. The exceptions came from voices that are more avowedly identified with the Left or the Right. I adduce two examples that each deal with Grossman's *See Under: Love*. The "politics" of that novel are by no means clear, but because Grossman revealed his own distaste for the occupation of the West Bank and Gaza in *The Yellow Wind* (Hazeman hatsahov), which was written after *See Under: Love* but published in translation in America before it, a kind of invitation existed to connect the politics of one book with those of the other. In a long review in *Tikkun* (Mar./Apr. 1990) Adina Hoffman makes the connection by averring that although Grossman warns against the costs of forgetting the Holocaust, "[e]qually fierce . . . is Grossman's admonition against an understandably but woefully misguided reliance on the past as eternal justification for the present. No doubt he would contend that the bankrupt moral state of Israel's present policies is the result in part of the too-frequent sounding of Holocaust alarms designed to drown out the din of Israel's own aggressive actions against others." On the other side of the political spectrum, Ruth Wisse invokes *The Yellow Wind* in a review in the *Sunday Boston Globe* to identify, in a far more nuanced way, a problem that is explicit in the journalism but implicit in the novel. While praising the novel on many scores, Wisse finds Grossman's artistic inventiveness cut off from an awareness of how the human condition is embedded in history. His shortcoming lies in his readiness to substitute "imagination for moral engagement."

> For all its invention, there is no moral tension in this book of the kind that derives from the decisions of protagonists who must take reality into account in the conduct of their lives. Instead, the author pits his imaginative will and his will to innocence against the human condition. In fact, readers familiar with The Yellow Wind . . . will recognize here the same dilution and avoidance of moral complexity that distorts his reportage of Arabs and Jews on the West Bank.

### Do Books About the Holocaust Receive Special Attention?

The answer is yes, they do. On a sheer quantitative level, one is struck by the notice taken in a large number of journals of Badenheim 1939 and See Under: Love as opposed to Israeli novels whose focus is contemporary Israel. These are two impressive works of fiction, but the breadth of their reception cannot be explained by their inherent artistic achievements alone. It has been pointed out that good Israeli writing routinely received serious attention in some of the central forums of American intellectual life, especially the New York Times, the New York Review of Books, and the New Republic. Yet despite the salience of this attention, it was rarely broad. This changed when Badenheim 1939 appeared in 1980. Publications that had previously barely acknowledged the existence of Hebrew literature wrote—often glowingly— about Appelfeld's novel. Newsweek, The Christian Century, Jewish Spectator, The Nation, National Review, Partisan Review, Present Tense, Punch, Sewanee Review, Tradition, the Voice Literary Supplement, the Wilson Library Bulletin, and World Literature Today represent an incomplete list of publishing venues to be added to the list of both Jewish and general usual suspects. In the case of See Under: Love, one can add to the list the following: the American Book Review, the Boston Review Commonweal, The Los Angeles Times Book Review, the London Review of Books, the London Observer, Review of Contemporary Fiction, and the West Coast Review of Books.

What is most telling about the reception of these books is that for most reviewers the fact that they are written in Hebrew by Israelis from within the enterprise of the Israeli literate is largely irrelevant and often unsaid. To be sure, Nehama Ashkenazi (*Tradition*, summer 1982) pointed out Appelfeld's connections to the Hebrew writers Y. H. Brenner and S. Y. Agnon; Hillel Halkin (*New Republic*, May 15, 1989) placed Grossman's Holocaust novel in the context of his previous non-Holocaust writing and identified the Hebrew stylistic devices and period echoes in the work; and I placed the novel within the framework of the problematic of the Holocaust in Israeli culture.[14] When all is said and done, however, most reviewers approached both novels in terms of the solutions they offer to the problem of representing the Holocaust in literature. It is as if these novels are contributions made to world culture by Israeli literature in which the origin of the gifts, although perhaps noted, is not terribly important. It is also a very privileged circle to be allowed to join. Edmund White concludes his review of *See Under: Love* in the *New York Times Book Review* (Apr. 16, 1989) with this encomium: "In a few mythic books, such as Faulkner's *Sound and Fury*, Gunter Grasse's *Tin Drum*, Gabriel García Marquez's *One Hundred Years of Solitude*, large visions of history get told in innovative ways. *See Under: Love* may be a worthy successor to this small but awesome canon."

*Baddenheim 1939* is everywhere compared to Kafka, and after calling the book a "small masterpiece," Irving Howe, also in the *New York Times Book Review* (Nov. 23, 1980), identifies Appelfeld as a "spiritual descendant of European modernism, though he lives in Israel and writes in Hebrew."

It may be pointless to try to prize apart the two components of this phenomenon: the fact that these are books about the Holocaust and the fact that they are significant literary achievements that depart from the conventions of Israeli literature. It may be fair to say, however, that no work of Hebrew fiction whose subject is Israeli society, no matter how outstanding its artistic realization, is likely to garner the volume of attention and admiration won by Appelfeld's and Grossman's Holocaust novels. In this sense, what is true about Hebrew literature and the world works to confirm what is generally true about the Jewish people and the world: it is holocaust rather than homeland that evokes admiration and empathy.

IF IT'S SO GOOD, WHY DON'T PEOPLE READ IT?

If this extended sojourn among the reviewers has proven anything, it is that in at least one place in American culture, even if that place is not a broad avenue, Israeli literature is being taken seriously and is being written about thoughtfully. What I have sampled here is only a selection of early books by key writers; the volume of critical discussion would be amplified considerably if I went on to include later works by Oz (*Perfect Peace, Black Box, To Know a Woman,* and others) and Yehoshua (*Late Divorce, Five Seasons, Mr. Mani, Open Heart*), Appelfeld's many novellas, Meir Shalev's *Blue Mountain* and *Esau,* Grossman's *The Book of Intimate Grammar,* and others.

Having documented this solid critical reception, I am brought back to the disproportion described earlier between this kind of success and the relative failure of Israeli literature in translation to sell books and to have an impact on the American Jewish community. I conclude this introduction with some interpretive conjectures about why this is so. These explanations must remain conjectural because I know of no hard evidence that describes the attitudes of Jewish and non-Jewish Americans toward Israeli literature in particular rather than toward Israel as a political entity in general. Although it is possible to assemble the body of published critical responses to this literature and to make coherent analytic statements about it, it is another thing entirely to explain the behavior of the final link in the chain of reception—the reader/consumer, who, in this case, more often than not elects not to receive the message. With these caveats, then, I offer the following salutatory observations.

The relative success of Israeli literature in European countries in comparison to America, to begin with, can tell one something about the reading habits of Americans in general. Because Europe is divided into small countries, European readers have long been accustomed to reading in translation, not to mention the fact that many can read in another language altogether. If one is Dutch or Swiss or even German or French and a reader of literature to begin with, one will as a matter of course find oneself reading translations of serious literature. This is the result of a number of factors. Among them is the awareness of an interdependent European identity and the plain fact that the literary systems of smaller countries are expanded and enriched by translations into that language. The result is that European publishers and readers are not just open to but are often eager for translations of good works of fiction. And this eagerness is completely separate from whatever interest in Israel and the Jews is satisfied by these works.

Americans are very skittish about reading literature in translation, and publishers know this better than anyone. The world of published books already written in English is perceived to be so extensive and so polymorphous that, given the limited time Americans have for reading to begin with, there is no pressing need to look farther afield. Reading literature in translation also reminds Americans of college courses in which they were required to read difficult works of European modernism or long continental novels. This attitude applies to American Jews, as well. Even if they buy more or read more books and even if they are interested in Israel and the Jewish world, there is, nowadays, no lack of domestically produced books to answer their needs.

American Jews who wish to engage Israel through reading fiction, moreover, do not have far to look. Beginning with Leon Uris's *Exodus*, there has been a steady stream of popular novels that have continued to cover this territory. More recently, one sees an increase in multigenerational family sagas written from the point of view of female protagonists. What is common to most of these works is a focus on heroic moments in the history of the state of Israel: its founding struggle against the background of catastrophe and world war, the capture of Adolf Eichmann, the Six-Day War, the raid on Entebbe, and so forth. In reading these paperback sagas, American Jews are using literature to connect to Israel in a way that characterizes a much larger pattern; they are using Israel to buttress their own identities. The glow of the heroic-romantic version of Israel abets this process; the moral realism of the Israeli literature I have been discussing here apparently does not.

From its inception Hebrew literature has always seen itself as a truth-telling literature. In this it is really no different from the serious literature of all advanced cultures that propose to offer a critical representation of the way we live now. As a genre, the novel itself from the days of the knight from La Mancha to the present has taken as its goal replacing illusion with reality. Whatever the perfection of artistry and literary form, truth-telling is an appealing quality only to those who want to know the truth. For American Jews, reading Israeli literature in translation must feel like eavesdropping on the internal squabbles of a family whose dirty laundry one does not want to see because it is too troubling to one's own purchase on purity.

Israeli literature is likely to remain important to those who have a different kind of relationship to Israel, to those who have discovered these writers in college courses, and to serious readers of fiction generally. The circumscribed compass of that aggregate reflects a larger truth about the Jewish people at the beginning of the twenty-first century—the drifting apart, in what seems to be an irreversible tectonic process, of American Jewry and Israeli Jewry.

## NOTES

Originally published in *Translating Israel: Contemporary Hebrew Literature and Its Reception in America* (Syracuse: Syracuse University Press, 2001), pp. 1–44.

1. I thank Rona Sheramy for her help in preparing the materials for this essay. I am grateful for the helpful suggestions made by Naomi Sokoloff, Gilead Morahg, and James Diamond.

2. Unfortunately, it seems nearly impossible to obtain reliable sales figures. Publishers regard these figures as proprietary information, and, for a variety of reasons, they are not willing to disclose them. What figures mean altogether is also rather slippery because the number of books *shipped* to book stores is often many more than the number actually sold, and this discrepancy is further complicated by subsidiary rights of various sorts. In the end, because authors are paid only for the books sold, it is only from royalties that sales figures are derived. The availability of information depends upon authors' willingness to share it and their recordkeeping. I wrote to the authors mentioned later in this introduction with the hope that I could shed more light on their relative success in America. Some responded sympathetically, some not at all. But none was able to provide the information I was seeking.

3. For a useful summary of these attitudes, see Eytan Gilboa, *American Public Opinion Toward Israel and the Arab-Israeli Conflict* (Lexington, Mass.: Lexington Books, 1987).

4. I am grateful to the Institute for the Translation of Hebrew Literature and its director, Nili Cohen, for its generous help and for sharing the information about the sales of Hebrew literature in Europe.

5. I know of only two of her major stories that are widely available in English. "Na'ima Sasson Writes Poetry," a moving and beautiful story, can be found in *Meetings with the Angel: Seven Stories from Israel*, ed. Bejamin Tammuz (London: A. Deutsch, 1973), 225–49, and in *Ribcage: Israeli Women's Fiction: A Hadassah Anthology*, ed. Carol Diament and Lily Rattok (New York: Haddassah, the Women's Zionist Organization of America, 1994), 48–70. "Bridal Veil" can be found in *New Women's Writing from Israel*, ed. Risa Domb (London: Vallentine Mitchell, 1996), 90–108.

6. An exception is Hillel Halkin's English translation of *Sippur Pashut* (A simple story) (New York: Schocken Books, 1985); I also hope that translations of some of the shorter texts escape this fate, such as those collected in *A Book That Was Lost and Other Stories* by S. Y. Agnon, ed. Alan L. Mintz and Anne Golumb Hoffman (New York: Schocken Books, 1995).

7. Alan L. Mintz, "Fiction: A Major Israeli Novel," *Commentary* 88 (July 1989): 56–60.

8. An additional subject should be mentioned in passing without making it a separate category—the tendency to compare Israeli writers to better-known Western writers. Oz is compared to Hemingway, Camus, Pavese, and Sylvia Plath and is even called a Levantine Jane Austen; the heroine of *My Michael* is called an "Israeli Madame Bovary." In Yehoshua's case names invoked include Kafka, Mann, Chekhov, Faulkner, Simenon, Gide, Hawthorne, and Pinter. Shabtai reminds reviewers of Proust, Balzac, Faulkner, and Joyce. Appelfeld evokes Edward Hopper, Mann, Kafka, and Proust; *Badenheim 1939* is called a "scherzo on a theme by Arendt." In Grossman's case it is Garcia-Marquez, Faulkner, Rushdie, Melville, Joyce, and Kafka, in addition, of course, to Bruno Schulz. The purpose of all of this glorious name calling is both to domesticate the foreignness of these writers by comparing them to familiar masters and to make claims for their nonparochial importance.

9. Although the focus of this survey is on the reception of Israeli literature in America, where it is appropriate I have occasionally brought in comments from English reviewers, mostly from the *Spectator*, the *Listener*, and, as here, the *Times Literary Supplement*, Dec. 7, 1979.

10. James S. Diamond, "The Israeli Writer as Mass Psychotherapist," *Conservative Judaism* 32 (Winter 1979): 95–102.

11. Writing of *The Lover* in a similar kind of journal, the *Reconstructionist* (Apr. 1979), David Rabi concludes his review along similar lines: "[*The Lover*] warrants reading because of its sincere and penetrating look at modern Israel as well as its prophetic vision of Israel in the future."

12. The real breakthrough came in the introduction of the character Naim in Yehoshua's *The Lover*. This represents the first time in Hebrew literature, to my knowledge, that the inner life of an Arab character is explored and the character is allowed to speak in his own voice. Yet this genuine innovation goes largely unnoticed in the review literature.

13. The anonymous reviewer in *Choice* (May 1977) offered this caution about *Early in the Summer of 1970*: "One admires Yehoshua's noteworthy technique, but his negativistic, almost nihilistic, philosophy makes one hesitate to recommend this work to a general college audience, and then only after they had been exposed to other writers, such as Agnon."

14. See *Translating Israel: Contemporary Hebrew Literature and its Reception in America* (New York: Syracuse University Press, 2001), chapter 8.

# CHAPTER 11

# Haim Gouri at 90

Last October I attended a gala celebration of the poet Haim Gouri's 90th birthday thrown by the city of Tel Aviv. Although Gouri has lived his adult life in Jerusalem, Ron Huldai, the mayor of Tel Aviv, was intent on appropriating this milestone for his city, as Gouri was born in Tel Aviv and, the mayor argued, hadn't Gouri written innumerable poems about the White City? The large auditorium in the new wing of the Tel Aviv Museum of Art was filled to capacity, and, as a group of actors and musicians alternately declaimed Gouri's poems and played musical settings of them, the audience sat in rapt attention, at home with dozens of texts for which only the titles were given in the program. Finally, the poet himself was helped to the stage. Although Gouri was a little unsteady on his feet, his voice was confident as he honored his hosts, evoking the heady days of Tel Aviv's literary cafes and reciting stanzas of its great poets from memory.

The Israeli literary supplements last fall were full of long interviews with Gouri conducted by such well-known writers as Meir Shalev, Ariel Hirschfeld, and Nir Baram. Over the holidays last fall, the great critic-scholar Dan Miron published a seven-part series on the inner development of Gouri's poetry in *Ha'aretz*. The Bialik Institute together with Kibbutz Hame'uchad put out two large volumes of Gouri's prose.

It's hard to exaggerate the importance of poetry in 20th-century Israeli culture. The willful disengagement from Orthodox beliefs and practices that accompanied the Zionist revolution left the spiritual needs of secular Israelis unattended to, and the writing and reading of poetry have often become a kind of sacrament filling that void. Beginning in Eastern Europe and continuing in Palestine, Hebrew readers looked to poets not only to illuminate their private experience but also to serve as secular prophets.

Each generation of the Hebrew literary public has further sought to invest some figure with the real if unofficial status of "national poet." It began with Bialik and was passed on to Natan Alterman. For some, the awesome Revisionist poet Uri Zvi Greenberg bore the mantel. Later in the century, that distinction belonged to Yehuda Amichai. But Amichai, who is very different from his contemporary Gouri as a poet and a public figure, died in 2000. Since then, Gouri has taken the position, and there are many who would say that it has been his all along. The only other living contender is Natan Zach, age 83, whose brilliant, stripped-down existentialist verse revolutionized Hebrew poetry in the 1960s. But Zach doesn't fill the bill for two reasons. To be a national poet, it hardly bears saying, one has to evince sympathy for the nation, and Zach has long distanced himself from the Zionist enterprise. Moreover Zach never followed his stylistic break-throughs of 50 years ago with accomplishments that connected with the poetry-reading public.

Here is where Gouri has shone. Rather than marching in place or remaining content to recycle his favorite themes, at the age of 86 in 2009 Gouri published a book-length cycle of poems called *Eyval*—more on the meaning of the title and the significance of the work later on—that was regarded by readers and critics alike as perhaps the best thing he had ever written. Gouri thus spared the public the embarrassment of having to celebrate him at 90 as a literary relic—the kind of grand old man of letters whose only recent achievement is his longevity. Instead, the new late-in-life book stimulated public discussion about the shape of Gouri's career and how it moved from its initiation in the War of Independence through several discernable stations to arrive at this late consummation.

**That Haim Gouri is not well known to us in America is regrettable but hardly surprising.** Here the contrast with Amichai is instructive. Amichai served in the British army in World War II, admired and was influenced by Auden, and made his living by teaching American Jews studying in

Jerusalem. He was a popular visitor on American campuses and, because he knew English well, was able to supervise closely the translations of his poems, most of which appeared on these shores. Gouri, on the other hand, was oriented toward Europe, to the degree to which he looked beyond Palestine/Israel at all. He spent a year at the Sorbonne after his studies at The Hebrew University and remains more comfortable with French culture than with English or American. The only book-length sampling of his poetry in English is a bilingual selection translated by the late Stanley F. Chyet, *Words in My Lovesick Blood: Poems by Haim Gouri*.

Interestingly, there is one hidden point of connection between Gouri's poetry and American Jewish culture. Anyone who attended Jewish summer camps or participated in Zionist youth movements in their heyday probably remembers singing the haunting Hebrew song "Bab El Wad" around the campfire. The lyrics are by Gouri and the melody by Shmuel Farshko. The title (literally, the gate to the wadi; Sha'ar Hagai in Hebrew) refers to a narrow corridor 23 kilometers from Jerusalem on the road from Tel Aviv. In 1948, during the siege of Jerusalem, the only way to get supplies to the city was to push makeshift armored vehicles through the blockade. Many Jewish soldiers lost their lives in the effort, and the burnt-out shells of these vehicles, which have been maintained as a memorial, can still be seen on the drive between Jerusalem and Tel Aviv. (Many versions of "Bab El Wad" can be found on YouTube; I recommend one by Shlomo Gronich because of the contemporary photographs that accompany the words.) This is one of a number of song lyrics that Gouri wrote in the eye of the storm in '48 that became instant classics by brilliantly realizing the mood and spirit of the Yishuv in the midst of the struggle and its immediate aftermath. Here is the chorus and one of the stanzas from "Bab El Wad."

> Bab El Wad, forever remember our names!
> Convoys broke through on the way to the city.
> By the side of the road lay our dead.
> The iron skeleton is silent like my comrade.
>
> And I walk, passing here in utter silence.
> I remember them, each and every one.
> Here we fought on cliffs and boulders,
> Here we were one family.

The atmosphere of sacrifice lies heavy upon these lines. The dead are freshly dead, laid out awaiting transport for burial. The comparison of their silence to the burnt-out shells of the armored vehicles expresses outrage and grief. Yet the horror is mitigated by the supremely meaningful nature of the deaths and by the fact that they were not, and will not be, alone. Not only did they fall defending their brethren in a desperate war of survival, but their efforts succeeded. The blockade was breached and Jerusalem resupplied. The soldier who survives, the "I" who walks in silence, justifies his own survival by a vow to remember the name of every fallen comrade because they were not merely comrades-in-arms but members of one family.

Split from their music, such lyrics can seem stilted and over-laden with emotion, but they make sense when they are sung, and in the decades that followed they were sung very often indeed, performing the function of a communal rite of remembrance on the part of the surviving, belated members of the national "family." Gouri himself regarded them as lyrics rather than poetry and did not include them in his collected verse. But the iconic status of these early songs had a paradoxical effect on his career. It gave him recognition far beyond the circles of readers of serious poetry, but at the same time it associated him indissolubly with the moment of 1948 and the high pathos of struggle and sacrifice attached to it.

Gouri's first published book of verse, *Pirḥei eish* (Fire Flowers, 1949), did not do much to shift the perception of Gouri as a war poet. To be sure, these were highly accomplished poems in their own right, not song lyrics. Yet, within this higher literary register, they performed a similar elegiac function and projected the feelings of tragic renunciation felt by a generation called by destiny to give up the normal prerogatives of youth—first love, studies, travel—and afterward felt unworthy when measured against those who had made the ultimate sacrifice. Although the voice in these poems was Gouri's own, the style of the poetry owed a great deal to Natan Alterman, the great eminence in Hebrew literary circles in the 1940s and 1950s. The lush figurative language and the neo-symbolic pathos Gouri borrowed from the master were oddly fitted to the experiences of violence and sudden loss on the battlefield. Within a few years, when Amichai and Zach began to turn the poetics of Hebrew verse upside down, Gouri's debut came to seem more like an homage than a new departure.

To understand Gouri's literary growth it's useful to know something of his origins. He was born in Tel Aviv in 1923 to parents who had emigrated from Russia. Committed Zionists, they came to Palestine already speaking perfect Hebrew and spoke no other language in the home, not even when they wanted to keep secrets from their children. The atmosphere of the home was utterly secular: no Shabbos candles, holidays, or bar mitzvah. Gouri recalls his mother saying that for the human heart there are no fixed observances.

His schooling reinforced Zionist socialist values. General subjects were studied, along with Bible and Hebrew literature, but there was little about the millennia of Jewish life in Europe. The past in general, except for periods of ancient biblical glory, was deemed irrelevant. It was all about the promise of tomorrow. The walls of the clubhouse of the Maḥanot Ha'olim youth movement, to which Gouri belonged, were festooned with placards carrying such slogans as: "You are the rock upon which the sanctuary of the future will be built." The violence surrounding the Arab revolt of 1936–1939 was a formative experience during his adolescent years. After two years on a kibbutz, Gouri attended the elite Kadourie Agricultural School in the Lower Galilee, where Yitzhak Rabin and Yigal Allon were classmates, before joining the Palmach. He participated in paramilitary actions aimed at hastening the British withdrawal from Palestine. In 1947 he was sent to Hungary and Czechoslovakia to organize the illegal aliyah of the remnants of Zionist youth movements. In the War of Independence he served as a deputy company commander on the southern front. After the war, he studied at The Hebrew University and the Sorbonne before undertaking a career as a journalist for labor and left-wing newspapers.

Gouri was a member of the first truly native generation, born in Palestine, raised wholly in Hebrew, and formed in the crucible of the struggle for statehood. This is, to be sure, the heroic stuff of modern Jewish history, but it is also a formation that entailed significant blind spots. Blacked out is the life of the Jewish people in the diaspora, not just the shtetls of Eastern Europe, but the vast, adaptive civilization of the Jews from the Babylonia of the Talmud to the golden age of Andalusia and Maimonides and then to the rabbinic and mercantile elites of Ashkenaz and Poland. Early on, Gouri began to come to terms with these limitations. The year he spent in Central Europe after the Holocaust was an education, exposing him not only to the enormity of what had taken place but also to the human faces behind it. His studies in Jerusalem helped him fill in the not-inconsiderable cultural space between the Bible and Bialik. As it happens, it was through

Bialik and Rawnitzki's great anthology of rabbinic legends *Sefer ha'agada* that Gouri encountered the spiritual world of the Talmud. He also read the great medieval Hebrew poets and delved into the High Holiday *maḥzor*. Gouri is the kind of poet who makes room for new influences rather than divesting himself of old commitments. The discovery of diaspora Jews and their culture surely affected his sabra attitudes, but rather than renouncing that core identity he simply became a *larger* poet.

The attention given the Holocaust in Gouri's work makes him unique among the native writers of his generation. As harsh as it is to say, Zionist ideology had made the destruction of European Jewry into the chronicle of a death foretold. No one had foreseen the specific mechanisms of its execution or its national source—that it came from the enlightened West rather than from the Slavic East was a surprise—but the disappearance of Europe's Jews through pogrom or assimilation had been considered inevitable. This certainty derived from a scathing critique of the physical passivity and moral corruption of diaspora Jews. When the predictions became fact, the catastrophe engendered a deep sense of shame and confusion in those who had been raised in the youth movements of the Yishuv. What stance could be taken by young people who were preparing for the defense of their land and people toward their brethren who, as it was commonly thought at the time, had passively submitted themselves to death?

This may be familiar territory, but it's worth recalling in order to gauge the singularity of Gouri's response. The year Gouri spent in Europe after the war working with survivors when he was 24 was the beginning of a long process that reached its climax when he covered the Eichmann trial in 1961 for *Lamerḥav*, the newspaper of the Labor-left Aḥdut Ha'avoda party. His dispatches are fascinating documents because of the tension they record between the trial testimony, which he dutifully describes, and his subjective responses as a native Israeli. Early in the trial, for example, a witness named Morris Fleischman related how, as an act of public humiliation, he and the chief rabbi of Vienna were ordered to go down on their hands and knees and scrub the sidewalks, and how the rabbi, dressed in his tallit, endured this as an act of God. Gouri's immediate response is disgust: "I had no desire to listen to this broken, decrepit man go on and on about his afflictions. . . . I would prefer attending the Nachal (the army pioneer corps) ceremonies taking place today at the stadium and seeing strong young people." And yet, he writes, "Morris Fleischman's testimony grabs me by the throat with incredible force and says to me: 'Sit down and listen to every word!'" Gouri's honesty is bracing, and it allows those of us who are often caught up in our own righteous hindsight to understand just how difficult this moral readjustment must have been for Israelis.

Gouri persevered in his engagement with the Holocaust. Stepping out of his métier as a poet, he published in 1965 a stunning short novel called *The Chocolate Deal*, which stages an encounter between Ruby and Mordy, two survivors in an unnamed German city several months after the war's end. Ruby is all activity and mobility unburdened by shame and self-reflexive memory; he is busy with schemes for cornering the market on surplus Allied chocolate. Mordy is flooded by memories of suffering, not only his own but those of others who sought to hide him. Gouri stretched himself in another direction when he was asked in 1974 by the members of Loḥamei Ha-getaʾot (The Ghetto Fighters) to prepare a documentary film for the kibbutz's Holocaust museum. Despite having no experience in filmmaking, Gouri worked over the next 13 years to produce a trilogy of well-regarded films: *The 81st Blow*, *The Last Sea*, and *Flames in the Ashes*.

This is how Gouri ends a poem ("Inheritance," translated by Stanley Chyet) written in the 1950s about the Akeidah, Abraham's almost-sacrifice of his son:

> Isaac, we're told, was not offered up in sacrifice.
> He lived long,
> enjoyed his life, until the light of his eyes grew dim.
>
> But he bequeathed that hour to his progeny.
> They are born
> with a knife in their heart.

Although the Holocaust is not explicitly mentioned, it doesn't need to be. Already at the end of the 11th century, survivors of the crusader massacres called attention to the somber fact that, compared to Abraham's uncompleted act, the sacrifice of their martyrs had been fully consummated. So too in Gouri's retelling of the Akeida. Even though the angel intervenes and the knife drops from Abraham's hand and Isaac goes on to live a long and happy life, the intended wound takes on a life of its own. Like a Jewish version of original sin, each new generation is born with a sense of dread. For a member of the heroic cadres that fought for the establishment of

Israel, this is no small admission. It is one of the things that makes Gouri a great poet.

The poetic "I" that speaks in most of his poems, though firmly planted in its home ground, is open to contemplating antagonistic arguments and points of view. But this is hardly a simple liberality of spirit or a Whitmanesque embrace of a world of contradictions, as indicated by the title of another poem from the 1950s, "Civil War," translated here by Stanley Chyet:

> I'm a civil war
> and half of me fires to the last
> at the walls of the vanquished.
>
> I'm a court martial
> working in shifts,
> its light never dimmed.
>
> And those in the right fire on the others in the right.
> And then it's quiet
> a calm composed of fatigue and darkness and empty shells.
>
> I'm nighttime in a city open
> to everyone who's hungry.

In the temporary calm that comes from exhaustion rather than resolution, the speaker compares himself to an open city using allusions that pull in two directions. The last two lines allude to Roberto Rossellini's 1945 film *Open City*, about war-torn Rome as a defenseless space open to looting. Yet Gouri closes the poem in a surprising note of generosity with the familiar Aramaic phrase from the Passover haggadah that offers the "bread of affliction" to all who are hungry.

This poetic conceit became very real at an important juncture in Gouri's career. After the Six-Day War, Gouri signed a manifesto supporting the Movement for a Greater Israel, a circle of secular writers and intellectuals—these were not the messianists of Gush Emunim—who advocated incorporating Judah and Samaria into the state of Israel. Gouri's participation was solicited by Natan Alterman, who overcame the younger poet's hesitations by laying out a vision of a single state with a Jewish majority—achieved by mass aliyah from the West—in which the Arabs would form a respected minority with full religious and national rights. Gouri was not a man of the right, but he had been formed by a Zionist youth culture that imbued him with a deep connection to the Land of Israel in its totality (all parts of which were accessible when he was growing up) and esteemed the value of *hulutsiyut*, pioneering and self-realization through settlement on the land.

In 1975, thousands of supporters of Gush Emunim occupied the old Turkish train station at Sebastia, deep in the Shomron. Until that point, the IDF had been removing settlers as soon as they established themselves, but this demonstration was bigger, and it took place against the background of Arafat's defiant, gun-in-holster appearance at the United Nations and the resolution condemning Zionism as racism. Gouri had been reporting on this tense confrontation between the settlers and the army when he was prevailed upon by the settlers to serve as a go-between between them and the Rabin government. He brokered a deal that allowed 30 persons—later interpreted as 30 *families*—to remain at Sebastia legally, the first in a series of concessions made by the Labor government that allowed settlements to spring up.

In time Gouri came to regret this as one of the greatest mistakes in his life. He had crossed the line between objective journalist and active participant. More disturbing were the violent excesses of the settler movement in the years to come. Nor did Gouri foresee the heavy moral price paid by Israel, especially by young soldiers as they policed Arab population centers, in ruling another people.

Yet rather than blaming the extremists, Gouri turns the light of moral scrutiny upon himself and his generation. It is this kind of grand self-reckoning, a *heshbon hanefesh*, that is the burden of *Eyval*, a cycle of 86 poems that has been widely celebrated as the late fruit of Gouri's career. The title comes from the covenant ceremony in Deuteronomy 27, in which Moses delivers the blessings concerning Israel's future on Mount Grizim and the curses on Mount Eyval. The place name conveys the somber mood of the composition. Gouri looks back and finds his generation—his comrades from the Palmach and the youth movements who forged the institutions of the new state—responsible for a fundamental error. In the heat of their bravery and in their heartfelt identification with the Land of Israel, they were blind to the trauma and disenfranchisement Palestinian Arabs had undergone and to the consequences their ordeal would eventually bear. Gouri sees no guile or malevolence here; the error was an unintended—but not necessarily unforeseeable—result of the legitimate goal of creating a Jewish homeland.

Gouri is no post-Zionist. Israel's enemies and their evil intentions are real. There are no fantasies of undoing history, and no rosy visions of resolution. All we can do, says the speaker of *Eyval*, is to open our eyes, renounce self-congratulation, become aware of the chances we missed, inhabit our regret with courage, and await judgment. What saves this reckoning from prophetic righteousness is Gouri's refusal to stand apart from his peers. The "we" that prevails in the poems is not moral camouflage but a generational collective for which Gouri takes full responsibility. In *Pirḥei eish* (Fire Flowers), his debut collection in 1949, he had spoken in the first-person plural and afterward spent decades on his own poetic subjectivity, apart from the collective. In *Eyval*, 60 years later, Gouri returns to "we," but on terms that are noticeably different.

Any summary of the political argument of *Eyval* is destined to sound crude, not because it simplifies the nuances of analysis but because it is beside the point. What is most real is the experience of regret, not its source. The poems explore what it's like to abide the uncertainty that is created when the principles that have guided one's life have been severely questioned. After admitting that "Almost all the holy cows have been slaughtered," the poet confesses:

> It's difficult for me personally without those cows.
> For years and years I pastured them.
> I am coming to resemble Methuselah,
> Another holy cow that has been slaughtered.

A great and much celebrated poet, a national institution, Gouri could have cruised into the last, late phase of his career. There is something breathtaking in his choice to knock his halo askew and forfeit the pose of the vindicated prophet.

*Eyval* demonstrates how great, luminous poetry can be made out of remorse. Gouri's persona in the poems manages the neat trick of accepting responsibility for his past actions and at the same time not taking himself too seriously. A gift for self-irony and wit leavens the gloom. There are antic shifts between wildly disparate registers of Hebrew; a rare biblical term will share a line with a conversational catch phrase or a piece of army lingo. For a poet so schooled in secularity, there is also an unexpected reaching out to the language of Jewish prayer. The experience of awaiting judgment is the fundamental mood of *Eyval*. The desire to know who will withstand this scrutiny is expressed by the question "Kama ya'avrun?" (How many will pass?); the echo of the U'netaneh Tokef prayer of Yom Kippur is unmistakable. References abound to the Ne'ilah service that brings the holiest of days to its conclusion. Here, at the end of Gouri's long career, he ranges over the entire Hebrew and Jewish tradition to create a poetry of wisdom.

NOTE

Originally published in the *Jewish Review of Books* (Summer 2014), pp. 36–39.

# CHAPTER 12

# Viva Voce

## *Vicissitudes of the Spoken Word in Hebrew Literature*

In the kulturkampf that raged between Hebrew and Yiddish at the turn of the twentieth century, Hebrew, despite its aristocratic lineage, was at a pronounced disadvantage when it came to representing speech. The deficit was less noticeable in poetry, but when prose writers sought to convey the fullness of the lived life, including the way people conversed with one another, they had few models to imitate. If no one really spoke Hebrew at the time, it might be said that in the case of Yiddish *all* people did. The givenness of natural speech in Yiddish was indisputably the great asset in creating a modern literary language. In this area Hebrew literature had to play catch-up during the course of the long twentieth century. I will first attempt to define the contours of the challenge and then discuss several exemplary stations along the way toward naturalizing speech in Hebrew literature.

The invention of a modern Hebrew literature, to begin with, necessarily entailed an inversion of the relationship between writing and speaking in the classical tradition. During the formation of Judaism in Late Antiquity, the continuing relevance of the written Torah was guaranteed and extended on the strength of the oral Torah. This *Torah shebe'al peh*, which was held to have been revealed to Moses at Sinai, was transmitted orally from one generation of authorities to another, and it was from this privileged oral wisdom that sacred texts could be endowed with supplements of meaning. Torah sages, especially during the time of the Mishnah, were scholars who were adept not only in interpreting the law but in transmitting it accurately through memorization and accurate repetition. Surely expense was a factor; scrolls were largely reserved for canonical texts, not the belated exegesis of them. When teachings are eventually committed to writing, whether Yehudah Hanasi's Mishnah at the end of the second century C.E. or in Maimonides's Mishneh Torah one thousand years later, it is always in response to a crisis in the reliability of oral transmission whether because of dispersion or persecution. And it is always second best. Even after the Guttenberg revolution, the written, now printed, word remained suspect. The reputation of a great personage, whether a Talmud scholar or a Hasidic rebbe, was established by making disciples, who in turn disseminated the words of the master. It was usually only after his death that the teachings were collected, written down, and published abroad. Epistles and responsa, documents written by hand and intended for immediate circulation for pragmatic or controversial ends, belong to an in-between category; and they illustrate how tangled and shifting was the relationship between the spoken word and the written word as Jewish culture moves into the early modern period and beyond.

That relationship was clarified and inverted with the emergence of the Hebrew Haskalah. At the center of the Haskalah stood the concept of literature in all its glory. *Sifrut* is the term that was coined in the nineteenth century as a Hebrew equivalent for "literature" (German: *Literatur*, Italian: *letterture*), referring to written works considered to be very good or of lasting importance. Letters, books, and the act of inscription are woven into the etymology of both "literature" and *sifrut*.[1] The very idea of literature presupposes the superiority of written words over spoken words. In the Tradition, authority is founded upon God's creative word embodied in Scripture, which in turn is interpreted orally and then, only reluctantly, written down. In literature, it is human utterance in written form that unapologetically creates meaning and demands devotion; and that is why literature, no matter how domesticated, will always—and correctly—be perceived as a threat to Orthodoxy.

The primacy of the written word is reflected in the *Sitz im Leben* of the new Hebrew literature. Aside from Odessa in the late part of the nineteenth century, there was no literary center where writers or readers interacted face to face. Young men scattered across Lithuania, White Russia, and Galicia wrote poems and penned sketches that they hoped to have published in periodicals such as *Hamagid*. They viewed their literary work as a sacred act, and publication in print was the means by which they could make contact with other communicants. This was a motley group of doubting yeshivah students, principled maskilim, merchants with a smattering of European culture, and lovers of Zion who were drawn together into a community that remained largely virtual and invisible, living on and from the letter alone.

We often point with pride and wonderment to the fact that modern Hebrew literature emerged nearly a century before organized Zionism and the settlement of the Land of Israel and even the beginnings of a critical mass of Hebrew speakers. This is indeed a confirmation of the power of the linguistic dimension of the Jewish national idea to take hold at a time when its territorial realization was only a dream. Yet the early success of modern literary Hebrew can draw our attention away from the difficulties imposed by the absence of communities in which Hebrew was spoken. Because of the eventual triumph of spoken Hebrew, moreover, we sometimes locate signs of its ascendency too early, as if it was already always there. Even once the main producers and institutions of Hebrew literature had been trans-ferred to Palestine by the mid-1920s and Hebrew had become the official medium of the Yishuv, the number of people speaking it on a day-to-day basis in their private lives was quite small. At home most people spoke Yiddish or Russian or Polish, because being "at home" in Hebrew remained an unnatural thing. No greater proponent of the Hebrew renaissance than Bialik famously quipped: *Habreyish redt men; yidish redt zikh* (One speaks Hebrew; Yiddish speaks itself). The real naturalization of Hebrew began with the children born to these immigrants, especially those who grew up in agricultural settlements and youth movements.

Which is to say that the problem of representing speech in Hebrew prose began early and lasted for a very long time. Hebrew writers, to the extent that they aspired to write mimetically, had to find ways to express in Hebrew conversation that took place in other languages, typically Yiddish or Russian. For much of the nineteenth century, the normative solution was to appropriate models of dialogue from the Hebrew Bible, where they can be found in great variety. This practice worked well for the maskilim for both ideological and rhetorical purposes. They viewed biblical Hebrew much in the way Greek and Latin were viewed in the Renaissance as pure, foundational classical languages worthy of serving as a basis for a renewed culture. The elevated diction of the Bible further aligned nicely with their conception of the decorum befitting literature written in Hebrew. The great exception to this rule is the maskil whose audacious masterpiece is just now getting the attention it deserves. Josef Perl's *Megaleh temirin* [Revealer of Secrets, 1819] is instructive for the purposes of this inquiry precisely because it stoops to conquer. In order to ridicule the superstitions and inanities of Hasidism, Perl parodies the coarse and ungrammatical Hebrew, replete with Yiddishisms and Germanisms, used by Hasidim in their correspondence. Because it is epistolary in its conception, *Megaleh temirin* is made up wholly of letters exchanged by its Hasidic correspondents, and Perl's own proper maskilic Hebrew is nowhere to be found. Yet in a way Perl could not have anticipated, the tables are turned. The parodies of Hasidim end up delivering the kind of boorish and even bawdy vitality that was entirely lacking in the overly refined Hebrew of the Haskalah. To complicate things, this contribution is made by what might be called the Yiddishizing of Hebrew. Although such epistles were regularly written in *loshen koydesh*, their Hebrew is a transcription of Yiddish syntax and thought patterns. This was indeed how people truly spoke and thought, hastily and roughly transcribed into Hebrew.

Tracing the representation of human speech in Hebrew literature would be a rewarding but ambitious undertaking. For the purposes of this essay, I've chosen two early examples that convey different responses to the challenge. It is important to point out at the outset that positing a naturalistic representation of speech, conversation, or discourse as a goal is more complex and elusive than may first appear. One factor, which has been mentioned, is that the very object of representation is going through many changes as speakers switch languages—with many hybrid combinations along the way—and Hebrew itself becomes adapted to actuality and thereby more serviceable as a pragmatic mode of communication. The other factor is a universal consideration about what writers do with dialogue in fiction. The representation of speech, no matter how authentic, is always critical and selective and never a transcription of the phenomenon itself. Writers strive for the *effect* of the authentic by artful compression and stylization aimed at conveying the essence of a character. Hesitations, repetitions and banalities may sometimes be used for strategic purposes but not out of fidelity to "reality."

My first example is taken from Abramovitch's story "Hanisrafim" [Burnt Out, 1897]. The story describes the encounter between Mendele the Bookseller and a caravan of Jews from his native town Beggarsburg (Kabtsiel), who have taken to the road to beg for alms after a portion of the town was destroyed by fire. Whereas the first part of the story skewers the Beggarsburghers for their primitive sanitation and their avoidance of responsibility for their woes, the second part pivots and assails the Jewish community for failing to come to the aid of their brethren. In this selection, taken from the second part, Mendele converses with Yehieh-Mordechai, described as a "good and honest man and learned in Torah."

> "Tell me please, Reb Yehiel-Mordecai, how you found nourishment and sustenance in the bad times that rose up and beset you?"
>
> "Blessed be our God, who has done miracles for us and sustained us, for in His goodness do we live," answered Reb Yehiel-Mordecai, raising his eyes to the heavens in praise and thanksgiving. "What does a Jew need for nourishment and to keep his soul alive? A bushel of potatoes from one sabbath eve to the next. We made do with little and trusted in His great name, may He be praised, and in the mercy of our Jewish brethren."
>
> "And did our Jewish brethren come to your assistance from their homes and dwellings?"
>
> "From one city and from the nearby villages they sent a few wagons full of bread right after the fire, and from the rest of the cities came nothing except some personal contributions, and they were few."
>
> "Why were you not diligent in informing them of your troubles in writing, telling them you were in great distress?"
>
> "We wrote, Reb Mendele, we wrote. We also sent special delegations to Jews all over, to gather contributions for us, and neither voice nor answer, has come from them all! When we saw that no help came from our brethren, and we could no longer sustain ourselves, we followed the maxim of our Rabbis, 'Judge not thy friend till thou art in his place,' and now we are walking to our friends' place, with our children and our old people, our sons and our daughters, and perhaps they will take pity on us. Perhaps they will have mercy. And what is your opinion, Reb Mendele? Will our journey succeed?"[2]

In this passage, Mendele gently maneuvers his interlocutor away from pious sentiments about making do with little and being reconciled to God's judgments, and he succeeds in moving him toward an indictment of communal hard-heartedness. When it comes to language, it is important to point out that "Hanisrafim" is part of a group of stories Abramovitch wrote in the 1890s originally in Hebrew. This was a departure from earlier works composed in Yiddish and then translated by Abramovitch himself or, later, by Bialik. So that even though the exchange between Mendele and Yehiel-Mordechai would have taken place in the "real world" in Yiddish, the Hebrew text before us is the primary representation of the exchange rather than a translation of an already existing Yiddish literary model.

Abramovitch's approach to rendering a Yiddish conversation in Hebrew might be called preemptive compensation. He seems intuitively to understand that it makes no sense to try to imitate the timbre, syntax, and intonation of Yiddish speech. (There may be something of that in "We wrote, Reb Mendele, we wrote.") Instead of a wan simulacrum, Abramovitch chooses a different mode altogether: rabbinic Hebrew. In a departure from his maskilic predecessors and from his own early practice, he abandons biblical Hebrew and shifts into what historians of the Hebrew language call *leshon ḥakhamim*, with its distinct syntax and semantics modeled on the Mishnah. It is an option open to Abramovitch in this passage because both interlocutors are at home in traditional texts. (Mendele is no *talmid ḥakham*, but he knows his way around the curriculum of the *ḥeder* and *beit midrash*.) To be sure, in a real-life encounter between two such figures their Yiddish would likely have been studded with *lomdish* Hebraisms. But the medium in which these bits of Hebrew erudition were embedded would have been distinctly Yiddish.

And yet. Abramovitch's switching out Yiddish for rabbinic Hebrew implies a provocative possibility. Is there perhaps some deeper link between these two languages, if for the moment we consider rabbinic Hebrew as a language separate from biblical Hebrew? We think of as fundamental to Yiddish speech that a sentence has the tonality and shape of a question. But is it not possible that the provenance of this phenomenon is in truth the give-and-take of talmudic argument? If Yiddish is indeed drinking deeply from that well, then what Abramovitch is doing is not translating so much as using as an equivalent language system, one that provided the original source for some of Yiddish's essential features.

The real compensation comes in the form of a witty, even wicked, play with textual allusions. This is of course not the monopoly of Hebrew; contemporaneously, Sholem Aleichem is doing the same thing with Tevye's artfully mangled quotations. But it is the proper domain of Hebrew. It's as if Abramovitch is saying to his readers, "Since I can't give you the verve and feel of real Yiddish dialogue, then you at least deserve entertainments of a different order." As in Tevye's case, the allusions are not erudite but rather familiar to any Jew of the time who attends synagogue. In the passage above, these are all clustered in the last paragraph. When Yehiel-Mordechai says that there was "no voice or answer" [*ein qol ve'ein 'oneh*] to their troubles from neighboring Jewish communities, he is invoking the contest between Elijah and the priests of Baal in I Kings 18:26, and not so subtly associating the apathy of the Beggarburghers' supposed brethren with heathen delusions. In the case of his own townspeople, Yehiel-Mordechai makes a far more positive association when, echoing Exodus 10:9, he declares that they are marching forward "with our children and our old people." Like the Children of Israel confronting Pharaoh, they will not be deterred.

Abramovitch's most gratifying gift to his Hebrew readers is surely the citation from Avot 2:4, "Judge not thy neighbor till thou art in his place." In its context among a number of statements in the name of Hillel, this maxim urges a tolerant moral empathy. You cannot truly take a man's measure until you have stood in his shoes. Placed by Abramovitch in Yehiel-Mordechai's mouth, the dictum is turned on its head by literalizing the word place. Rather than connoting circumstance or situation, place is now taken to mean the physical locality in which your neighbor lives. With this revised meaning established, the saying from Avot now becomes a piece of winking, pragmatic guidance: If you want to succeed in getting something from reluctant neighbors, then the best thing you can do is travel to where they live and place yourself in their faces. And, having taken to the road to beg for alms, this is precisely what the Beggarburghers have done, and all with the approbation of the ancient sages.

The other example is taken from Y. H. Brenner's first novel *Baḥoref* [In Winter, 1904]. Although it appeared only seven years after Abramovitch's story, the gap between the two texts is enormous. Brenner's world-weary autobiographical narrator, writing retrospectively from his early twenties, has already cycled through all the major phases of the late nineteenth-century Jewish drama: small-town poverty, yeshivah study as a breeding ground for exposure to the Haskalah and Hebrew literature, the down-and-out life of an extern in a Russian metropolis, a tortured relationship to women, self-exile to the provinces to make money as a tutor. In the following passage, the narrator Yirmiah Feuerman is sitting among a party of fellow students in the Russian city in which the middle portions of the novel take place. While the buzz of conversation takes place around him, conversation that recirculates the same tired slogans and declarations, Feuerman "speaks" to himself in the form of an interior monologue. Only the last sentence is said aloud.

> Who are these people sitting here with me? Why did they come? Why don't they leave me to myself? But what difference does it make? . . . Ah, at last I am able to think about my own inner affairs. . . . Like a child idiot. . . . Absorbed in small-mindedness. . . . Small-mindedness—then what is large-mindedness? Yes, yes, yes, it is hard to live, life is hard, a life like this. . . . My room is full of spider webs. . . . A lizard sucks the brains of flies. . . . It's cold, cold living without God. . . . Cold—but bourgeois warmth, what help is it to me? . . . . If this means living for the true and exalted, isn't all life the same? . . . "Should"—that familiar should. . . . "Afflictions"—which afflictions? . . . " Courageously"—what courage? What am I doing putting on airs to myself? . . . Ohhh, all my thoughts are purposeless . . . There is no "should." . . . It's all one, one, one. . . . A total wasteland . . . "Wasteland"—What wasteland? No, no, no. . . . "Nothingness!" I suddenly cry out with a loud laugh.[3]

One cannot understand the chain of associations here without understanding the theological and existential crisis Feuerman undergoes in *In Winter*, which I have described elsewhere.[4] Feuerman has already thrown off the yoke of Torah in a heroic gesture modeled on such Haskalah heroes in the autobiographical tradition as Moshe Leib Lilienblum. The romance of apostasy has worn off, and he is now reckoning with the true bleakness of life in the void. He sees through the shallowness of "bourgeois warmth" [*hahmimut ha-"ba'al-batit"*], and he deconstructs the platitudes that have been thrown at him about the need to face one's afflictions with courage. Finally, he shouts out the word "Nothingness!" [*re'ut-ruah*]. The young people sitting around him, having no context for his outcry, think he is crazy, while we the readers, privy to the internal monologue, understand his negation as a profound, and profoundly distressing, description of the philosophical-existential cul-de-sac he finds himself in.

The use of interior or internal monologue is familiar to all readers of modern fiction, but it is surprising to learn that Brenner (and Gnessin) were deploying it before it became current in European literature. The earliest works of Joyce and Woolf using this technique come more than a decade later. Interior monologue is related to but distinct from free indirect discourse, which presents the thoughts of a character in the third person. Interior monologue is a variety of speech rather than thought; it is unvoiced speech spoken by a character to himself. Why Brenner had recourse to this technique in the absence of evident literary models is the result of the interplay of a number of factors. The fundamental choice to write in Hebrew at a time—and a place—when it was not spoken entailed the challenges described above. Perhaps the bigger problem is not the language in which conversation takes place in life but the very possibility of real conversation. It may not be possible to converse—that is to share feelings through speech with another person—for someone like Feuerman who has lived through the collapse of the metaphysical security of traditional belief and sees through the pretentions of Haskalah rationalism and Socialism and Zionism to replace what has been lost. He has nowhere to go but inside himself, and when it comes to speaking his thoughts, he himself is the only one who can listen.

Because Feuerman does not have to make himself intelligible to anyone other than himself, his speech has the thrilling effect of the real. It is, of course, a kind of mad discourse. The abundant use of ellipsis indicates the compression of a mind that is thinking in spurts and leaps. Brenner relies on our familiarity with the turmoil of the times to fill in the gaps, and so there is no need to unpack ideas and offer explanations. What is most exciting, to my mind, is the creative hodgepodge of languages. In the real-life mimetic situation, Feuerman would be speaking Yiddish; but the Hebrew speech we have before us is not a translation but a thing unto itself. Although it is written in updated modern literary Hebrew, the question-and-answer pattern harks back to the dialectic of Talmud study. The analytic exegesis that was once trained on sacred texts is now applied to deconstructing the sententious slogans of modern existential moralism; every term contained in exhortation that "one must bear affliction and live with courage" is taken apart, examined, and vitiated. Significantly, Yiddish is not erased. *Haḥmimut ha-"ba'al batit,"* which I've rendered as "bourgeois warmth," is an awkward Hebrew equivalent for *balebatishkayt*; by putting quotation marks around the term, Brenner is indicating that it has not been domesticated, as it were, into Hebrew, and he is signaling to the reader to recognize it or to translate it back into the familiar Yiddish concept, for which there is no real Hebrew equivalent. To indicate his distracted and constricted state of mind, Feuerman uses *qatnut* (small-mindedness), a Hebrew term borrowed and psychologized from kabbalistic and hasidic thought. To deliver the summary negation, the utterance that finally explodes into voiced speech, Feuerman appropriates the term *re'ut-ruah*, which is paired with *hevel* throughout Kohelet. Detaching *re'ut-ruah* from its better-known twin has the effect of dulling the gloss connected to biblical terms and focusing on the power of a Nietzschean or Schoperhauerean undermining of all received values.

These examples from Abramovitch and Brenner reveal some of the ways in which Hebrew literature dealt with the absence of a living, mimetic model for Hebrew speech. One might assume that it was just a matter of time until life and literature could catch up with one another. For the dissemination of spoken Hebrew was so successful in the Yishuv, and then the state, that it has provoked criticisms of the erasure of the many language cultures that the immigrants brought with them. By mid-century there should have been plenty of real-world material to be represented in literature. But I would argue that this appropriation was never fully successful. We lack, so far as I know, a sustained critical inquiry into the representation of speech in modern Hebrew literature, something much to be desired. In the absence of such research, I put forward the following speculations.

It may well be that Israeli literature—in tandem with the society it writes about—is conspicuously non-dialogical. There is abundant speech but little true conversation. The most characteristic form of speech is therefore the monologue, public and external as well as the interior variety written by Brenner. The monologue is a way—in spoken words—of making statements and mounting arguments and verbalizing states of mind; it presupposes the existence of a listener or audience to whom the discourse is addressed, but it does not expect or make room for responses leading to an exchange of views or feelings. A clarifying example is the well-known story "Haderasha" [The Sermon, 1942] by Haim Hazzaz, in which Yudke, a kibbutz member, hijacks a community meeting and launches into an extended discourse about Zionism and the meaning of Jewish history. The great virtuoso of the monologue is of course A. B. Yehoshua, whose debt to Faulkner has been often acknowledged. His debut novel *Hame'ahev* [The Lover, 1977] is composed entirely of dramatic monologues, each a first-person refraction of a complex family dynamic. The monologues lack any identifiable interlocutors, in the way in which Pani Shalom Aleichem is importuned by Tevye or the rabbi to whom Yentl brings her pot. Yehoshua's monologists, like Faulkner's, simply speak, leaving us the readers as the inferred audience. Yehoshua refined and intensified this strategy in *Gerushim me'uharim* [A Late Divorce, 1982] by devoting each chapter in the book to a different player in the family drama and according to each a highly idiosyncratic and differentiated style of speaking. The cultivation of oral performance finds its apotheosis in *Mar Mani* [Mr. Mani, 1990] with its famous half-conversations spoken by five characters in five different languages. Yehoshua's supplying us with only one half of these conversations—a decision brilliant and annoying in equal measure—nicely dramatizes the preference for monologue over dialogue. David Grossman would seem to be Yehoshua's brilliant disciple in this regard, as can be seen from many aspects of *'Ayen 'erekh: ahavah* [See Under: Love, 1986] and from the extraordinary speeches of Ora in *Ishah borahat mibesorah* [To the End of the Land, 2008].

Which leads me to a final and even more presumptuous speculation. Hebrew writers can be divided between the writerly and the speakerly. By their deepest temperament, some writers like S. Yizhar, Amalia Kahana-Carmon, and Amos Oz seek to paint exquisite word pictures by exploiting the far-reaching resources of the Hebrew language. Other writers, of the sort that have been described here, find reality most vividly revealed in the idiolect of individual human voice, and they devote their talent to distilling it on the page. This is a binary not special to Israeli literature; I see it at work in American Jewish fiction, where it can distinguish between Cynthia Ozick and Philip Roth. But why it is the monologue that is the great achievement of Israeli literature is a subject worth further exploration.

## NOTES

Originally published in *In Geveb* (June 2020). Reprinted with permission from Susanna Morgenthau.

1. The Aramaic term *safruta* refers to the craft of the scribe.

2. The translation is by Jeffrey M. Green, in *The Literature of Destruction*, ed. David G. Roskies (Philadelphia: The Jewish Publication Society, 1988), 142.

3. This citation is taken from the Shtybel edition, *Kol kitvei Y. H. Brenner*, vol. 1 (Warsaw, 1924), p. 74. The translation is mine.

4. See my *Banished From Their Father's Table: Loss of Faith and Hebrew Autobiography* (Bloomington: Indiana University Press, 1989), ch. 6, p. 171 on this passage. The Hebrew source can be found in *Yosef Brenner ketavim* [The Works of Yosef Brenner] (Tel Aviv: Hakibbutz Hame'uchad and Sifriat Poalim, 1978), vol. 1, p. 193. The translation of the passage is my own.

# CHAPTER 13

# Knocking on Heaven's Gate

*Hebrew Literature and Wisse's Canon*

## ARGUING THE MODERN JEWISH CANON

It is perhaps inevitable that at the turn of the millennium Ruth Wisse should have mounted a counter-attack against the assault on the canon that had been building during the last two decades of the old century. Although *The Modern Jewish Canon* is, of course, principally concerned with Jewish literature, the position it takes about canon making was mobilized in reaction to the turmoil in American Studies that came to a head in the 1980s. This was a heady time when oral narratives by slaves and American Indians were being discovered and great numbers of unknown or forgotten works by women, African American, Asian American, and Chicano writers widely published. The curricular cartel of Poe, Hawthorne, Melville, Twain, James, Faulkner, and company had to be cracked open, it was claimed, to embrace, or at least to represent, the diversity of American literatures, which no longer deserved to be relegated to separate categories labeled minority or ethnic. In the face of this claim, figures such as E. D. Hirsch and Harold Bloom reasserted the need for a common core of literary works whose universal interest and unimpeachable aesthetic achievement would provide a coherent basis for a shared national culture.[1]

When Wisse set out her vision of the modern Jewish canon, she was turning in two directions at the same time: toward the conservative camp in the culture wars in the American academy and toward her colleagues in Jewish studies. In the case of the former, Wisse generally applauded the will to set standards and to assign to great books an authoritative role in culture and schooling. Yet, as a Jew engaged in the study of Jewish literature, Wisse had to demur when it came to the universal and deracinated portrayal of the human condition in most versions of the western canon. National context is not merely background and setting for strong works of art but the deep soil in which they grow and make sense and in which human struggle becomes most human. In presenting a modern *Jewish* canon, then, Wisse did not see herself filing a report from a provincial outpost of Western literature. Rather, the Jewish works she presented in her volume are great precisely because they are entangled in the parochial predicaments of a group whose transactions with modernity should be of interest to all.

A related kind of entanglement gave Wisse reason to contest positions held by some members of her own party in the national debates about the canon. She had no problem joining the chorus of voices deploring the manipulation of the curriculum to further (radical) social ends, and she did not disagree with advocating allegiance to enduring aesthetic standards. But she would not join Harold Bloom in declaring that true essence of the canon rests only upon the sovereign autonomy of the aesthetic and the private pleasures of reading. The best works of Jewish literature are wholly embroiled in the ferment of Jewish historical forces and ideologies, and their extra-literary dimensions cannot be extracted without doing violence to their integrity.

Yet, after the fashion of a family feud, Wisse's fiercest polemical energies are brought back home. Although modern Jewish literature may enjoy recognition in both the public mind and Jewish studies, it is nevertheless set apart in a gauzy aesthetic zone of its own and denied the authority accorded to works of Jewish history and thought. Wisse sought to upend this hierarchy by demonstrating through strong readings of strong texts that it is the modern Jewish novel, as a complex and multivocal act of historical understanding that, in fact, provides the fullest and most profound account available of modern Jewish experience. "It is the most complete way of knowing the inner life of Jews," Wisse avers.[2] Although Wisse does not gainsay the pleasures of the novel—its humor and aesthetic effects—she does insist on its ultimate seriousness.

As such, in Wisse's view, the modern Jewish novel legitimately deserves to be called canonical in something more than a figurative sense. When modern literary scholars talk about the canon, whether to debunk or defend it, they are usually borrowing a figure from the codification of the Hebrew and Greek scriptures to suggest the sway implicitly exercised by works of art. To be sure, some books may be enshrined in school curricula, but the use of the term canon is at most an image or a *façon de parler* used to convey the way a consensus of taste privileges some works over others. For Wisse, by contrast, the way in which the twenty-four books of the Hebrew Bible were drawn together and sealed into an authoritative package is more than a metaphor. It is, after all, *our* bible, and Wisse sees in the flowering of Jewish literature in many languages in the nineteenth and twentieth centuries a reemergence of the same kind of imaginative creativity displayed in the Hebrew Bible. It is as if some deep-running wellspring of national imagination had been unstoppered. The fact that the products of this upsurge are modern works of art rather than inspired religious scriptures does not mean, to her lights, that we are free to treat the former with less rigor and seriousness of purpose than the latter.

With this new gift of spirit come responsibilities. Like the members of the Sanhedrin in antiquity, we cannot shirk our duty to decide which works of modern art—analogues, perhaps, to the vexing border cases of Job and the Song of Songs—deserve, or do not deserve, to be essential components of the cultural patrimony we transmit to future generations. "This modern list," Wisse opines, "will probably never be as firmly redacted as the twenty four books of the Hebrew Bible, because no contemporary community is as confident as its ancestors, and because moderns are generally warier of any process that smacks of authority" (4). Yet despite these obstacles, the critic-scholar is not free to desist from the kind of critical argument that would draw lines and enforce distinctions rather than erase them.

*The Modern Jewish Canon* is a powerful instance of a scholar discharging this responsibility. In her vigorously argued analyses of Sholem Aleichem, Brenner, Kafka, Babel, Agnon and many others, Wisse lays out the justification for including each work according to her dual criteria: each is an accomplished work of art that succeeds in representing the historical experience of the Jewish people in its age. Wisse is no theorist, and although the introductory chapter of her book adroitly explains her approach to her project and makes various qualifications and clarifications that affect her choices, she means for the proof to be in the pudding. Rather than appealing to a set of abstract principles, Wisse is content to let the interpretive argument wrapped around each canonical work bear the burden of persuasion.

Canon making, at least of the sort practiced by Wisse, is a combination of drawing the list and then mounting arguments to defend the choices. As a scholar who does not speak on behalf of an institution—however much she may feel accountable to the Jewish people—she is free to make her own nominations to the modern Jewish canon. "My criteria are largely aesthetic and personal," Wisse admits. "In this book I set out some of my favorite Jewish works as a way of inviting others to continue discussion over them" (5). Yet beneath the breezy rhetoric of personal preference lies a bold assertion of power. Give heed and obeisance, it proclaims, to these—my decisions about those works that most urgently deserve to be transmitted to the future and those that do not. Without the willingness to make these assertions—and to accept the exposure to resistance and criticism that unavoidably goes along with it—there is ultimately, Wisse would argue, no culture. Yet the hard work of canon making lies not in listing the choices but in defending them. The greatness of *The Modern Jewish Canon*, to my lights, lies less in the probity of the list than in the critical discussions that justify the choices and connect them together into a grand argument. The fine intelligence and committed passion of these arguments are the truest sources of authority for the claims made on behalf of the works.

In the spirit of these spirited arguments, it strikes me that one can discover something of the rough-and-tumble democracy found in the Talmud. Even though they are treating matters of grave import, the sages see no need to wear kid gloves as they search for the truth by knocking one proof against another to see which rings true. Being in the game means being willing to have your position scrutinized for consistency, utility, and elegance. The goal is not the triumph of individual authority but the clarification of God's will through the instruments of human ingenuity. In *The Modern Jewish Canon* Wisse plays by similar rules. Although she is not shy about projecting her opinions, her goal is not to seal the impress of her authority and secure humbled assent. Rather, she writes to provoke other serious minds into serious argument about serious matters of Jewish culture. She would, I think, prefer to be shown wrong in her championing of a particular work of literature if the counterargument shed expanded light on the enterprise of the Jewish imagination. She seems ready to take her chances with all comers—if only they would come.

In the spirit of this dialectical openness, I propose to think about Wisse's canon from the vantage point of a student of modern Hebrew literature. It will be generally conceded, I think, that modern Hebrew literature from the Haskalah through the founding of the State of Israel on into the present is a crucial, even privileged, corpus within the catholic embrace of modern Jewish literature. Yet the student of modern Hebrew literature has to take some deep breaths upon discovering just how catholic Wisse's conception truly is. Hebraists and Zionists of the old school would claim that the revival of the ancient national tongue and its blossoming into rich modern literature deserve to be regarded as the one great drama of Jewish literature. Yiddishists of the old school, pointing to Yiddish as the great indigenous flower of the diaspora, would make a similarly exclusivist claim. Although she is a native daughter of the latter and profoundly sympathetic to the former, Wisse would tell the proponents of each camp to simmer down and get used to the fact that Jewish literature has moved on to circulate in a wider orbit that includes Russian, German, Polish, French, Italian, and, most of all, English. Wisse's canon is a meritocracy in which there are no protected slots reserved for works in Jewish languages; each place is awarded solely on the strength of a work's aesthetic assets and its imaginative power in representing Jewish historical experience.

Even playing by these rules, Wisse's treatment of modern Hebrew literature is deeply problematic. Part of the problem stems from the criteria Wisse has established for the shape and nature of her canon, and part of the problem stems from her deep ambivalence to Israeli literature. I will take these up under three heads.

The first is Wisse's seigniorial decision to limit her canon to novels and to exclude poetry, short fiction, and drama. True, it is Wisse's canon and she can lay down her own principles, and surely the novel is a legitimate and formidable genre. Yet if the goal is to represent what is greatest in modern Jewish literature–here and throughout I will use the test case of modern *Hebrew* literature—it must be admitted that a great deal of greatness is left out if the novel is the only entry ticket. When it comes to a critical argument justifying her decision, there is none to be found aside from a fleeting assertion that the novel "more than poetry pronounces its social context and cultural affinity" (5). Now, from the rich readings of individual works in the body of her book, a serious reader, equipped with a little learning from the abundance of critical work on the history of the novel, would not have much trouble inferring nuanced claims Wisse might make on behalf of the novel's special place in modern Jewish culture. Yet, regrettably, these are arguments that are never undertaken.

As estimable a cultural achievement as is the novel, it is not the genre through which the greatest works of Hebrew literature were realized. Hebrew literature does boast some fascinating novels, but, like Brenner's astonishing *Bahoref* [In Winter, 1900], their artistic force is purchased by a self-conscious parodic play with conventions of the novel that are recognized at the outset as irrelevant to Jewish society. The novel as a phenomenon in European culture was perfected in the nineteenth century in such national cultures as France, England, and Russia, where a settled social order was being destabilized by forces that allowed individuals to move across class lines. Against the background of the "hum and buzz of implication" in the manners of social institutions, novelists explored themes of individual will, romantic love, marriage, property, and family. However, because East European Jewish life at the end of the nineteenth century was characterized by pauperization, crumbling religious authority, anti-Semitism, and mass immigration, the conditions that nurtured novels were simply not present. The exact nature of those enabling conditions remains a tantalizing object of scholarly discussion. My notions on the subject were formed by the work of Ian Watt, Georg Lukacs, and Lionel Trilling, but more recent scholarship has productively barked up many different trails. Investigations of the role of female readers as consumers of novels have been particularly illuminating. Yet even as our knowledge of the origins of the novel grows, the stubborn fact of the genre's stunted appearance in Hebrew literature remains.

That the novel is not Hebrew literature's long suit does not mean that it lacks brilliant examples of prose fiction. These are ample, but they are forms of *short* fiction, including the sketch, the short story, the long short story, and the novella, and, as such, do not qualify for the canon. Take, for example, the case of Micha Yosef Berdichevsky, the prolific polymath who engaged in provocative Semitic scholarship in addition to writing some of the most important fiction of the Hebrew Revival. Although Berdichevsky's work is not analyzed in the body of *The Modern Jewish Canon*, his novel *Miriam*, his only novel and a problem work, is included in the list of recommended books in the volume's appendix. (The novel has been translated into English, another necessary condition in Wisse's scheme, about which more shortly.) The fact is that any one of a dozen stories of Berdichevsky's is far superior to *Miriam*. But wanting to do the right thing by this writer, as she should, Wisse is stuck with a lesser example of his fiction because it is a novel. At least Berdichevsky has a novel to be chosen. Pity the case of Uri Nissan Gnessin and Devora Baron, the finest Hebrew prose writers of the early part of the twentieth century, who have only their superb short fiction to offer. There are profound historical and aesthetic reasons for the superiority of short fiction over the novel in classic modern Hebrew literature and a strong case to be made that the short forms are the truest and most characteristically Jewish prose expressions of the age. Yes, the novel has prestige, but it can also be seen as a form alien to the Jewish imagination at this time. Superimposing a novel-based schema upon the vitality of Hebrew literature means, by definition, that its finest achievements cannot shine forth. From what I know of Yiddish literature, moreover, the case is similar. When it comes to picking a work of Sholem Aleichem's for analysis, for example, Wisse declines to go to works like *Stempenyu*, which are truly novels and rely on the conventions of sentimental fiction; instead, she writes one of the most brilliant chapters of her book on the cycle of the Tevye stories. Although this may indeed be Sholem Aleichem's masterpiece, calling this series of monologues a novel requires a prodigiously elastic conception of the genre.

The largest problem by far is the case of poetry. Aside from Brenner and Agnon, many would agree that the greatest Hebrew writers of the twentieth century are Chaim Nachman Bialik, Shaul Tchernichovsky, Uri Zvi Greenberg, Natan Alterman, and Yehuda Amichai. They happen to be poets. Again, it is not happenstance but serious historical and aesthetic conditions that account for the unequal distribution of greatness among the genres of modern Hebrew literature. These poets are great for some of the same reasons that Wisse is drawn to the novel: their poetry embodies the historical experience of the Jewish people and provides deep insights into the inner lives of Jews. Yet the poetry does something that the prose rarely does. It stages the most acute confrontations in modern Jewish experience (tradition v. modernity, particular v. universal, individual v. collective) *within* the drama of language. The language, of course, is Hebrew, and, as anyone who has read a Bialik poem knows, the ability of the modern Hebrew poet to play the variegated historical layers of the language in concert and in conflict with one another produces extraordinary possibilities of meaning. Similarly, no one who is familiar with Wisse's scholarly career could seriously think that she is unsympathetic to poetry or undervalues the great Hebrew poets. Her exclusion of poetry from her canon project, one assumes, has to do with the fact that it does not travel well in translation and cannot be presented in a way that will be persuasive to a general reader. Be that as it may—the issue of translation will be addressed directly—we are left with a modern Jewish canon that does not mention Bialik, Tchernichovsky, Greenberg, Alterman, and Amichai.[3] The problem is not so much that Hebrew literature is not given its "due credit," but that the meaningfulness of the entire endeavor is diminished by the absence.

The second major issue is the decision to include only works translated into English. Writing in America and addressing an English-speaking audience in an era in which English has become a global medium, Wisse need make no apology for the priority of English. But the translation-only policy requires more clarification, and one wishes that Wisse had been more self-reflective on this critical decision. From the outset, one infers, Wisse conceived of her project as an act of public education and public responsibility. The implied reader of *The Modern Jewish Canon* is a general reader who, however intellectually curious and broadly cultured, comes to the book without specialist knowledge of Jewish literature and without Jewish languages. Students of Yiddish and Hebrew literature may have a lot to learn from this book, but they are not its intended audience. Hence the rationale for hewing to works translated into English; even if the translations are not currently in print, of which quite a number are not, they exist in libraries and can be accessed. Now, this is a perfectly understandable and principled stance that speaks to the vocation and responsibilities of the scholar and public intellectual. Yet the overall success of the enterprise must be judged by the integrity of the final product. By integrity I mean the question of whether the public account of the modern Jewish canon bears a true relationship, as to proportionality and emphasis, to the account given by scholars in the field after all the adjustments have been made. Speaking, again, from the perspective of Hebrew literature, it seems to me that, once one eliminates poems and short stories and all works that have not yet been translated into English, the result runs the danger of conveying a distorted map of modern Jewish literature. Although the intelligible and stimulating public presentation of Jewish culture is a goal of paramount importance, the question is whether this approach does or does not end in becoming a classic case of *yatsa sekharo behefsedo*, the gain being erased by the loss (Mishnah Avot 5:11).

What would happen, it's very much worth wondering, if the English-only stricture were breached? Let us say, for argument's sake, that Wisse shared my view that Brenner's as-yet-untranslated first novel *In Winter* is superior to his last novel *Breakdown and Bereavement*, which has been translated, and she then went on to make a stirring case for the importance of his early novel while mentioning along the way the writings of Brenner's—stories in addition to the late novel—that could be found in English. In addition to producing a more accurate account of Brenner's achievement, an intellectually stimulating discussion of the untranslated novel would likely create a buzz of interest that would eventually result in the novel's being translated and published in English. Ruth Wisse on the ten greatest untranslated Jewish novels—now that would be a formidable list indeed! One should never underestimate the efficacious curiosity of intelligent readers who have been told that something valuable has been withheld from them. Sticking only to works available in English means accepting the extant map of Jewish literature as conveyed under this severe and potentially distorting limitation rather than preparing the ground for a fuller and more accurate account. Admittedly, the loss of immediate access is a disadvantage, but considered on balance, there is a strong argument for seeing here the possibility of reversing the lamentable scenario mentioned above and turning it into a happy case of *yatsa hefsedo bisekharo*, the loss being redeemed by the gain.

Even within the general audience to which *The Modern Jewish Canon* is aimed, Hebrew plays a privileged role that it would be a shame not to exploit. Although the "demographic" of the audience can never be precisely known, it is safe to say that among the younger lay and professional leadership cadres of the American Jewish community a certain amount of Hebrew literacy can be assumed. While I would not exaggerate what average day school graduate or Jewish Studies major can accomplish in Hebrew, I would say that there are many who, with the help of annotation and translation, could grasp the meaning of a contemporary Hebrew poem or a short prose text. Hebrew is the only language of the many tongues represented in Wisse's volume about which this can be said, and it is, of course, no coincidence. As a community, we have not invested in German or French or even, for that matter, in

Yiddish; but we have invested considerable resources in Hebrew literacy because we see in Hebrew an irreplaceable link both to the classical past and to Israeli culture and society.[4] We are unique in this regard; I know of no other community in America in which numbers of young people can read their ancient texts in the original. Yet there remains a disconnect between this inchoate knowledge of Hebrew and Wisse's great books. For if there is one thing that our Hebrew-literate American Jewish leader is unlikely to be able to do is polish off a Hebrew novel whole. If this version of the modern Jewish canon had room for poems and short stories, there would be putative points of entry, and many aids–and why not computer-assisted aids?–could be devised to make this first-hand encounter with great Jewish culture accessible. But if the only real currency of Jewish culture remains the novel, then the encounter is destined always to be mediated through translation.

My third and final animadversion concerns the perplexingly scant attention given to Israeli literature. Now, admittedly Wisse has set out to assemble a canon of individual great books and not to write a history of Jewish literature. Her intention absolves her of the need to draw maps of literary movements, trace connections among key figures, and mark off periods of development. Nevertheless, she must take responsibility for the fact that, like it or not, a narrative account of modern Jewish literature emerges from her project. Rather than analyzing the substance of this narrative, I will suggest its contours by contrasting it to a very different account. Israeli historiography points to the gathering body of creative Hebrew writing from the period of the Yishuv through the founding of the state to the present and argues that, taken together, it represents, not to put too fine a point on it, the greatest flowering of Jewish culture since the time of the Bible and the Mishnah. There are many assumptions, of course, that are packed into this assertion and many ways that one could disagree with it. Yet any refutation would have to come to terms with the brute fact of the scores upon scores of Hebrew writers who have populated Israel's active literary life. Wisse accords places to six in her supplemental list (Yehuda Amichai, Aharon Appelfeld, Shulamith Hareven, Amos Oz, Yaakov Shabtai, and A. B. Yehoshua) and discusses only Shabtai in the body of the book. Yet letting my eyes graze over my office bookshelves and overcoming the strong urge to include scores and scores of poets and playwrights, I see the names of not a few Israeli prose writers who have won deserved places in the national literary culture: Eli Amir, Gavriella Avigur-Rotem, Shimon Balas, Hannah

Bat-Shahar, Haim Be'er, Hanoch Bartov, Yehoshua Bar-Yosef, Yitzhak Ben-Ner, Yosel Berstein, Orli Castel-Bloom, Amir Gotfreund, David Grossman, Yehudit Hendel, Yoel Hoffman, Amalia Kahana-Carmon, Yehudit Katzir, Yehosua Kenaz, Etgar Keret, Yeshayahu Koren, Abba Kovner, Saviyon Librecht, Ronit Matalon, Aharon Megged, Sami Michael, Haim Sabato, Dan Benaya Seri, Natan Shaham, David Shahar, Meir Shalev, Moshe Shamir, Yuval Shimoni, David Shutz, Dan Tsalka, and S. Yizhar. The point of this very partial list—on which, it should be added, there are many translations into English—is not to impress with numbers but to indicate that, even with sundry reservations and qualifications, there is something undeniably huge going on here.

The title Wisse gives to the final chapter of *The Modern Jewish Canon*, which is devoted to Israeli literature, is "A Chapter in the Making." After tracing the miraculous invention of modern Hebrew and the establishment of a full and proliferating literary culture in Israel, Wisse concludes that it is too soon to establish a canon of Israeli literature; she gives her chapter the title she does "because it would require another book to contain the subject of Israeli literature" (29). Although the chapter contains a brilliant comparison between Abramovitsh's *Di klyatshe* ["The Mare," 1873–1909] and Shabtai's *Zikhron devarim* ["Past Continuous," 1970], Shabtai's novel remains the only work of Israeli literature discussed in the volume. This is, to my mind, as if an entire galaxy had somehow slipped off the map of the heavens. Moreover, the acknowledgment that another book would be required fails to convey a profound or promissory sense of conviction. My perplexity stems from the difficulty in squaring this vague absence with Wisse's universally recognized advocacy of Israel. She is, simply, the most articulate American intellectual on behalf of Israel. What, then, are we to make of this gap? Does she believe that Israeli literature, like Israeli politics, should not be criticized or assessed by Jews living outside the country? Does she contend that the critical politics implied in much Israeli fiction undermines its literary force? Does she feel that the broad failure of Israeli literature to engage Jewish tradition similarly disqualifies it? One is forced to look for answers between the lines, and on this subject there are, alas, few lines to read between. But one imagines that this discreet recoil from Israeli literature derives in the end from the not-so-discreet recoil of Israeli authors from the use of Jewish power. It is no secret that from its origins in the Haskalah Hebrew literature has been an "enlisted" literature that takes as its vocation the critique of national and social institutions, and in this quality it resembles nothing so much as American and British literature and many another national literature. One's stance toward Hebrew literature will depend largely on whether one views it, as the maskilim did, as a continuation of the prophetic tradition of being a "watchman to the house of Israel" or whether, like Wisse, one views it as a betrayal of the intellectuals. Wisse's position is clear, principled, and consistent, yet, to my mind, it is reductive in a way that demands renouncing extraordinary aesthetic achievements that shake us up and make us continually rethink our positions. I am repulsed, for example, by many of the political positions dramatized in the poetry of Uri Zvi Greenberg even as I am enthralled by the imaginative power of his verse. Figuring out such a contradiction is the work we literary scholars have to do.

Taken together, all the issues I have raised are by way of wishing that Wisse had written an even larger and even more ambitious book than the already imposing volume she has produced. I am aware of the niggardliness entailed in ignoring the splendid and shining chapters on Sholem Aleichem, Babel, the Singers, Bellow, and many others in favor of an argument on behalf of other, perhaps alternative, goals the project might have accomplished. Although as a specialist rather than a general reader I am not the main audience for *The Modern Jewish Canon*, I feel inspired, challenged, and goaded into seeing my role as a scholar in a new way. Wisse's volume joins together with the essays gathered by David Stern in *The Anthology in Jewish Literature*[5] to create an awareness of how thoroughly our work as scholars is permeated by acts of selecting and excerpting and the critical arguments that justify our decisions. Every time we teach a class or prepare a syllabus we are participating in the central endeavor of picking and presenting that has characterized the making of Jewish culture since the books of Proverbs and Psalms. There is virtually no aspect of our work as scholars that is untouched by the anthological impulse and, inevitably and ineluctably, we make our canons as we go.

What Wisse has done is to take this everyday act and write it large and write it with force. On the one hand, she has simply—oh that it were so simple!—taken a wonderful university course that has been developed and refined over time and invested with enormous intellectual passion and turned it into a book. On the other hand, she has done what few others of us Jewish literature professors have done: she has projected her views into the public realm and called it a canon. This is an exercise of power that should be neither underestimated nor unappreciated. Wisse is not, to be sure, of the party of Michel Foucault and his disciples, who see the iron fist of hegemony at work in every institutionally sanctioned cultural norm. When it comes to motives, she would prefer to see herself as sailing under the motto from Deuteronomy, "Thou shall teach them diligently unto thy children," which actually appears on the opening page of her Introduction. Nonetheless, make no mistake. *The Modern Jewish Canon* is a work of great entrepreneurial force. When all is said and done, Wisse gets to tell the canon *her* way.

It is just this willingness to be willful that is the shining example to all of us. I will conclude with an example from my own work. For some years now I have been studying the American Hebraist movement; these are the writers, critics, educators and especially poets who, beginning in earnest around World War I, attempted to create a serious Hebrew culture in America. The American Hebrew writers hoped to play an active role in a global Hebrew literature centered in the Yishuv even as they worked to raise a younger generation of Hebraists in America. Instead, they incurred a double rebuff. They were ignored in the literary journals and cafes of Tel Aviv, and at home their efforts were thrust aside by the galloping steed of Americanization. By the time the founding of Israel engendered in American Jewry a new excitement about spoken Hebrew, the decades of Hebrew creativity in America had either been forgotten or come to be viewed as a quaint Haskalah survival. I came to this literature because I was fascinated by the encounter it stages between the Hebrew language (and all it brings with it) and American history and the American landscape. Dusting off these tomes and reading them afresh, I found much to admire on aesthetic terms and much to take hold of as the work of my precursors here in America.

Here's the rub. As much as I believe that the double marginality endured by these writers is unfair, as much as I believe that fruits of American Hebrew literature should be widely available to American Jews and appreciated by them, and as much as I believe that anyone teaching Hebrew literature in the United States, be they Israeli or American, has the duty to place these cultural artifacts before their students, believing all this does not make it so. Railing against injustice and undeserved obscurity persuades no one that the American Hebrew writers warrant inclusion in some division of the modern Jewish canon, be it modern Hebrew literature or American Jewish literature. The only way to achieve this goal is to gather, republish, anthologize and translate their works, to create occasions and venues where scholars can become familiar with them, and, most of all, to write critical studies that demonstrate their aesthetic and historical interest. To whine about the justice of inclusion and exclusion is to behave as if someone other than ourselves is in charge of the canon. As Ruth Wisse has shown us, the canon belongs to all of us who take the trouble.

## NOTES

Originally published in *Arguing the Modern Jewish Canon: Essays on Literature and Culture in Honor of Ruth R. Wisse*, ed. Justin Cammy, Dara Horn, Alyssa Quint, and Rachel Rubenstein (Cambridge, MA: Center for Jewish Studies, Harvard University, 2008), pp. 23–35.

1. Harold Bloom, *The Western Canon: The Books and School of the Ages* (New York: Harcourt Brace, 1994); E. D. Hirsch, *Cultural Literacy: What Every American Needs to Know* (Boston: Houghton Mifflin, 1987).

2. *The Modern Jewish Canon*, 4; henceforth referred to simply by page numbers in parenthesis in the body of the text.

3. Amichai's novel *Lo me'akhshav, lo mikan* ["Not of This Time, Not of This Place"] (1963) is included among the supplementary works in the appendix, "Suggested Reading from the Modern Jewish Canon" (384). But, again, the novel template forces Wisse to ignore the enormous achievements of a writer's verse in favor of an anomalous and far from successful prose work.

4. Of Wisse's commitment to Hebrew there is no mistake. See her "The Hebrew Imperative" in Alan Mintz, ed., *Hebrew in America: Perspective and Prospects* (Detroit: Wayne State University Press, 1993), 265–76. The essay first appeared in *Commentary* 89, no. 6 (June 1990), 34–39.

5. Oxford University Press, 1974. The book began as several special volumes of *Prooftexts: A Journal of Jewish Literary History*.

# CHAPTER 14

# Modern Hebrew Literature and Jewish Theology

*Repositioning the Question*

Once the world was contained by the Torah; now the Torah is contained by the world. Once the life of the Jew was regulated by the rhythm of chosen days and appointed times; now the flux of experience is shaped by different forces. Once Zion was an otherworldly ideal; now it is an exigent and complex actuality. Once the soul of the individual Jew was bound up in the collective life of the people; now the space of the self, subject to perpetual analysis, recedes inward away from the community.

This great transformation, which goes by many names, marks the experience of the Jewish people in the modern era. Although many peoples and cultures have undergone a similar crisis, the instance of the Jews is unique on two counts. In Western Europe the process of secularization unfolded over the course of several centuries; for most Jews the ordeal was accelerated and compressed into one or two generations. While the exposure to modernity has been equally jolting for many Third World cultures, it is only in the case of the Jews that this confrontation has involved a high literary and intellectual culture not in the sole possession of a hieratic class.

What happened? How did it happen? Differing and related answers to these questions are offered by the responses of the Jewish people to the crisis of tradition: modern Jewish history, politics, literature, philosophy, and the branches of academic study which have arisen to interpret them. For the purposes of this essay I wish to concentrate on one of these responses, modern Hebrew literature, and make a case for its special powers in illuminating the great transformation in Jewish life. It is my contention that this literature can serve not only as an explanatory account for the dilemmas of modern Jewish identity, but as something much more: a resource for restoration. In its very secularity, modern Hebrew literature can be a source for Jewish theology.

There is, to begin with, the mystery of the Hebrew language. Mystery is not a term that sits comfortably in Jewish theological discourse, and I use it for its strangeness and perhaps its aptness. That Hebrew *literature* should be revived and take on new forms is astonishing, but it is not beyond belief because of the continuous and creative employment of the literary language down through the ages. That the *spoken* language should be brought back to life and become a natural and ambient medium for a significant portion of the Jewish people, literate and nonliterate alike—this surpasses astonishment. If many of the original visions of Zionism have failed or been compromised, the revival of the Hebrew language has succeeded beyond any imagining. For any religiously sensitive person there are signals of hope to be picked up here.

If the deep cleavages within the Jewish people are one day to be lessened, it will be due in part to the power of the Hebrew language. It is that language—and it seems sometimes that it is *only* that language—which constitutes an arc of continuity between the tradition and the culture of the modern Jewish state which has supplanted it. Lodged deep within the recesses of the Hebrew language are both the meanings that have been lost and the resources for their reappropriation and transformation. So, while most of the remarks that follow refer to Hebrew literature in the sense of the kinds of writing we conventionally understand as literature (poetry, fiction, drama, essays), we must never lose sight of the fact that these creations are constructed out of the more fundamental material of language, and it remains the Hebrew language and its rebirth upon which everything depends.

It is both the discontinuity and continuity of Hebrew that make it a special case. Modern Hebrew literature is "modern" because of the new ends for which Hebrew began to be written at the end of the eighteenth century and the new forms in which this program was realized. Make no mistake: Before this time Hebrew had had a vital and unbroken history as a compositional medium, not just in the chain of post-Biblical interpretation, not just in the vast corpus of liturgical poetry and in the flowering of the Spanish Golden Age, but in many modes and genres less conspicuously sacred or secular—historical chronicles, romances, treatises on logic and on astronomy, essays in philosophical consolation, travel literature, ethical wills and personal correspondence.

What changed at the beginning of the modern era was that Hebrew was made into the chief instrument of the *Haskalah* (Enlightenment) movement to modernize Jewish life. For the first time Hebrew was pressed into use (through parody and satire) as a medium for social criticism. Moreover, beyond their didactic function, the novels, ballads, and lyric poems written in imitation of Western models claimed for themselves nothing less than the autonomous dignity of art itself. When the hopes of the Haskalah foundered on the realities of Russian anti-Semitism at the end of the nineteenth century, Hebrew became the language of romantic nationalism and embodied the vision of establishing a Jewish homeland. The revival of a people was inconceivable without the revival of its language. Yet once revived, Hebrew could not be limited to this proper civic mission. A generation of intellectuals had been born into the world of faith only to be banished from it by the disintegration of Jewish life in Eastern Europe at the close of the century. The new Hebrew literature became the modernist medium through which their uprootedness and dislocation were explored. By the late 1920s, the venue of Hebrew literature—its writers, periodicals and publishing houses—had been transferred to Tel Aviv and Jerusalem. From that time forward Hebrew became, largely but not exclusively, the literary (as well as popular) culture of a particular society, first the *Yishuv* (the Jewish settlement in Palestine) and then the State of Israel.

I have adduced the provenance of modern Hebrew literature in order to make an obvious but important point: In confronting the dilemmas of identity and belief, to write in Hebrew represented *a* choice *not* to write in a Western language.

A language like German provided such Jewish authors as Freud, Kafka and Walter Benjamin with a powerful lexicon of modernity and with immediate access to the advanced questions of culture. Their contributions to modern culture were truly awesome; yet insofar as they sought to address the crisis of Jews and Judaism, their linguistic medium kept them on the outside. For Hebrew writers, on the other hand, no matter how cut off they felt from the world of piety out of which Hebrew had emerged, and no matter how artificial and unsuitable Hebrew must have been at first for engaging issues of modernity, the choice of Hebrew was a choice to work from the inside. To write in Hebrew, especially before the success of the Jewish national enterprise, was itself a statement of faith and a declaration of where one stood within the hermeneutical circle of modern culture. But it was far more than a matter of allegiance. Because Hebrew literature had become both the repository of classical Judaism and the record of a reawakened people's adventure in modernity, Hebrew was thought to possess the internal resources to negotiate the mediation between old and new. Substitution, retrieval, containment, synthesis, reconciliation—all the dynamics of cultural change could take place *within* Hebrew literature, because in that medium alone did the old meanings and new meanings exist simultaneously.

Granted the importance of Hebrew literature, what account does it render about what happened and how it happened, about the great transformation of Jewish experience and consciousness? As befits the complexity of modern Jewish history, the explanation turns out to be not one, but two. In literary history—the branch of criticism that studies literature across time—there have been until recently two principal models for explaining the origins and development of modern Hebrew literature. These explanatory accounts are important because they close certain options and open others in the endeavor of making literature "available" to Jewish thought and theology.

The first is the Rebirth Model associated with the ideas of Joseph Klausner and Simon Halkin. It views the appearance of the new forms of writing in modern Hebrew literature—novel, short story, essay, lyric, epic, idyll, ballad—not as an imitation of "fallen" Western models but as the expression of a newly expanded and invigorated national life, at the center of which stand the themes of love, nature, power and art. This argument holds that the Jewish soul, released from prolonged constriction, has been freed to appropriate the full reach of its humanity. This is to be understood as a rebirth rather than a modern creation *ex nihilo*, because the new forms of the imagination are extensions or delayed outgrowths of ancient, Biblical forces which lay quiescent through the long night of exile.

There is a radical and a conservative version of this rebirth model. The aim of the new literature, according to the radical version (M. Y. Berdichevsky, 1865–1921), is to revolt against the old, usurp its place, and stop at nothing less than a total "transvaluation of values." In the conservative version (Ahad Ha-Am, 1856–1927), the new culture can evolve from the old by translating the religious values of the past into usable spiritual and ethical ideals through a process of hermeneutical recovery. Common to both of these approaches to modern Hebrew literature is a conception of sectors of experience and imagination which have been newly appropriated or restored. A spatial image may help us. The "house" of the modern Jewish spirit, we might say, has been enlarged; new rooms have been built on and inhabited. In the meantime, the old rooms remain standing, esteemed but unused, and from them the objects deemed still valuable have been taken and installed in the new living space.

According to the second approach, the Catastrophe Model associated with the work of Baruch Kurzweil (1907–1972), the house of the Jewish spirit was destroyed, its foundations razed, and in its place was erected a totally new and flimsy structure whose claim to connection with what preceded it is a lie. The total usurpation envisioned welcomingly by the young Berdichevsky had, in Kurzweil's eyes, sadly come true. Modern Hebrew literature was the medium that documented and described the collapse of the world of Torah and the disinheriting of the Jewish mind. In the vacuum created by this disaster, eros had become demonic sexuality and belief self-deluding ideology. Modern Hebrew was a significant literature when it dramatized these transformations as acts of evasion and bad faith (Bialik and Agnon); it was a trivial literature when it represented the new life of the Jewish people in Israel as a healthy redemption from a benighted past (Palmah Generation writers).

Kurzweil's stance is neither reactionary nor nostalgic but tragic, with full awareness that the term tragedy is alien to the Jewish tradition. The wholeness of the world of Torah is irretrievably lost, and man's life in the aftermath can be nothing other than absurd. Signs from the past are, of course, not wholly absent in modern Hebrew literature: Biblical motifs, allusions to classical texts, transformed religious symbols. According to the rebirth model, these are consoling survivals and markers of cohesion, which support the status of the new literature as the legitimate successor to the classical civilization of the Jewish people. According to the catastrophe model, however, they are the flotsam of a great shipwreck which reveal both the hollowness of the rescue and the impossibility of complete divestiture.

In the face of these two models, I wish to argue that the question of religion and literature can be put otherwise. To say that, in the life of the modern Jewish imagination, religion has been either tragically lost or absorbed and superseded, is to miss some of the unexpected directions in which this translation can move. Both approaches hew close to the bone of modern Jewish history and take literature as a record of the pathos of that history. This linkage is accomplished, it seems to me, at the expense of the "literariness" of literature. By this I mean the way in which literature, especially modern literature, in addition to holding up a mirror to reality, determines an autonomous space of its own, at the level of both the literary object and the literary system as a whole. In this space of its own certain maneuvers become possible, as well as certain experiments in the mimicking of transcendence—and this precisely because the grip of history is held at bay.

There are potential materials here for use in the construction of a modern Jewish theology, but that ambitious undertaking is hardly my purpose in these pages. Rather, I wish to present an itinerary of four locations where such materials may be found, indicate what they might look like, and by so doing support my claim for a repositioning of the question as a whole. The tack I shall *not* take is the one most commonly followed in such discussions: selecting a motif like the *akedah* (the binding Isaac) or a Biblical figure like David, and tracing its persistence and transformation in modern literature. These are useful exercises, to be sure, but they often reflect more on the ironizing energies of modern texts than on an engagement with the theological meanings represented by the motifs and figures. In that sense, the issues I wish to raise are adjacent to, but not part of, the widely discussed topic of modern Hebrew literature and the Jewish tradition.

## TEXT AS SCRIPTURE—SCRIPTURE AS TEXT

To begin with a phenomenon which is admittedly not unique to Hebrew literature, but which is nevertheless central to our theme: It has been commonly observed that the modern literary text has come more and more to resemble the Bible in the way in which it is read. What was once regarded simply as an object of appreciation and evaluation, is now approached by contemporary literary critics as a hidden universe of infinite complexity and inexhaustible meanings. The hallmark of the modern literary text—let us call it simply "the text"—is its polysemousness, its "many-signedness." Constructed of multiple intersecting sign systems, the text does not necessarily yield up its meaning when one traces the surface sequence of events and gestures. In ways which resemble the midrashic techniques of the rabbis, the decoding of the text requires nonlinear procedures which make connections among different systems of signs at different levels of meaning.

The very proliferation of meanings, and the impossibility of fixing their number or containing the text's production of them, are reasons why some "strong texts" we call classics seem to have something to say, often something different to say, in each generation. The fact that the meanings of the text are not just *there*, but can be realized only through interpretation, has placed new emphasis on the role of the interpreter. Far from being an ancillary or subsidiary activity, interpretation and the aggregating body of discrete interpretations have enlarged the conception of the text and blurred the sharpness of its boundaries. If the text cannot be realized without interpretation, then the text must come to include within it the history of its interpretations. Not all texts possess the surplus of meaning that makes them worthy of this kind of intensive reading. Those that do are said to be part of a canon, and although the canon of modern literature is open to change in a way in which the Biblical canon is not, the aura of canonization privileges the text in not dissimilar ways.

Finally, as an object the modern literary text has undergone changes in status that recall the vicissitudes of Scripture in the hands of its students. A period in which the text was regarded as the ineffable creation of genius was followed by a period in which the text's sources of influence were searched out and its philosophy elucidated. The focus next moved inside the text to discover there a complex organic unity, only to have that structure challenged by today's widespread claim that the text's meaning is produced by shifting codes of signification whose turbulence makes the idea of a single, stable organization impossible.

How are we to take this analogy between Scripture and text? I think we should be suspicious of those who would urge too close a historical tie between the two. This position takes the form of the argument that the new status and methods of interpretation represent either a secularization or a displacement of the ways in which the rabbis of the midrash read the Bible. There is a necessary presumption here of historical influence or transmission which is simply not defensible. Even if the rabbis could be claimed as precursors of the critics—and this is doubtful—to suggest their influence is to ignore the many cultural transformations that mediate between then and now. The Scripture/text analogy is evocative, moreover, precisely because its two terms are ontologically unassimilable one to the other. The modern work of art, no matter how mystified or demystified its metaphysics may be, is clearly grounded in humanly produced meanings, whereas the Bible and some of its commentaries claim for themselves a different kind of sanction.

The Scripture/text analogy nevertheless remains interesting, though on other grounds. It is the nature of man as a sign-producing and meaning-generating creature to set apart certain beautiful and powerful artifacts, to reverence them, and to make their interpretation a guarantee of the continuity of culture. In an age in which God no longer speaks audibly to man, endowing texts with the authority of His utterance, it should not be surprising that the need persists to be in the possession of such texts and to approach them in ways which mirror, even mimic, the ways the Bible was once approached.

The whole question, in fact, needs to be reversed. Rather than looking to the rabbis to teach us how to read modern literature, we should look to modern literature to teach us how to read the rabbis and *their* great text, the Bible. What could be more ironic and more wonderful than that the late fruits of secular humanism, in the form of literary criticism, should help us to recuperate our relationship to the founding texts of our religious tradition?

The phenomenon I speak of is not a speculative proposal, but a fact that is being repeatedly demonstrated, with impressive results, in the current study of the Bible and midrash, and being tentatively extended to other bodies of traditional material. Some of the names that come to mind in this regard are Meir Sternberg, Robert Alter, James Kugel and David Stern. The application of these methods is more than a happy accident. It was because students read Eliot and Faulkner, Agnon and Zach, because they trained on the devices of the modernist text, because they learned about point-of-view, metaphor, allusion, gap filling, and analogical structure—in short, it was because of the creation of this new sensibility of reading that it became possible to take up the text of the Bible and rediscover in it a religious drama which had been missed for a very long time.

This is much more than a simple case in which "modern methods" have been usefully applied to ancient texts. Form criticism, archaeology and comparative semitics have in their time yielded much useful knowledge about the Bible and its world. But little has approached literary theory in recovering the primary inner excitement of the experience of reading the text of Scripture. To speak of excitement in this context is not out of place. The original source of this excitement for modern readers was not the Bible but modernist texts. It was in the deep analysis of the poem and the novel that the revelatory power of the text was first re-experienced. The shimmering overdeterminacy of the text, the serious play of meanings, the significance and inseparability of interpretation, the drama of sequential reading—all of these were factors in reconditioning the faculty of wonder in the presence of the aura of the text. It was only then that this sense of discovery could be retrojected in a way which makes us into the kind of readers the Bible and midrash truly deserve. It is not my intention to demote the importance of studying modern literature by making it merely propaedeutic to the "divine sciences." Yet that function has in fact been served, perhaps incidentally, and it provides us with a suggestive illustration of how signals of transcendence may be imbedded in the secularity of the modern text.

## NEGATION AND CREATIVITY

Let us now return to modern Hebrew literature proper, to ask what its complex history can tell us about the possibilities of belief and disbelief. A starting point is the fact that the emergence of modern Hebrew literature ineluctably presupposed a rejection at some level of the metaphysics of normative Jewish belief: the sovereignty of God, the covenant with Israel, the divine origin of the Torah, the authority of the commandments. Doctrine, to be sure, was not necessarily at the center of this movement; the target of rejection was the whole fabric of traditional Jewish life in Eastern Europe. Yet the failure of belief was inseparably part of things, whether conceived of as a patrimony outgrown and pushed aside (the rebirth model) or as a structure of plausibility that collapsed and was lost (the catastrophe model). It is the *moment* and *process* of negation that need to be more finely examined; for, as it is represented in the life of Hebrew literature, apostasy is a complex experience in which negation and creativity are intimately entwined.

A good example is to be found in the very originating moment of modern Hebrew literary history. In 1819 a Galician *maskil* (a proponent of the Hebrew Enlightenment) named Joseph Perl published a satire of Hasidic tales called *Megalleh temirin* ("The Revealer of Secrets"). The work is made up of imaginary letters allegedly circulating among Hasidic leaders and adherents concerning frantic efforts (including bribery, blackmail and other reprehensible measures) to locate the whereabouts of the German manuscript of a book revealing damaging information about the inner workings of the Hasidic movement. The literary material being parodied, incidentally, was the writings of Nahman of Bratslav, whose parabolic tales are today so admired by students of literature. What for Perl was so ridiculous and discrediting about this material, in addition to its obvious distastefulness to Enlightenment principles, had to do with language: The Hebrew in which it was written was crude and vulgar, awkwardly translated from Yiddish speech with many Yiddishisms still intact. Ironically, it turned out to be precisely the uncouth and graceless stylistic qualities of Perl's satire which, unbeknownst to him, made the work significant. The revival of Hebrew as a modern literary language heretofore had been based on the purity of high Biblical models and conducted according to the most elevated and ornate stylistic principles. The artificiality of this medium made it hardly suitable for dealing with the real business of life. Therefore Perl's parodying of the "fallen" models of Hasidism infused Hebrew with a vitality, resourcefulness and raw humor which, though essential to the growth of the new literature, could not be acquired "legitimately."

A more thematic example comes from the late nineteenth-century confessional novel *Le'an?* ("Whither?") by M. Z. Feierberg. The work is set in the heart of pious Ukrainian Jewish society of that period and traces the intellectual coming-of-age of the young protagonist as he passes from the first inklings of childhood doubts to a tragic sense of permanent loss in young adulthood and, finally, to an impassioned affirmation of a nationalist rebirth in the East. From a compositional viewpoint, what is striking about the novel is the disproportion between its main sections and the proto-Zionist declaration at the end. The sections describing the journey toward apostasy are marvelously realized; by focusing on the child's fantasies and daydreams, Feierberg succeeds in presenting disbelief as a process which unfolds from within the tradition and is linked to the development of the moral and spiritual imagination. These richly evoked reveries contrast sharply with the depleted rhetoric of the closing visionary passages. The difference is more than simply the difference between what is known and what is yet to be, and it characterizes the autobiographical genre in Hebrew as a whole. The story of the struggle to disengage from the toils of the tradition inevitably makes for better art than the life of disengagement that follows.

Rejection draws its strength from the power of the object rejected, and disbelief lives off the strength of the culture of faith. From the examples above and from many others that could be furnished, it becomes clear that although modern Hebrew literature is a secular literature of revolt, in its genesis—and at crucial moments in its development—it drew its creative force from the very tradition against which it revolted. Victory did not come without costs; the emancipation of Hebrew literature from its embroilment with faith and tradition has at times left it perilously denuded of subject and vitality. The struggle between faith and apostasy is, then, an embrace in which a secret exchange of strengths takes place, an exchange which lasts, of course, only as long as the struggle is joined.

## ALLEGORY AND THE THEOLOGICAL LIFE OF LITERARY FORMS

Literary genres possess their own theological suggestiveness. The lyric poem presupposes the possibility of presence represented in the fresh articulation of the human voice. Epic implies the cohesion of the created social world and its rapport with a transcendent order. Narrative guarantees temporal duration and the successiveness of experience; the more self-conscious forms of the novel play on the analogy between God's providence and the flawed but protean authority of the narrator, or implied author, over the world of the novel.

Allegory, however, is a special case because, unlike lyric, epic and novel, it is not a modern, Western genre but a literary form found throughout classical sources of Judaism and, for that matter, of Christianity as well. From the prophetic and wisdom literature of the Bible, the rabbinic *mashal*, and the rationalist hermeneutics of medieval philosophy, to the extravagant symbolizations of the Kabbalah, and the tales of Nahman of Bratslav mentioned earlier, allegory has provided a way of speaking otherwise about matters which do not lend themselves to being spoken about directly. The modern Hebrew tradition is a rich one as well: the verse dramas of S. D. Luzzatto, the satire of Erter, the long poems of Bialik, the existential fables of Agnon, the theater of Hanoch Levine, and the fiction in the 1960s and 1970s of Amos Oz, A. B. Yehoshua and Aharon Appelfeld.

It would be easy to take Agnon as an example, that great classicist-modernist who made such obvious use of the parabolic materials of the tradition. But to demonstrate how deep this tendency runs let us turn instead to the fiction of A. B. Yehoshua, whose work is fully domesticated into the milieu of secular Israeli society. In Yehoshua's short fiction of the 1960s the hero is typically a well-educated, often nameless, native-born Israeli male (a high school Bible teacher, a philosophy lecturer, an aging university student) who is isolated from family and friends even as he moves among them. Deprived for so long of confirmation by others, and unaware of his own desperation, he momentarily loosens the controls that bind him to civilization and longs to participate in and even precipitate a cataclysmic disaster, only to recede in the end back into his isolation, unchanged. Yet even though these figures seem to embody the quintessence of individual alienation, the stories manage at the same time to speak of much larger issues: the effects of perpetual war on Israeli society, the image of the Arab in the Israeli mind, the relationship to the Diaspora. In such stories as "Facing the Forest," "Early in the Summer of 1970" and "Missile Base 612," the connection is made through subtle devices of background detail and submerged systems of reference rather than through the one-to-one correspondences we are used to associating with allegory. The centrifugal forces of allegory, which point us in a direction beyond the story, are held in close balance with the centripetal forces of textuality, which focus our interest on the workings of the story itself. The reader becomes aware of the allegorical possibilities only after the first reading and, in contrast to classical allegory, there may be no single "solution" but rather an ambiguous set of alternative interpretations.

In good hands, allegory provides a defense against the solipsism of the modern work of art. It is a defense against nakedness as well. Nietzsche observed that it is in the nature of modern knowledge to seek to rip off the veils surrounding truth and lay it open to direct description. In permitting the possibility of speaking otherwise, allegory "clothes" its difficult truths in narrative forms whose textures make us want to touch and feel them, and thereby draw close to what they encloak. For the Israeli writer, allegory has proven itself to be an alternative to the techniques of socialist realism with its insistence on the representativeness of fictional characters. Through allegory the writer can keep faith with the great national themes without sacrificing fineness of focus and symbolic movement. In modern Hebrew literature the national focus inevitably takes the form of a critical assessment of the state of Israeli society and the Jewish people as a whole. This preoccupation with the commonweal is the most significant aspect of Israeli literature as a *Jewish* literature. The allegorical mode represents a strong link between this contemporary concern and the dominant themes of classical Hebrew literature. It may no longer be transcendental realities that are pointed to by the allegorical counters; nevertheless the "otherness" enforced by allegory, even as a modern device, cannot help performing a function which in the end is not so very different.

## TRUTH-TELLING AND CRITICAL THEOLOGY

The eclipse of traditional faith in the late nineteenth century created a vacuum which a variety of ideologies rushed to fill, functioning in turn very much like religions. The devotion and enthusiasm with which Jews committed themselves to communism and socialism—and many other movements, Zionism among them—bear witness both to the internal weakness of Judaism in that moment and to the tenacious persistence of the need to believe. The nature of these "de-conversions" from traditional religion to an ideological surrogate is complex, and it has been the role of the best literature written in the West to examine the phenomenon with particular reference to the deformations that result from this displacement. In the case of modern Hebrew literature, it was of course Zionism which had to be submitted to scrutiny. In this context Zionism means not so much the Zionist *idea* of the establishment of a national homeland in Palestine as the potent blend of Zionist-socialist *ideology* brought from Russia by the young settlers of the Second Aliyah in the years just before the First World War. It was on the basis of this ideology that the kibbutzim were founded and the major political and educational institutions of the Yishuv were set up. Although much had changed by the time of Ben Gurion and the establishment of modern Israel, the originating impulse was still evident in nearly all sectors of the new society.

At the very beginnings of Zionist ideology, Hebrew fiction was already there and involved in preparing a critique of the hubris of Zionism. The critique was an internal one, conducted in Hebrew within a broad consensus on national goals. Yet the fact that it took place "within the family" did not make it any less radical or acrimonious. At issue was the claim of Zionism to solve the problem of the modern Jew, both as Jew and as modern man, and to offer a framework of belief and action which effectively replaced the piety of "exilic" Judaism. The founding figure in this truth-telling tradition was Yosef Haim Brenner, whose magisterial novels from the period of the Second Aliyah present the soul of the Jew, in the extremity of its theological and existential dispossession, as untransformed by the experience of the new land. Brenner was prophetic about the dangers of acting as if man had already been redeemed; the actual consequences of this presumption could only be observed at a remove in time.

In the fiction of the 1960s Amos Oz examined the later life of this ideological inheritance as it was realized in that most rationalist of utopian experiments, the kibbutz. In *Elsewhere, Perhaps* and *Where the Jackal Howls and Other Stories*, Oz finds the kibbutz an endangered community, not only prey to the forces of hatred at large in the world but, more significantly, vulnerable to the turbulent passions of the unreconstructed human material contained within. Oz's stories are particularly insightful regarding the costs paid by the sons for the ideological purity and romantic self-dramatization of the fathers. Although the kibbutz in Oz's fiction is intended to be a metonymy for the Zionist enterprise as a whole, it remains a special case.

Vividly presented in the late Yaakov Shabtai's novels of the 1970s, *Past Continuous* and *Past Perfect*, the cityscape of Tel Aviv cuts even closer to the bone. Although his characters may have fantasies of going off to a settlement to put themselves back together, they are mired in the degraded aimlessness of their urban lives. The psychological space occupied by these figures is a vacuum created, again, by the passions, ideological and otherwise, of the generation of the founders. The absence left behind becomes in turn entropic and demonic.

To speak of these writers as having theological ambitions would be inappropriate, if not ridiculous. Yet if we have learned anything from literary theory in recent years, it is that the significance of a text depends on the interpretive community that reads it. So, while such writers as Oz and Shabtai may have no intentions in this direction, there is nothing illegitimate about a desire to make theological use of their work.

What I have in mind relates to the tradition of negative theology in medieval Jewish philosophy; this is the position which holds that, because of God's transcendent otherness, we are limited to making statements about what God is not, rather than describing His positive attributes. One of the roles of modern literature, I would submit, is to tell us where in the world God is *not*. This is not simply a way of labeling all social criticism as essentially religious. It applies specifically to literature which investigates the consequences of systems that have usurped the role of religion and operate in its place. Hebrew literature makes wonderfully good reading in this regard. If the picture drawn of Israeli society is unpretty, it need not be depressing. The demystifying and truth-telling force of this literature is welcomed by all who believe that the future of the Jewish people depends on an honestly renegotiated relationship to the religious heritage of Judaism. In that endeavor, knowing where God is not is valuable intelligence.

In searching modern Hebrew literature for sources of theological insight, I have not drawn upon the most obvious instances: the magisterial figures of Bialik, Agnon and Uri Zvi Greenberg. In their writings the problem of tradition and the crisis of Judaism are directly engaged and made the explicit subject of their best art. There is much to be learned there, of course, and students of modern Jewish culture must return to their work over and over again. But the question I have sought to pose rests on a more severe base: What can we learn from modern Hebrew literature in the modernity of its detachment from the tradition? To seek this learning, that is, to view modern literature theologically, is not the same as theologizing it. Beware the voices which declare that all the departures and rebellions of modernity have been anticipated by our sages! If Hebrew literature is to help us in shaping a vision of the Jewish spirit in the future, it will do so only from within its own stubborn secularity.

NOTE

Originally published in *Orim* 3, no. 1
(Autumn 1987).

# CHAPTER 15

# Hebrew in America

*A Memoir*

Only much later in life did I become aware of the contours of the Lithuanian-Zionist-Hebraist complex into which I was born. Worcester, Springfield, Providence and other fading industrial cities in New England, not to mention the metropolis of Boston, had been colonized at the beginning of the twentieth century by young Jewish educators with a fierce allegiance to the newly revived Hebrew language. Because later in that century Zionism became indissolubly identified with Israel, it's hard for us to imagine a time when the territorial dimension of Zionism was largely a romantic fantasy while its cultural dimension was real and revolutionary. As a vehicle for Jewish modernity, Hebrew had already been hard at work as a literary language and a cultural program for over a hundred years. Hebrew, after all, was the portable component of the Jewish national idea, and that quality made it highly suitable for export in the shabby valises of passionate young men who arrived on these shores from the cultural centers of Eastern Europe.

These bearers of the Hebraist torch had to dim their light in order to make a go of it in America. For all its freedom and waywardness, American Jewry, especially in its New England embodiment, was surprisingly traditionalist in public life, and synagogues stood at its center. The Hebraists began by establishing free-standing schools—supplemental, afternoon schools, of course—based on a culturalist curriculum emphasizing Bible, Hebrew language, and Jewish history, as well as the new folkways developing in the nascent Yishuv (the Jewish Community in Palestine before 1948). It was realized early on that concessions would have to be made to the moderate religiosity of the immigrant communities. Boys would have to be taught to recite kiddush, kaddish, and haftarah and the Four Questions for the seder; the laws of the Sabbath and the holidays—flying under the colors of "customs and ceremonies"—would have to be duly conveyed. The accommodations were made, but it was not long before these institutions lost their independence and were folded into the supplemental schools of (mostly Conservative) synagogues. The fact that these synagogue schools were called Hebrew schools and not religious schools is more than a semantic vagary. It signaled the success of the Hebraist agenda; the curricula of these schools continued along recognizable nationalist principles.

Yet the accommodation between religious belief and practice and the Hebraist-nationalist program remained a fragile entente. The great events of mid-century—the murder of European Jewry and the establishment of Israel—exerted stresses on this marriage of convenience. On the one hand, the fact of statehood on the heels of the Holocaust brought all the synagogue denominations in American Jewish life into the Zionist consensus. On the other, Hebraism was ill-equipped to deal with the questions of religious meaning that arose in the wake of the Holocaust and as a result of the growing prosperity and consumerism of American Jewry. These tensions were hardly explicit, and I was certainly not conscious of them when I was a pupil in the Hebrew school of the Congregation Beth Israel in Worcester, Massachusetts, in the late 1950s. But later on, the contradictory and complementary relationship between these two formations—Judaism as structure of value and experience and Hebrew as a language and literature—would play a deepening role in my life.

The shift in Jewish education was played out in my own family. My father, Nelson Mintz, who was born in Worcester in 1909—his father had emigrated from Lithuania in the 1880s and died in the influenza epidemic of 1918—was sent as a boy for a few years to an independent institution called, rather grandly, the Hebrew National School 'Ivriyah rather than to the local Talmud Torah. When the time came for my schooling, the 'Ivriyah no longer existed, and Hebrew education had been taken over by Beth Israel, the city's Conservative synagogue. But the Hebraist markings were still unmistakable—strengthened, I think, by Israel's recently won independence—and the curriculum marched to the beat of the Bureau of Jewish Education in Boston with its strong ties to the Boston Hebrew Teachers College (HTC). It was the personalities as much as the subjects that impressed on us the value of Hebrew. The rabbi of Beth Israel, Abraham Kazis, who had grown up in Chelsea and graduated from HTC before studying for the rabbinate at the Jewish Theological Seminary (JTS), was himself an accomplished Hebrew speaker. He gave his full backing to the ideological severity of Harry (Zvi) Plich, the principal of the Hebrew school. *Mar* Plich, as we called him, had grown up in Russia and then joined the *halutsim* in Palestine. His medical studies in Belgium were cut short by the Nazis, and he lived the second half of his life as a Hebrew educator in America. His devotion to Hebrew was implacable; this was a stern allegiance that brooked no contradiction.

My earliest memories of Hebrew are in fact connected to pleasing these figures of authority. Studying Hebrew pleased adults, and I was a child who wanted acknowledgment. Hebrew enjoyed prestige, and I was aware that this prestige came from two sources rather than one. Hebrew was conspicuously the language of the prayers and the Humash in the weekly round of my life, but I was also conscious that it was the language spoken by Israelis in Israel. Yes, my teachers spoke Hebrew to us and to each other, but I knew that a different kind of Hebrew was being spoken over there.

As I approached adolescence, Hebrew came to serve me as a private secret language. My parents had Yiddish as their secret language, and I had Hebrew. Not that there was anybody much to share it with, but that didn't matter. I looked around at my classmates in the public school I attended and saw no one else who knew any classical language. Even the Roman Catholic kids were no longer being taught Latin, and here I was taking Latin in school and mastering the language as well or better than they. The kids from Greek and Armenian homes may have known a smattering of their heritage languages, but nothing approaching real literacy. I was swelled with unspoken pride over my ability to read portions of the Old Testament, as it was called, in the original tongue. Knowing the rudiments of Hebrew was like possessing a secret decoder ring that allowed me to uncover the hidden meaning behind the utterances and behaviors that shaped my life as a Jew. Others in junior congregation might recite the prayers mechanically, but I could parse the words—well, at least some of them.

The inkling that Hebrew was the key to unlocking the secrets of Judaism began to take shape in me. Learning that most Hebrew words are based on three-consonant stems was a further revelation that made the map of Hebrew come alive with unexpected interconnections between remote contexts. To discover the kinship between the root of a word used in the biblical books of the Prophets and one that appeared in the Sabbath liturgy was interesting enough, but to see a connection between one of those ancient texts and modern spoken Hebrew was exciting. Even the tedium of grammar had a pay off. There was little fun in rehearsing the *binyanim* and the nominal suffixes, but once you had some of that under your belt, the inner springs of the language became more discernible, and the stubborn perplexity of classical Hebrew became more forgiving. Once you learned the rationale behind the formation of the words, it became possible, even if in the most tentative way, to form your own words and write or speak sentences in which the verb was conjugated correctly and the nouns agreed with one another in number and gender.

I well knew that Hebrew was a spoken language, but in practice I had never heard it spoken without a European or American accent by anyone who did not seem ancient to me. That's why in the summer following ninth grade attending Camp Yavneh, a camp sponsored by the Boston Hebrew Teachers College, was so eye opening. Added to the usual cast of aging Hebraists were real live Israelis, as well as college students returned from a year of study in Israel. Speaking Hebrew, which had long been associated for me with pleasing my idiosyncratic elders, suddenly became cool. Although we campers did not speak Hebrew among ourselves, the official life of the camp indeed took place in Hebrew, which had the effect of making the language come alive as a genuine medium of oral communication. That summer I took my own first strokes swimming in that medium. In one memory that has stuck in my mind, I recall returning from an unsuccessful errand and reporting to the counselor who had sent me, "*Lo 'alah beyadi.*" Of the various ways in spoken Hebrew of saying that something didn't work out, I had chosen the most elevated and literary, parroting, presumably, the official Hebrew I was hearing around me.

Summer living under the banner of Hebrew also had an interesting social dimension. At camp, as with Hebraist institutions generally and as with the famous "status quo" in Israel, the population was much more variegated then what I was used to in my congregation in Worcester. One of my bunkmates was Nahum Twersky, whose father was the principal of the Hebrew school at Bnai Moshe in Brighton; his uncle, if I remember the family relations correctly, was Isadore Twersky, the son of the Talner Rebbe. I spent the following Simḥat Torah as a houseguest of Nahum's family, and the holiday spent in the orbit of the Talner shul, with its aura of a Hasidic court, proved a significant event in the development of my adolescent religiosity. I was exposed to a very different face of Orthodoxy in the hair-raising stories of the vicious pranks played by yeshiva boys on their teachers, told by another bunkmate after the lights went out. That too was something to remember.

Ironically, my first visit to Israel the following summer contributed to my Hebrew much less than the season at Yavneh. My trip, which was sponsored by United Synagogue Youth (USY), the Conservative Movement's youth arm, was aptly called Pilgrimage. We did much more davening than learning Hebrew. This priority reflected the values of synagogue life in America—not just in the Conservative stream—which cared much more about conforming religious practice than about imparting the Hebrew-language skills that would open up a meaningful engagement with Jewish texts. There was little Hebrew on the trip, but on my free days I managed to lose myself happily amidst the babble of native speakers on the streets of Jerusalem, and I did my best to converse with my adult cousins in Netanya. Seeing my interest in Hebrew, my cousins gave me the poems of Raḥel (Bluwstein) as a gift. I was gratified to see that I could understand some of the poems, and I recognized one or two that had been sung around the campfire the previous summer. Although I didn't learn much Hebrew that summer, I did come away with an exposure to what Hebrew was like in its "natural habitat," as well as an intimation of the difference between nativeness and near-nativeness in the knowledge of Hebrew, a distinction that would become important to me later on. For me at that moment, hearing Hebrew spoken by Israelis was like listening to a live performance of a piece of music I had heard only on the phonograph.

It was as a USYer that I spent most of my extra-curricular hours during high school, rising eventually to become the organization's national president. And here too Hebrew played a role. Most of the teenagers involved in the leadership, as enthusiastic as they were, had not had the benefit of a strong Jewish education. I had. My knowledge of Hebrew gave me the confidence to speak about Judaism with authority, and I used that asset to my advantage. If when I was younger Hebrew had served as a secret language of self-importance, now it became a public demonstration of my worth. Under the right circumstances, Hebrew could be admixed with power, I learned. Grandiosity was not far behind. Each year the national organization would chose a key Jewish value as its annual theme and put together a booklet with relevant sources. The year I was president the theme was family harmony, and emblazoned on the front of the printed booklets was the traditional but grammatically incorrect Hebrew term for that estimable ideal: *shalom bayit*. It should be *shelom bayit*, with a *sheva* under the *shin* because of the possessive construction, I self-righteously lectured the adult professional staff. I have no excuses for my behavior other than to say that the adults running USY, lay and professional, encouraged young people to mimic some of the less appealing, hierarchical features of Jewish organizational life, and I turned out to be no exception.

Hebrew played a more beneficent role during my teenage years when it came to my inner life. I was but one in a very long line of young people for whom reading the Hebrew text of the Song of Songs was an entrée into thinking about love and the body while staying within the precincts of sacred literature. I was naturally attracted to the kabbalistically inspired hymns in the prayer book, such "Lekha Dodi," "Yedid Nefesh" and "An'im" Zemirot, whose figurative language, so gendered and embodied—how unimaginable were those terms then!—turned the staid text of the liturgy into vibrant and intense poetry. Even in the secular poems of Raḥel in the volume I had received from my Israeli cousins I found a lyric attunement to the moments of anguish and ecstasy in my adolescent sensibility.

During my university years at Columbia, first as an undergraduate in the College and then as a doctoral student in the English Department, Hebrew continued to be a rich resource for an important but hidden part of my life. Whether it was taking courses at the Jewish Theological Seminary or later studying Jewish texts as a member of the New York Havurah, I led a Marrano-like double life. Hebrew and English, each with its own imposing cultural formation, occupied separate spheres, and I ran back and forth between them, only occasionally catching glimpses of common threads. At Columbia I read the Great Books as part of its famous core curriculum, and at JTS I studied the Bible, the Talmud and Hebrew literature. The JTS courses were taught in Hebrew, and in the late 1960s there was still something left of the ideological fervor that had made JTS's Teachers Institute/

Seminary College a flagship of Hebraism during the interwar period. What was new to me was the nexus between Hebrew and the critical method. I was used to Hebrew as the discourse of Jewish nationalism and its culture, yet here I was excited to find the latest methods in the humanities, not the old Wissenschaft ideas, being used by the younger faculty members—Yochanan Muffs, Avraham Holtz, and David Gordis among them—to unpack ancient and modern texts in new ways.

The moment that stands out is my first exposure to the stories of S. Y. Agnon. It occurred during the spring of my freshman year in an introduction to modern Hebrew literature taught by Avraham Holtz. The course required writing an interpretive term paper—in Hebrew of course—and I chose to write on Agnon's 1935 novella *In the Heart of the Seas* (Bilvav yamim), a story about the adventures and tribulations of a group of Galician Hasidim in the early nineteenth century seeking to settle in the Holy Land. I had never before read anything so lengthy in Hebrew, nor, for that matter, had I written a paper in Hebrew. Where I found the ambition to do so is beyond me. Judging from the squall of red markings on the paper when it was returned to me, I had a very long way to go when it came to writing proper discursive Hebrew. But as regarding Agnon, a bond had been formed, and I continued to read his works with pleasure and fascination. It was with my discovery of Agnon that I first saw a bridge to the Western canon we were reading at Columbia. Here was a modern master, I thought, who deserved membership. Although I no longer have that freshman paper in my possession, I know its substance because I cannibalized it to write an article, this time in English, that I contributed to the inaugural issue of *Response Magazine* in 1967.[1] Because my research interests in recent years have been pledged to Agnon, this early connection is particularly dear to me.

After my third year in graduate school, I underwent a crisis that was precipitated by my failing efforts to sustain both spheres of my life. I was increasingly involved in the New York Havurah and in Jewish student politics just at the time that my English literature studies were threatening to turn vocational. Although I thoroughly enjoyed studying English—I was concentrating on Victorian Studies—I could see looming on the horizon the inevitable moment when I would have to take a job and devote all my energies to making a career in that field. I discovered that for that path I lacked the requisite depth of personal commitment. Instead, I wanted to use whatever resources of mind and imagination I possessed to make a contribution to Jewish culture. To which field of Jewish culture I did not know at first. I started with midrash and then tried *piyyut* and medieval Hebrew poetry before finally arriving at modern Hebrew literature. The process involved several *Wanderjahre* spent in Cambridge, MA, Jerusalem, and New York.

And as the saying goes, that, my friends, is when my troubles began. As long as I did not aspire to be regarded as a Jewish Studies scholar, my facility with Hebrew, the accoutrement of an *amateur*, was regarded as impressive and noble. But once I decided to profess Hebrew, the rules of the game changed demonstrably. The glass that had been half full, or at least filled up part of the way, seemed, in my eyes, proportionally empty. I underscore "in my eyes" because much of the anxiety I experienced as an American Hebrew speaker came from my own sense of exposure to the judgment of others. Whether this judgment was a fact or largely a projection is something I'll never know, and it is beside the point. My transition from graduate student in English to aspiring professor of Hebrew and Jewish Studies did entail spending several years among mentors and colleagues in Jerusalem, presenting conference papers in Hebrew, and making my debut writing an academic article in Hebrew. The self-exposure was real, even if the judgment was a web I spun myself.

There were two dimensions to my difficulties. The first had to do with the limits of my Hebraist upbringing. When I was drawn to the study of midrash and thought of making it my professional destination, I ran up against the fact that I lacked the grounding in the Talmud and rabbinic literature that comes from a yeshiva education. I had studied the odd Talmudic tractate, but the Hebraist curriculum that had formed me, following in the footsteps of the Zionist-nationalist conception of Jewish history, was strong on the Bible, history, and literature, but scant attention had been paid to the great swath of rabbinic learning. My ego had already been rendered fragile by the move into Hebrew studies; taking on the Talmud seemed beyond my strength. It has taken decades of amateur Shabbat-afternoon Talmud study to begin to make up for what I missed. Although I chose modern Hebrew as my field, I wanted to remain connected to the classical breadth of Jewish literature. David Roskies and I started *Prooftexts: A Journal of Jewish Literary History* in 1983 with two convictions in mind. The ideological partition between Yiddish literature and Hebrew literature was no longer relevant and needed to be superseded by a comprehensive concept of modern Jewish culture in many languages. Similarly, the cleavage between the classical and the modern could productively be overcome by using literary studies as a lens and encouraging literary approaches to the Bible, the Talmud, Midrash, and medieval texts. In creating a new journal, moreover, we were seeking an alternative to the fractious and sometime vicious scholarly culture we had observed in the generation of our predecessors, especially in the Israeli academy. We wanted a collaborative editorial process that reflected a community of scholars working to elaborate the variegated meanings of Jewish culture. In this expanded vision, Hebrew literature, by virtue of the abundance and richness of its production, retains its pride of place, but it takes its position alongside other and earlier Jewish literatures. I take great pride from the role *Prooftexts* has played in creating Jewish literary studies in America.

The second difficulty was becoming myself a producer of Hebrew. With my colleagues in Israel and with my Israeli colleagues at American universities, speaking Hebrew has always been a self-conscious performance. I often think about what I want to say before I say it, pretesting grammar and word choice. The times I have made gross errors are etched into my brain and will never be repeated. There have been many gratifying times, too, when a felicitous phrase has come to me unbidden, but those moments are less well remembered. I once had occasion to examine the voluminous handwritten journals of Mordechai Kaplan in JTS's Rare Book Room. Kaplan was the dean of the Teachers Institute at JTS for several decades in the first half of the twentieth century. Although he presided over a faculty of veteran Hebraists, he himself lacked that kind of background; speaking and teaching in Hebrew were a challenge for him as well as a source of self-consciousness in his relations with his staff. It was a challenge that both invigorated him—about twenty percent of the journals are written in Hebrew—and filled him with anxiety. He was especially anxious at the beginning of each semester, when he had to make a formal address in Hebrew to the assembled faculty and students. To pump up for the occasion and tone up his Hebrew muscles, as it were, he spent days reading nothing but Hebrew as he got ready for the occasion and mastered his fears. I think of Kaplan working out in the Hebrew gym as a kindred spirit.

I know that I will never shake my American accent, and I know that my Hebrew—what the linguists call my idiolect—remains stilted and elevated in a way that marks it as non-native—charmingly so, I would like to think, but who knows? I will never have the ease enjoyed by natives in skipping intuitively from ironic banter to street Hebrew and back to academic discourse within a few beats. For me, writing in Hebrew is the hardest thing. When I'm taking part in a conversation or giving a talk, there are no expectations of perfection; I can phrase and rephrase, and I can use affect and gesticulation to enhance the message and create a bond with my interlocutor or audience. But putting pen to paper feels like swimming with weights, and I am thrust into a black awareness of all that I can achieve in English that seems beyond me in Hebrew: humor, irony, nuance, understatement, and, most of all, the deft idiom, the apt colloquialism, the *mot juste*. In Hebrew I am scourged of subtlety and artifice. I stand naked without my finery.

When it comes to interpreting literary texts for the purpose of publication or teaching, I am chastened by an awareness of how many echoes will never be picked up by my ear. With the help of concordances, dictionaries and other reference works, I can identify allusions to classical sources and parse rare words. But when I stumble over a bit of doggerel or a nursery rhyme or a pop song or an army acronym familiar to nearly every child raised in Israel, I am undone. When it comes to slang and colloquialisms, forget about it. Take a small example: The great poet Natan Zach ends a poem with the line in which a woman wishes a man that the good *yinasheq lekha*, literally, "kiss you." I have to be told in a note by Arieh Sachs in *The Modern Hebrew Poem Itself* that in colloquial Hebrew of the era the verb *lenasheq*, when used the dative, means the opposite of what you think it would mean. It means "to kiss off" or "kiss my ass." If you've missed that, alas, you've missed the poem. No one reader, I well understand, can approach becoming the "ideal reader" or "super-reader" who catches all the references and tonalities; we each bring our lenses and the limited set of our receptivities. Nonetheless, it is sobering to know that there will always be things that you can never get.

Looking back over my life with Hebrew, there is a term I have grown to loathe and a term I have grown to embrace. The one I loath is "fluency." When people find out that I teach Hebrew literature, they invariably remark, "Oh, you must be fluent." It is an observation that can be made only by someone who has no serious experience with learning a foreign language. Etymologically "fluent" is related to the Latin word for river and designates fluid or speech that bubbles up and flows freely. Fluency is an imagined state of effortless, spontaneous language production that has little to do with the imposing, arduous, and desultory process of mastering a language. For people who use the term, fluency implies a state of arrival achieved by a fixed amount of exertion. You begin by not being fluent; you work hard at it, and then—you are fluent. Well, I've been working hard at it for many decades, and I'm still waiting. And I'm not in a hurry. I keep learning new words, some old and some newly coined; I'm forever looking to integrate snappy idioms into my speech; and I'm always trying to nudge my novel reading to move a little faster. If the term had not already been turned into a lame cliché, I would say it's truly a matter of lifelong learning. The one thing that has changed, thankfully, over the course of my life is that I am less anxious. Now when I learn a Hebrew word or phrase, I don't think of it as plugging a hole or making recompense for a chronic insufficiency. Rather, I feel as if I've been enlarged. Students of foreign-language acquisition shun the term fluency and prefer proficiency. Proficiency is a word that encourages no mystification and proposes as a goal becoming good enough to function in a language for a variety of pragmatic goals. When it comes to learning a foreign language, moreover, instead of one proficiency there are four separate skills: understanding speech, producing speech, reading comprehension and writing. Each of these skills is susceptible to infinite stations of progress from the absolute beginner to the most advanced student, and in every learner these skills are proceeding along separate tracks at different rates. The most, and the best, we can say is that we are on the path and we are moving forward.

The term I've come to embrace is "near native." I first came across it in job listings for university Hebrew instructors—it's used in all languages, not just Hebrew—that invited applications from those with "native or near-native" knowledge of the language. It's not clear to me whether the phrasing acknowledges a real parity between the two classes of candidates or whether native speakers are truly preferred but for legal reasons cannot be specified exclusively. I've never seen the word used as anything other than an adjective, but I see no reason not to make it into a noun. I therefore am pleased to declare myself a near native, who belongs to a small but happy (most of the time) band of other near natives. As Americans who speak and work in Hebrew, we near natives are indigenous to America—that is, for two or three generations at least—but not to Hebrew. The more you think about the concept of nativeness, the more it comes to resemble a boat springing leaks. Many of the Hebraists who taught my generation never ever lived in Palestine, yet their Hebrew was richer and more robust than most of their counterparts in the Yishuv. And in the Yishuv itself, aside from the strange case of Eliezer Ben-Yehudah's son Itamar Ben-Avi, the members of the first generation raised in Palestinian Hebrew were born only in the early 1930s and were likely to be the children of parents who had learned their Hebrew in the Tarbut schools in Europe. When it comes to Hebrew, in short, nativeness is an invention. A particular style of orientalized Hebrew spoken in the youth movements in the Yishuv in the 1930s and 1940s succeeded in conferring upon itself the designation "native." Other styles of Hebrew spoken in Europe and America were marginalized and deemed less authentic.

It was decked out in its supposedly native costume that Hebrew gained admittance to the university as a modern language to be taught alongside other modern languages. The price of admission was the need to package Hebrew as a foreign language spoken by inhabitants of a country in the Middle East and thereby obscure its provenance as the language of Jewish culture. There are the makings of a true *Kulturkampf* here. Should the Hebrew taught on university campuses be the Hebrew spoken in the present moment by literate speakers in Israel? Or is that Hebrew only one and only the latest of the manifestations of a larger conception of Hebrew, which includes the achievements of both secular and religious culture over a longer time frame and not just in Palestine/Israel? These are issues to be engaged on there own terms, but even from the terms of the debate it is easy to see why Hebrew has never been a comfortable fit in Middle Eastern departments. It is not until the 1920s that real Hebrew speech and literature developed in Palestine. So what is one to do with the hundred and fifty or so years that modern Hebrew was being created in Germany, Poland, Galicia and America before arriving in the Levant? Are Bialik and Tchernichovsky Middle Eastern writers? Truly? The isolation and demonization of Israel must sadly be added to the mix nowadays. The anti-Zionism in some Middle East departments is so thick that it has become nearly impossible to teach Hebrew and Israeli culture in any but a defensive and apologetic way.

Along these same lines, it should be obvious by now that, although I extol its achievements, Israeli literature is not identical to Hebrew literature in my eyes. In the dialectical necessity to throw over the old in order to create a new reality, Zionism jettisoned whole blocs of the Jewish classical heritage. The baby was thrown out with the bathwater and never taken back in. Israeli literature, which is the descendent of this rejection, has been hobbled by this deracination and has accomplished what it has accomplished despite being cut off from its roots. The great exception is the writing of S. Y. Agnon, and that is why his work has become so central to my own. Agnon provides a bridge that reaches in two directions. It connects Zion and the Jewish state to the culture of the Diaspora, and it connects modern Hebrew writing to the Talmud, midrash, *piyyut*, medieval philosophy, Hasidic tales and the other products of premodern Jewish civilization. For us American Jews, Agnon's expansive embrace is particularly relevant because, unlike our Israeli counterparts, we did not have the great either/or between religion and secularity forced upon us. The rapidly lengthening shelf of good translations of Agnon into English makes this an opportune moment to draw wisdom from the greatest Jewish writer of the twentieth century.

For these reasons I have felt fortunate to have taught at Brandeis and JTS, both institutions in which no apologies for Hebrew need be made. At JTS especially, I've been further fortunate to have the support and the students each semester to teach a literature class conducted in Hebrew. What was once a staple of the Hebrew colleges in all subjects of Judaica and not just literature—and certainly at JTS's own Teachers Institute—is now a rarity. You might put this down to lower standards of student preparation, but you would be off target. The reasons have to do with the collapse of Hebraist ideology and the scarcity of instructors confident enough to teach their subject in Hebrew and confident enough in the value of Hebrew to take the trouble. And make no mistake: it takes trouble. It is not easy to conduct a classroom in Hebrew. The already unbalanced playing field between instructor and students becomes even more unbalanced when students are at a disadvantage in their ability to freely express comments and questions. The different levels of Hebrew background and competence usually equal the number of students in the class. The pace of discussion often slows down frustratingly as students laboriously formulate their answers to questions.

Nevertheless, there is something wonderfully bracing in the very artificiality of the situation. Like me, most all of the students are American born and speak English in their everyday lives. Yet when we cross the threshold of the classroom, we enter into a compact to conduct our interactions in Hebrew. We take on roles and perform for each other in a language not our own. We impose this constraint on our naturalness out of a belief that the gains are worth the trade-offs. The prize is a special synergy that comes from reading texts in Hebrew and discussing them in Hebrew. This is not to say that there are not *other* things to be gained from discussing a Hebrew text in

English and thereby engaging in the exercise of transposing discourse from one system to another. But when it is Hebrew-to-Hebrew, there is an unmistakably unique intimacy. And there are secondary gains. Students develop a capacity for conceptual and analytic thinking in Hebrew that is hard to acquire elsewhere. New vocabulary is being added; the Hebrew muscles are being flexed and conditioned. There is the satisfaction of succeeding at something difficult and the joy of putting one foot before the other on the path, the lifelong path of Hebrew knowledge.

In America, alas, most often we must walk that road alone. We're not watching TV or reading newspapers in Hebrew, nor are we talking to service representatives on the phone and having fights with our spouses in Hebrew. I love my wife very much, but if she were an Israeli it would have done wonders for my Hebrew. That's why Hebrew-speaking summer camps were once so important and why I cling to my Hebrew classroom. Time spent in Israel is a necessary infusion of oxygen. I spent years studying the works of American Hebrew writers, and it is this quality of loneliness and aloneness that has stayed with me most indelibly. Those poor souls felt doubly abandoned. The new generation of Hebrew readers they hoped to foster at home never materialized, and the Hebrew readers of the Yishuv evinced little interest in literary gifts from the Diaspora. For Israel Efros, Avraham Regelson, and Shimon Halkin, the isolation was intolerable, and they each found their way to Israel around the establishment of the state. But most stayed on in America. Gabriel Preil, Eisig Silberschlag, Ephraim Lissitzky, Reuven Wallenrod, and many others continued to write Hebrew prolifically on these shores.

Yet no matter how quirky and perverse these figures may have been, they were not delusional. They were able to soldier on and create in Hebrew in the absence of readers because they were not dependent on them. There was something in the private relationship of each with the Hebrew language that provided the necessary nourishment. One can find a glimpse into that relationship in Regelson's magnificent ode to the Hebrew language *Haquqot otiyotaikh* (Engraved Are Thy Letters), which he wrote at the end of World War II before his move to Israel. There the poet describes Hebrew as a sublime yet nubile beloved whom he worshipfully courts like a troubadour and to whom he pledges eternal fealty. He praises her plasticity and polymorphousness, and he even writes a hymn to the *binyanim*, those verb paradigms that threaten to defeat novice learners. Regelson's ode is gorgeous, fulsome, and over the top, but it is right on target when it comes to identifying the gratifications experienced by the Hebraist in working the language and manipulating it. The pleasure is quasi-erotic and the fidelity quasi-religious. Despite the want of readers and despite the lack of honor, the Hebraist has no doubt that, where it counts, his or her affections are returned.

I may not be as ardent a lover or as great a believer or as erudite a possessor of Hebrew as my predecessors, but that does not prevent me from feeling something of those pleasures. Although I am a Zionist, I'm grateful that the revival of Hebrew and the establishment of Israel, though deeply linked, are not one and the same thing. As the portable component of the Jewish national idea, Hebrew is a source of nourishment and delight in the diaspora. Hebrew is dear to me because it gives me unmediated access to my religious tradition and enables me to make informed decisions about my Jewish life. The ability to read the Torah, the Prophets and Wisdom literature in Hebrew is an incalculable pleasure. Hebrew allows me to grasp the inner poetry of liturgy and ritual. Despite its historical layers and the influences of surrounding cultures, Hebrew is recognizably one language, and that fact makes it possible for me to savor the thrilling ways in which Hebrew roots do cartwheels and transform themselves over the ages. The very simultaneity of ancient and modern meanings is a wonder. I cannot fail to be exhilarated each time an allusion in Bialik or a metaphor in Amichai unpacks itself and shoots across the space between the holy and the profane. Israeli literature in its stories and poems and plays is an amazement, and I am profoundly grateful that in order to read it I am not dependent on the miniscule sampling available in translation. And even though Hebrew has its own life in the Diaspora, without it I could never hope to have firsthand knowledge of the greatest creation of the Jewish people in our times. For the very reason that my Hebrew is acquired rather than given to me in my mother's milk, it will always remain just a little strange to me. There is a lot that I miss by virtue of not being a native; but as a near native there is a lot that I can see that the native will never appreciate.

I am grateful that Hebrew is my daily bread. "Were not Your Torah my delight," says the psalmist, "I would have perished in my affliction" (119:92).

## NOTES

Originally published in *What We Talk About When We Talk About Hebrew (and What It Means to Americans)*, ed. Naomi B. Sokoloff and Nancy E. Berg (Seattle: University of Washington Press, 2018), pp. 211–226. Reprinted with Permission from University of Washington Press.

1. I returned to this early encounter with Agnon as part of a symposium celebrating the twentieth anniversary of *Prooftexts: A Journal of Jewish Literary History* in which the editors were invited to chose a work that had been important to them and discuss how their relationship to it had changed over time. See "In the Seas of Youth," *Prooftexts* 2001, vol. 21 (1), pp. 57–70.

# Packing Up an Office

*The Work of Mourning and the
Creation of an Archive*

BEVERLY BAILIS

> Archives reveal the passions of the collector. The remains heaped up in
> them are reserve funds or something like iron reserves, crucial to life, and
> which for that reason must be conserved.[1]

Alan Mintz was my doctoral advisor at the Jewish Theological Seminary.
Since his death, several of Alan's friends, colleagues, and family members
have reached out to me looking for a "student of Alan's" to work on a series of
projects to honor him and his work. Participating in these projects has given
me the opportunity to reflect on different ways to memorialize and to offer
tribute. One approach has involved gathering materials created by Alan to
help consolidate and preserve his academic scholarship. For instance, I was
asked to help prepare an edited transcript of a talk Alan gave at a conference
at Yeshiva University's Center for Israel Studies in the fall of 2016, entitled
"Agnon's Stories of the Land of Israel: Celebrating the 50th Anniversary of
S. Y. Agnon's Nobel Prize." Jeffrey Saks, one of the conference's organizers,
who is editing a volume based on the talks from the conference, invited me
to turn a video recording of Alan's talk, "Homeland and Hometown: The
Dialectic Between Eretz Yisrael and Buczacz in Agnon's Late Works," into
a written essay to be included in the book. Another project has entailed

working with David Stern in putting together this present anthology of Alan's essays. This has involved following the "life cycle" of articles to see if they had already made their way into a book and gathering together those that had not. From these gathered essays we selected for inclusion representative examples of his wide-ranging scholarly contributions.

Both of these anthology projects are attempts to make the ideas and thoughts of Alan and his scholarship more permanent and available to future readers. In this sense, they are evocative of the notion of *kinnus*, or "ingathering." This late 19th and early 20th-century enterprise, spearheaded in large part by Ḥayyim Naḥman Bialik, consisted of Jewish intellectuals collecting texts and artifacts of Jewish culture and creativity throughout the generations, and then organizing, anthologizing, and reevaluating them in a new light for the needs of the present and future. The act of gathering together aspects of traditional Jewish culture was central to the passing down and preservation of this tradition, and an attempt both to memorialize it and to keep it alive. The creators of such anthologies were frequently motivated by a sense of imminent loss, as well as the threat that aspects of traditional Jewish culture were on the brink of disappearing with the onset of modernity.[2] Just as facing a sense of cultural loss triggers a collective response to gather, preserve, and commemorate, the loss of an individual, a mentor and colleague, likewise activates a similar impulse to assemble and consolidate, to preserve the memory of the deceased.

However, the task that provided me the most profound, all-immersive opportunity to offer tribute and to mourn an advisor on a personal level was of an entirely different order. It entailed working over the course of a summer emptying Alan's office with his wife, Susanna, and his daughters, Amira and Avital. Emptying the office constituted a radically different kind of experience than the more overtly literary or scholarly projects. Most significantly, it marked a shift from the world of ideas to the world of tangible things. Books, papers, paintings—all the contents of an office—impress themselves on you, each individual thing demanding time, space, consideration, and decision. Dealing with these objects means confronting the memories connected to them, since the things that someone owns are part of him or her, a repository of some aspect of the owner's history and personality. There is something about the confrontation with tangible objects that can trigger melancholy. As philosophers and literary critics have noted, ". . . there is a melancholy to physical objects. Maybe not if they were to exist alone in the world without us. It is we who attribute the state of melancholy to them in their reminding us, or making evident to us in our perceiving them, that we and they are two in the world and not one, and we are, therefore, not whole. This knowledge is loss, and recognizing the loss provokes an unresolvable melancholy."[3]

Such a deep sense of loss, in effect, belies the very act of packing an office since it quite literally involves taking something that is ostensibly complete and full—full with a veritable accumulation of things—and then taking it apart, and finally emptying it. Alan died suddenly, and so his office was very much in the middle of being used. It was full of books, papers, works in progress, current syllabi and teaching notes; it contained a whole work-life. The act of emptying the office felt, in a way, like a form of violence, a dismantling and the dispersal of things, the creation of an absence or void out of former plenitude and completeness. All this went against all the other projects of memorial *kinnus*, of bringing things together to make them more permanent, concrete and "whole." The acuteness of this sense of violence and loss was expressed immediately by his daughter Amira, right after the first boxes of books were given to some friends and colleagues. While glancing at the many books on the shelves and taking in the seeming enormity of the task before us, she wondered if there was any way of keeping all the books together, of transporting the office, as it was, to a different location to keep her father's collection intact and whole.

As this work continued, though, it became clear that what was at stake was not simply emptying Alan's office, dispersing all of its contents, but getting each of these items to those who could find the most meaning in them. Much like the many books and letters circulating in Agnon's stories that carry some urgent, potentially redemptive meaning or message, we needed to get these things where they could be used, where they could go to the right recipient. There was both a literal and figurative weightiness to all of these possessions. And this act of distributing them, in and of itself, became a way of memorializing and passing on a literary tradition. It also provided moments of discovery, since the things Alan had, his collection of books and papers, revealed so much about him: not only about him as a scholar, but his quieter aspects and interests, his qualities as a person and a teacher.

The process of clearing the office with Susanna entailed different stages. First, we had to get to know the office. We needed to map it and to orient ourselves in it before we could start taking it apart. By reading the office as a kind of text, we could sense that how and where he placed his things held clues to their significance. Hanging on a wall, among other pictures, was an actual framed map of "The Holy Community of Buczacz," Agnon's home-town, which also appears in the English translation of *A City in its Fullness* that he edited with Jeffrey Saks. Alan and Jefferey designed it along with the graphic designer Elad Lifshitz, and it appears in the endpapers at the front and back of the book. He then had it framed for his office wall, along with another copy that he hung outside of his office. The map contains images of Buczacz's Town Hall, the Great Synagogue, Old Beit Midrash, Train Station, Market Well, and Castle Ruins, along with images from several of Agnon's stories, superimposed on an official map of the region. It also features frag-mented passages of Hebrew text from Agnon's stories embedded in the map, helping to create its texture. Alan was very proud of this visual mapping of Buczacz, and its placement in multiple locations indicates a kind of merging of the spaces represented in the map and his own physical work-space of the office. It highlights the internal intellectual space Alan occupied during the past few years he had dedicated to writing about Agnon's *A City in its Fullness*, and the centrality of this project in his scholarship.

On one side of the office were bookshelves dedicated to different writers and critics, including shelves organized alphabetically for Agnon, Appelfeld, Bialik, and other Hebrew authors, along with a shelf or two dedicated to the works of literary critics, such as Dan Miron and Gershon Shaked. On the other side of the office were shelves containing scholarship about the Holocaust, along with books about American Jewish history and other general literary criticism. The arrangement of the books slowly came back to me as I remembered how my husband, then a law student, and I had helped Alan unpack his library and set up his book collection back when he first came to JTS.

Then there was the filing cabinet. In the top drawer were papers deal-ing with courses, and the second drawer, the middle one, held many of the papers pertaining to his book on American Hebraists, *Sanctuary in the Wilderness*. Underneath the hanging files, stored at the bottom of the file drawer and never displayed, were paintings Alan had painted—vibrant water color landscapes and still-life pictures—in surprisingly rich blues, reds and purples. Their beauty is especially dynamic in the way they experiment with color and reflected light. But it was the third, bottom shelf that seemed to serve as a kind of inner sanctum, or holy of holies. Here he kept his original scholarship in the form of detailed handwritten notes on different authors, a collection of letters from a year he spent in Israel retooling from English literature to Jewish Studies, and papers relating to his past leadership role as president of the USY (United Synagogue Youth). In this third drawer he also kept pages and pages of notes from particular courses he had taken. One collection of notes was from courses Alan took with Ezra Fleisher, the Israeli poet and scholar at Hebrew University, who was noted for his scholarship on the Cairo Geniza. As Fleisher's obituary in the NY Times explains, a *geniza* is "a repository for worn-out texts traditionally kept in a synagogue because, under Jewish law, paper with sacred writing on it cannot be simply discarded."[4] The courses Alan took with him ranged from "Hebrew Poetry in Christian Spain and Provence," to "Religious Poetry in Spain," and a course on "Piyyut," or liturgical poetry. Alongside these course notes were other notes taken from courses with the preeminent scholar of Hebrew and Yiddish literature, Dan Miron. Some were marked with dates and some not, including, "20th Century Yiddish Fiction—The Line of Wit" from the summer of 1978, "The *Eretz Yisrael* Short Story," also from the summer of 1978, a course on the Israeli poet Natan Zach from the spring of 1985, "Hebrew Fiction from 1900–1920," and a course on the Hebrew poetry of David Fogel, Uri Zvi Greenberg, and Avraham Shlonsky.

While both Ezra Fleisher and Dan Miron are prolific scholars with no shortage of published material, the fact that Alan kept these notes suggests that they differed from other published work. They are unique in that they mark the transmission of knowledge from teacher to student in a moment in time. They are not edited and perfected into the solidity of a book, or polished as a published essay, but they record the immediacy and intimacy of an exchange of ideas, a conversation. The elegance of Alan's penmanship, in both English and Hebrew, with a complete absence of doodles or anything extraneous, attest to his focused attention and love of the subjects he was learning. The only drawings to be found in the notes were illustrations of some of the different tree-like and pitcher-like shapes in which medieval Hebrew, Arabic and Castilian poems sometimes appeared. While the location of these notes in the bottom drawer are evocative of the kind of sacred texts stored in a *geniza*, unlike such buried texts, I suspect that Alan periodically went back to this drawer, either for course ideas or for inspiration, because these courses were really what set him on the path to

Hebrew literature. The way that he kept them in the bottom drawer of his filing cabinet therefore suggests that this was what literally and figuratively grounded his work, especially since Susanna's and my immersion in the world of physical things taught us that there is an order to emptying and filling a filing cabinet; it must be filled from the bottom first for it not to fall. Their location implied that they were not only a kind of treasure, something verging on the sacred, but also one of the quiet ways that he honored his teachers by keeping their spoken words close to him.

From the filing cabinet, we turned our attention to the papers on his desk, to the work disrupted *in medias res*. Confronting these papers marked the moment when the immediacy of a scholar's current work is suddenly turned into an archive. We needed to figure out how to manage this in-between space between the past and the present, and how and where to keep these things to orient them toward the future. Susanna and I developed a kind of "hevruta" for the study of things to determine their significance and where they should go, as we thought through each book, artifact, course packet, article, hand-written scholarly work, and letter. First, we asked "what is it?" as I translated titles from Hebrew and Yiddish, and deciphered handwritten dedications and inscriptions. Then we considered the context of the item, its relevance to Alan's work, and imagined what would Alan have wanted its fate to be. We pondered who could use these objects and where would other scholars look for them? Where could they do the most good and how can they get into the right hands? We also raised other questions: Would a "normal" person, a non-specialist in the field, want to read this? Which stories or books would most connect future readers to Alan, which works would he have wanted them to read? What would his daughters enjoy? Future generations of his family?

Along with these questions, a series of possible places emerged for the distribution of the books. They could be kept by the family, given to friends and colleagues, donated to the JTS library or other university libraries without a strong Judaica collection, sent to Beit Agnon in Jerusalem, or picked up by a family friend who is planning to open a Hebrew café in Brooklyn. While family, friends, and colleagues came and chose books, others were sent to these different destinations. Books by or scholarship on Agnon, Brenner, and Bialik were sent to Beit Agnon, while other more contemporary Hebrew novels and poetry, along with offprints of essays, went to the Hebrew café. Some of the untranslated Yiddish literature was sent to a friend in Ramat Gan, who had been a refusenik in Minsk, and who had not had access to Yiddish literature. A Hebrew slang dictionary and Avraham Regelson's Hebrew children's book, *The Journey of the Dolls to Eretz Yisrael*, along with an English translation of the story by Regelson's own daughters, Sharona (Regelson) Tel-Oren and Naomi (Regelson) Bar-Natan, were kept for future generations of the family. The other many books about American Hebraists were also kept intact for the family, except for those by Shimon Halkin; those went to his nephew, Hillel Halkin. Many of the other books went to the JTS library for the librarians there to consider.

Through this process of distributing and sorting books and the other items in the office, it became clear that there is a kind of hierarchy or system of ascribing value to things. On the one hand, libraries and other serious collectors want "gems" or "prized pieces" of collections. On the other hand, there are other things that have value since they might be useful to others. But there is an entirely different kind of valuable object, following the lead of Walter Benjamin, who explained that peculiar to the collector is "a relationship to objects which does not emphasize their functional, utilitarian value—that is their usefulness—but studies and loves them as the scene, the stage of their fate."[5] It was this last category of thing, the kind associated more with the "ephemera" of the office, that in many ways served as the most illuminating. Such papers, notes, and books were kept because they embody or illustrate an idea or sensibility; they reveal and preserve something of Alan.

Among the items kept were two copies each of the many photocopied stories that Alan either taught in his courses, or used in presentations or seminars. These stories were put aside and stored despite the fact that they appear in actual books, and thanks to the digital age they can be accessed online via Project Ben Yehudah or elsewhere in PDFs. They were saved for his daughters in commemoration of a longstanding tradition where their father would tear out stories from the *New Yorker* or other magazines and journals for them to read. He would select the story not necessarily because it was a "classic" or something they "should" read; these stories were not by their nature excellent, but they were singled out and presented with the words, "I think *you* would like *this* story." This practice of connecting readers to texts—implying a knowledge of something about the person that would connect to some essence of the story—was a form of communication and a gift. Their torn, fragmented state was part of what made them a compelling read, because they had been selected out of something larger, especially for their recipients. The way they were given as a form of communication was reflected in how his daughters chose books from his collection as well, such as when Avital asked, "Which Appelfeld should I read, which Yehoshua? Which did my father like the most, which do you and your students like?" as she and Susanna wondered which book or story he would have thought they were interested in.

Another series of papers that were kept were the many versions of syllabi, such as "Classics of Modern Jewish Literature," courses on Yehuda Amichai and on Agnon, "Israeli Literature," "Gender in Modern Jewish Literature," "Representation of the Holocaust," and "Varieties of Religious Experience in Literature." Along with these syllabi were printed out e-mails from other professors he had contacted for advice when developing these courses. The various iterations of these syllabi over time, coupled with these e-mails, underscore his efforts to really get the course right as he sought ways to bring people closer to the material and to share his literary passion. As an unpublished memoir-like essay by Alan emphasizes, "Great literary works are moments of collective understanding, but their necessity and beauty are often hard to appreciate," when he spoke about his vocation as both a "critic-interpreter" and teacher and how he strives to make these works' relevance "luminous."[6]

A small stack of other papers was salvaged from the recycling pile, namely several pages of downloaded e-mails to students offering them feedback on presentations they had given in Hebrew. He first related to their ideas and offered positive comments. When explaining to a student that he or she should speak slower, he wrote: "By slowing down you are saying to your listeners that you really want them to understand." He explained further that by taking the time to read cited passages of texts accurately, one "honors the listeners and the text." Susanna and I discussed how this feedback was not meant to diminish the students, but rather to mentor them and to show respect to their learning process; the overall effect of his communication to them created the sense that Alan was really listening. This feeling of being listened to reminded me of the first time I met Alan when I was applying to Ph.D. programs, and why I chose to study with him. Instead of just discussing the program and answering a few of my questions as I expected, he spoke with me for nearly two hours. He asked me exactly which books I had read, with whom I had studied at Hebrew

University for my master's degree, what exactly had been on each syllabus of each course, what I had chosen to write about, etc. Such thoroughness and interest made me feel that I had found a true mentor. And later, as his student, when he did have occasion to offer a critique of my work, it was somehow always uplifting. After handing in my first paper on Brenner's *Breakdown and Bereavement,* somewhat past the original deadline, he told me, "I would say that it was worth the wait if I didn't think it might give you the wrong kind of encouragement." The way he spoke with me and many other students enacted some of the key ideas Alan discussed in an article he wrote on the rabbinic approach to communication for *The Third Jewish Catalogue* back in 1980. Namely, that while according to Jewish law, there is a need to confront others when something is amiss and needs correction, such statements must be said in a way that others can hear them, and this must be done in "gradual steps" and "in a spirit of solicitude rather than accusation, with respect and dignity."[7]

Other articles featuring his more popular writing, including an essay "Sushi and Other Jewish Foods" that appeared in *Commentary,* likewise surfaced in the office. This essay offers a reading of the many Jewish cookbooks that emerged in the U.S., and how they reflect trends in Jewish food as a mode of cultural expression. He explores his own interest in the reenergizing of Jewish communal institutions and traditions by demonstrating how some of these cookbooks read as a truly collective literature, and an attempt to retrieve how "Jews cooked before the great dislocations and disasters of recent history."[8] Along with this was another, unpublished essay, "Cooking for Others: Fancy and Plain," which spoke about his own cooking, and how it changed when he was no longer cooking for himself alone, but for others. Here Alan spoke about how his cooking became a way of connecting with those close to him, specifically his family, which entailed paying close attention to what they liked and disliked, reading about and understanding the ingredients he used, and focusing on the aesthetic presentation of the food. His deliciously crafted meals also served as festive occasions for bringing family, friends, colleagues, and students together for holiday dinners. In fact, his approach to cooking and hospitality seemed to inform some of his more academic sensibilities, such as his view on what constitutes good academic writing. Alan would explain that a good academic article should come across as interesting dinner conversation; it should be intelligent and enlightening, as well as engaging and accessible, inviting others into the discussion. His interest and pleasure in cooking complemented his other acts of artistic creativity, including his watercolor paintings and his own writing, which was not bogged down by theoretical terms but executed with clarity, or as a reviewer of his first book on George Eliot put it, with "verbal grace."[9] These creative expressions were all part of an aesthetic sensibility, meant to convey ideas and feelings with a sense of artistic purposefulness.

In some ways clearing Alan's office has underscored his absence and has made it more tangible. Yet, the process of getting things—the objects of the field—to who can use them and find meaning in them, seems bound up with Alan's work in the field of Modern Jewish Literature, and his efforts to pass on and make accessible the creative expression of a culture. Just as scholarly efforts of assembling anthologies and other tributes, including this present volume dedicated to Alan Mintz and his scholarship, serve as a way of preserving and commemorating his work, packing his office has shared the similar aim of passing on the intellectual inheritance that Alan has left for all of us.

FIG. 6.1  "Teapot." Watercolor by Alan Mintz. Photograph by Amira Mintz-Morgenthau.

FIG. 6.2 "Winter Scene." Watercolor by Alan Mintz. Photograph by Amira Mintz-Morgenthau.

FIG. 6.3 "Cityscape." Watercolor by Alan Mintz. Photograph by Amira Mintz-Morgenthau.

## NOTES

Adapted from an article in *Prooftexts* 37 (2019), pp. 451–62. © 2019 Beverly Bailis. Reprinted with permission of Indiana University Press.

1. Erdmut Wizisla, "Walter Benjamin's Archive: Images, Texts, Signs," trans. Esther Leslie, New York: Verso Press, 2007, p. 2.

2. For more on the role of anthologies in the transmission, preservation and creation of Jewish tradition, see the double issue of *Prooftexts* vol. 17, no. 1 and 2, dedicated to the "Anthological Imagination in Jewish literature." These issues were then turned into a book, *The Anthology in Jewish Literature*, edited and introduced by David Stern. For scholarship on the specific notion of "*kinnus*," see Israel Bartal's essay "The Ingathering of Traditions: Zionism's Anthology Projects" and Stern's introduction to *The Book of Legends (Sefer Ha-Aggadah): Legends from the Talmud and Midrash*," eds. Hayim Nahman Bialik and Yehoshua Ravnitzky, trans. William G. Braude, NY: Schocken Books, 1992.

3. Walsh, Meeka. 2009. "A Pale Nimbus of Melancholy," *Border Crossings* 112: 12–13.

Here Walsh is summarizing some of the key ideas in Peter Schwenger's introduction to his book, *The Tears of Things: Melancholy and Physical Objects*, Minneapolis: University of Minnesota Press, 2006.

4. Ari L. Goldman, "Ezra Fleischer, Expert on Hebrew Poetry is Dead at 78," *New York Times*, August 1, 2006.

5. Walter Benjamin, "Unpacking My Library: A Talk About Book Collecting," *Illuminations*, ed. Hannah Arendt, trans. Harry Zohn, New York: Schocken Books, p. 60.

6. "Stalking Agnon," 18.

7. "Dissonance and Harmony; lashon ha-ra," *The Third Jewish Catalogue*, Jewish Publication Society, 1980.

8. Alan Mintz, "Sushi and Other Jewish Foods," *Commentary*, 1998 (43–47).

9. Julia Prewitt Brown, Review: "Work and Art: On George Eliot and the Novel of Vocation by Alan Mintz." *Novel: A Forum on Fiction*, vol. 12, no. 3 (Spring 1979), pp. 260–63.